RISING PRICES
EMPTY SHELVES

Warning Signs That Triggered The Deadliest Famines in History

৪০ • ৫৪

Bill Heid

Rising Prices, Empty Shelves: Warning Signs That Triggered The Deadliest Famines In History
© 2011 Bill Heid

A product of Solutions From Science

Published by:
Heritage Press Publications, LLC
PO Box 561
Collinsville, MS 39325

ISBN 13: 978-1-937660-04-8
ISBN 10: 1937660044

Table of Contents

൭•ര

ഇ•ൠ

INTRODUCTION

ာ • ၁

A
PERFECT
STORM

The average American doesn't spend a lot of time thinking about the possibility of famine. Many urban people are out of touch with where their food comes from; the process that gets the food from farmers to supermarket shelves is barely of interest to them. Barbara Kingsolver's book Animal, Vegetable, Miracle offered a rather poignant vignette which demonstrates this very phenomenon:

> *"When you say, 'the potatoes are up', what do you mean?" She paused, formulating her question. "What part of the potato comes up?"*
>
> *"The plant part," I said. "The stems and the leaves."*
>
> *"Wow," she said. "I never knew the potato had a plant part."* [1]

This ignorance about our food makes it difficult to discuss food policy in an intelligent way. Combine the ignorance with the nearly child-like trust that many Americans offer our leaders, our institutions, and our businesses and it's easy to see why few Americans fear the specter of famine. To the average person, hundreds of foodstuffs are available at the local supermarket, where they have always been available, and where they always will be available.

We've been taught that America is somehow exempt from a threat which has stalked mankind for as long as mankind has existed. Americans are over-exposed to the false idea of America's unyielding prosperity and richness, and the possibility of famine is completely ignored.

The question of whether or not famine is a potential threat in America is not new. Some of these issues have been in play since the early 20th century. We have been fortunate that the complex web of political, economic, social and agricultural conditions have not yet produced a famine in America—or the sort of global famine which could very well be on the horizons. But saying "they predicted a famine in the 1960s too, and that never happened," is like denying the Gulf of Mexico has everything it needs to produce a hurricane just because a season passes without one.

In truth, America has suffered various shortages of foodstuffs before, even if you don't acknowledge the idea of a full scale famine ever having touched her shores. There was, for example, a meat shortage in 1973. Howard Ruff, author of Famine and Survival in America, gives a vivid picture of what a simple shortage of even one staple food item can cause.

The meat market counters were empty. I was in the local supermarket, walking past the meat counter, when a butcher dumped a cart load of ground beef packages into the bin. I reached to pick up one or two and was almost trampled in the rush, as every woman in the store swarmed over me and started grabbing meat. I was elbowed, kicked, kneed, and generally roughed up. Catching the spirit of the occasion, I fought for my share. I got ten packages and headed for the check-out stand. Then the shock hit me as I realized what I had done. I had been caught up in mob panic. So I can understand how it can happen. Knowing that feeling, I don't want to be within a mile of a supermarket if a transportation problem cuts off urban food supplies! [2]

Famine does not, necessarily, mean that there "is no food." Many, many famines have happened even when the country was producing a good crop yield. Millions of people have still starved, however, as a result of government policies, oppressive governments, and all manner of strife. Sometimes, food has been slaughtered, burned, or left to rot while citizens starved in the streets. Having access to no food produces exactly the same effects as a lack of production. Prices that spiral out of control until a bag of beans is beyond your reach have the same practical effect as a drought which kills every crop in the nation. Even if you believe the propaganda that says our food supply is better than fine, it's important to realize that the quantity of food that a nation produces is not the only problem that can lead to disruptions in feeding its citizens.

If the idea of a famine still seems like a remote possibility to you, consider a scenario that's a little bit closer to home. In April of 2008, independent truckers, a group which makes up 90% of the nation's trucking network, threatened to strike over diesel prices. Truckers were paying as much as $1,200 to fill their tanks, and they were hoping to pressure lawmakers into cutting taxes on diesel [3]. The strike largely fizzled but, had it been successful, food prices would have skyrocketed overnight. Supermarket shelves, deprived of their suppliers, would have been completely bare in less than a week. Where, then, would the average American have gone for food when their own cupboards followed suit, especially given most homes have enough food to get by for no more than 3-4 days [4]? Even if you believe the United States produces so much food that we have to pay our farmers not to farm, the power of a single industry to cut you and your loved ones off from any food, indefinitely, should give you pause.

Trucker strikes have already taken place in other countries. Spain experienced massive food shortages all over the country due to a strike in June of 2008. The trucks stopped on Monday. By Tuesday, supermarkets, restaurants, and gas stations were feeling the pinch. Each quickly ran out of pork, beef, vegetables, fruits, and other goods [5].

Even short term disruptions can impact the food supply, locally if not nationally or globally. In Texas, during Hurricane Rita, with the memory of Hurricane Katrina still fresh on the minds of Gulf Coast residents, millions of people in Houston, Galveston, and the surrounding areas packed up their cars and attempted to evacuate. When the evacuation began Rita was a Category 5 storm. Satellite maps showed a massive, angry, seething mess of red and yellow that seemed to swallow the entire Gulf of Mexico. The eye of the storm seemed to be aiming directly at downtown Houston. Few people chose the "wait and see" approach.

With bumper to bumper traffic, anyone from the southern end of the city on September 22, 2005, soon discovered that it would take them up to 6 hours to get outside of the city limits. By midnight, restaurants were putting up "No Food" signs. Gas stations ran out of gas. Panicked people had cleaned most of the essentials from supermarket shelves before the stores themselves closed.

These smaller incidents help demonstrate the fragile nature of our food supply. We face a network of threats to the food supply, both nationally and globally. Rising unemployment could mean an inability to afford food right in front of you. The farce of American farm control, which has made us dependent on foreign nations for food imports, could be revealed for the house of cards it truly is in the event of a war, when those imports would no longer be available. The fuel prices could rise to the point where truckers either strike—or are merely run out of business for the inability to pay for gas. The government could take a dramatic shift for the worse and begin using food as a weapon to ensure the obedience of the populace. The foundations for such a shift are already in place, awaiting the circumstances that will allow the treasonous interests which have infiltrated our government to snap the trap shut. The damaging use of pesticides which weaken our crops while strengthening insects, and the farming methods which leave nothing but barren soil behind, could catch up with us at last. Our insistence on playing God and the frightening phenomenon of genetically modified foods, combined with the recently passed Food Patriot Act, could bring us a famine of nutrition—a scenario where we feel full but wind up eating nutritionally dead foods, or foods which act as slow poison in the body. The United Nations' open, stated policy of using food as a means to control nations could wind up turning against us. Or all of these factors could begin crashing together, propelled by one crisis that explodes into a massive tragedy of war, civil unrest, and destruction. Each threat is tied to all of the others in vital ways; the advent of one problem brings the high likelihood that the others will follow.

A study of the history of famine will uncover terrifying parallels between the circumstances which caused the famines of today and the conditions we see all around us. In some cases, the policies coming from the mouths of world leaders are chilling in their near word-for-word parallelism to the policies of leaders and countries who saw millions die of starvation in even our recent past. There truly is, as Ecclesiastes 1:9 reminds us, "nothing new under the sun." More colloquially, we Americans don't tend to pay attention to any history but our own, and are on the verge of being "doomed to repeat" the history of others.

The deck is stacked against us, and there is a campaign of subterfuge, misdirection, and downright lies meant to keep us from even seeing the cards. Big Government, Big Business, and Big Media all have a vested interest in keeping the truth hidden from you. Even those who suspect the truth might not be handling it in an effective way.

It's important to note that there are people on all sides of the political spectrum that are at least concerned about *aspects* of the way we handle our food, though each person may have their own pet projects. A conservative may focus in on farm control, collectivist thinking, and the death of personal responsibility as government gets ever bigger. A liberal may focus on the environmental and long-term impact of pesticides and GMO foods. Both are correct in identifying threats to the food source. Both are wrong in that they may be prone to discount all other sources of danger in the pursuit of their own goals. At the end of the day, however, the danger of famine and our food supply is neither a conservative nor a liberal problem, but a very human problem.

Throughout history there have been those who have faced down ridicule and ignorance in order to get prepared for times of trouble. Talking about famine, or any other potential disaster, is not about inspiring fear. The truth is, human nature and the cycles of human history mean that at some point or another, something is going to go wrong. Unfortunately, people are scared. It's easier to retreat into making fun of someone else's preparation efforts or to say, "it will never happen here" or "it will never happen to me" than it is to sit down and figure out how to deal with frightening situations.

As you continue through this volume it's good to be aware of how certain terminologies are used. "Famine" is the most common term used in this book, and much of the research focuses around this level of food crisis simply because it represents a "worst case" scenario. If you're going to get prepared at all, it's good to prepare for the most dire situation you can think of. "Food shortages," however, can be just as devastating to a family in the short term. Food shortages are short term. For whatever reason, there is less food available, and the market reflects this: prices rise and some food becomes unavailable. This can range from a sign in your local supermarket stating that there are no tomatoes due to a late frost to a scenario where civil disturbances happen as a result of the working man's inability to purchase food, or enough food. It doesn't become a famine until mortality rates take a sharp upturn as a result of starvation and the disease that accompany it [6]. These are definitions that historians use. In a practical sense, unless a shortage is truly minor and affects only one or two foodstuffs, the result can be exactly the same for any given individual. If you can't feed your family because a can of beans costs $50, you're in exactly the same bind you'd be in if there were no beans at all.

Reading this book will take courage. It will take courage to overcome that initial resistance in order to understand the problem. It will take courage to take action instead of dismissing the problem and deciding that everything will always be fine. It will take courage to understand that periods of "being fine," prosperity, and plenty are quite short and sparse in the course of human history. Once you make it this far, however, you'll be able to get prepared. Preparation is not a guarantee of survival, as much can still go wrong. It is, however, something that can allow you to face the future knowing that you were wise and responsible; a person who did all that he could.

PART 1

঵•঵

THE
HISTORY
OF
FAMINE

Developing a history of famine has two purposes. First, it's meant to provide evidence that famine and food shortage have always been with us, and, as such, there is no reason to assume that we will somehow become exempt from them. Several historians have noted that historical focus tends to be on the wars and politics of nations, but that the average person cares about food more than the movements of troops. Most of us are more fixated on feeding our families than on following every little action of our politicians.

The second purpose is to trace those factors in history which contributed to famines and food shortages. There are certain reoccurring mistakes, thoughts, and circumstances which can combine into that "perfect storm" of major crisis. Providing a demonstration of how these issues parallel the modern day, or how they would look in today's world, is therefore extremely important to taking the lessons from that history. If you know, for example, that the rise of a welfare state in Rome helped contribute to its eventual fall, then you have much more context to look at today's welfare state than you might otherwise have had. In addition, you will have, with the benefit of a historian's hindsight, the ability to take a look at the motivations of those who have gone before, as well as their follies and incidences of hubris. In many cases, the words that came out of the mouths of our forefathers and foremothers are coming out of the mouths of our contemporaries today, and are being treated as if they are brave new ideas. In reality, they are very old ideas, dressed up and presented in modern language and terms. You will find the parallels outlined for you in each chapter.

1.1 Famine in the Bible

ॐ • ☙

If you sat down with a King James Bible and searched for the word "famine" or "famines" you'd find the word is mentioned 90 times. The word "dearth," a synonym for famine, is mentioned seven more times [7]. Famine is so much a part of the human experience that you'll find it addressed at the beginning (Genesis) and at the end (Revelations) of human history. Individual places and people escape famine at given times, but the planet as a whole finds famine inescapable.

Certainly not everyone reading this book will necessarily believe in the infallibility of the Bible. If this is you, don't be quick to discount this chapter. At the very least, the Bible represents one of the largest compilations of historical record stretching back to before the "ancient" period of the Greeks and the Romans. It has plenty to say about the human condition, and the human experience as well. Not much has changed—the Bible records wars, plagues, strife, uprisings, famines, coups, acts of dire evil, acts of incredible honor, kindness, and love. Watching CNN today would outline the exact same experiences. In any time, in any place, humans are humans, and the world is the world.

Our earliest recorded famine, then, comes out of Genesis 12:10: *"And there was a famine in the land: and Abram went down to Egypt to sojourn there; for the famine was grievous in the land."* Not only is the famine just twelve chapters into the first book of human history, but it begins with Abram, who would become Abraham. Famine affects the righteous individual just as surely as it affects the unrighteous. You could even observe that God's redemptive plan truly began with Abraham—and here you see famine almost as soon as this Biblical hero is introduced.

Just one generation later, Isaac finds himself having to travel to a foreign country thanks to a famine (Genesis 26:1). This is before we even get to Joseph's famine (Genesis 41:53-56), arguably the most famous famine in the Bible.

It's also important to note that two out of these three early famines represented a major crisis. Abram's famine was described as "grievous." Joseph's not only lasted seven years, but was "all over the face of the earth." Egypt's storehouse and the preparations that Joseph made in obedience to God became a source of blessing and grace to those who were able to reach them, but you can imagine how many thousands of people must have died because they did not make it to Joseph's storehouses—even if you take "all over the face of the earth" to simply mean, "the entire section of earth that early Biblical writers actually knew existed."

Sometimes, famine simply happens—a result of natural weather, an over-abundance of insects, or bad planting years. Several such famines are listed in the Bible. This appears to be the case in the famine that began Ruth's story (Ruth 1:1). The Bible simply says, "it came to pass," without bothering to attach any natural cause or supernatural judgment to it. Famine is just a fact of life in a fallen world.

In other cases, however, a famine comes about because God is judging either the people or the rulers of the people. A ruler is like the head of a household. If the head of a household mismanages the house, even the children, who had no part of the mismanagement, suffer as a result. The case of 2 Samuel 21:1 illustrates why we should continue to be very careful and discerning about the leaders we choose, and why we should continue to be active in monitoring those leaders. This verse says: *"There was a famine in the days of David for three years, year after year; and David enquired of the LORD. And the LORD answered,' It is for Saul, and for his bloody house, because he slew the Gibonites.'"* The famine didn't even happen during Saul's time, but it was sent as a punishment for Saul's actions. Actions have a way of rippling into the future, even after the originators are no longer around to suffer their consequences. In fact, a 400 year old treaty colored these events; during the age of Joshua the Israelites entered into a covenant with the Gibonites, promising not to slay them (Joshua 9). Saul's mass murder was particularly grievous, not only because of all the lives that were lost, but also because it broke the covenant of a nation.

The Bible does not spare us any gruesome image of famine. In our state of comfort, our imagination gives us some version of what it's like when we miss a meal or two: hunger pangs, and perhaps the dizziness and irritability of low blood sugar. Yet the physical effects and the pain of famine go so much deeper than that.

Deuteronomy 32:34 vividly records the fevers brought on by malnutrition: *"They shall be burnt with hunger, and devoured with burning heat, and with bitter destruction"*. Lamentations 4:8 and 5:10 describe blackened skin, most likely due to Niacin deficiency. They also discuss the skeletal limbs that are somewhat familiar to us from photographs and television. Those photographs and videos don't do starvation justice, however: some individuals were so ravished by starvation that they were literally unrecognizable: *"…not known in the streets."* In Egypt and Canaan during Joseph's famine, people literally fainted in the streets (Genesis 47:13), in spite of all of Joseph's preparation. Death, of course, is a given, though you will find verses specifically recording this consequence as well.

The Bible packs a lot of information into very short sentences, so short that their impact can often be lost to modern audiences. The Bible gives us in one or two verses what we might devote an entire article to. It therefore takes some imagination and careful focus on the relevant passages to get the full impact of the desperation and devastation of those who sought food during Biblical famines.

In 2 Kings 4:39-40 you find a story which records a group of people attempting to eat wild herbs during a famine in Elisha's time. Now—wild foods are a viable option for gathering foodstuffs in times of famine. It's something we'll cover ourselves in Part 4 of this book. But most people don't have the knowledge to tell a dangerous plant from an edible plant. In this verse, *"the men went out into the field to gather herbs, and found a wild vine, and gathered thereof wild gourds his lap full, and came to shred them in a pot of pottage: for they knew them not. So they poured out for the men to eat. And it came to pass, as they were eating the pottage, that they cried out and said, O thou man of God, there is death in the pot. And they could not eat thereof."* Ignorance is a poor companion when foraging for food, but many people will attempt to eat anything green when hunger truly sets in.

A few passages later you see people throwing silver at the most disgusting of items just for the tiny bit of nourishment those items might offer: anything that might so much as *resemble* food. *"An ass's head was sold for fourscore pieces of silver, and the fourth part of a cab of dove's dung for five pieces of silver"* (2 Kings 6:25). It's a sobering picture for those who might put their trust primarily in hard currency like gold or silver, thinking that will see them through any time of crisis or collapse. During a famine, nobody cares about gold or silver, because you can't eat gold or silver, and possession of a donkey's brain might make you the richest man in town.

Those who are wealthy now really need to sit up and take notice. Your current wealth will matter little in the event of a famine. The current "housing crisis" does not even begin to compare with the crisis born of famine. In Nehemiah 5:3 it says: *"We have mortgaged our lands, vineyards, and houses, that we might buy corn, because of the dearth."* In some famines, the price of a loaf of bread has risen as high as a single day's wages. To put this into terms you can understand, take a 40 hour a week job at minimum wage. That means a loaf of bread alone would be $60.00. One could well imagine people having to take out home equity loans (if they were even available to at that point) or selling their homes at cut-rate prices just to buy groceries. At the *average* American income of $46,326 a year [8], you'd be looking at a loaf of bread for $178.00! This single loaf would allow each member of a five person household to have one slice a day, per day, for four days, with a single slice left over to divide into careful strips, perhaps to serve as a treat on the final day.

Of course, there's one group that won't come out too badly—the super-rich. In Revelation 6:5-7 the black horse of famine intones: *"A quart of wheat for a denarius, and three quarts of barley for a denarius; and do not harm the oil and the wine."* Traditionally, the oil and the wine would be the foods of the very wealthy. The common laborer could spend one day's wage (a denarius) for a quart of wheat, or he could choose to spend three day's wages for some barley, but the very rich continue to enjoy their luxuries. People who can afford yachts and golden parachutes will hardly be troubled by a $3000 grocery bill.

Who are these people in our country except for the politicians, the heads of the mega-corporations, and the bankers? Are these really the people you'd put your trust in to make sure you are fed? Given their current record, one of two things is likely to happen: either they will make the clueless statement that everyone who is starving simply lacked "personal responsibility" and deserve what they get as they turn their back, ignoring any role they themselves might have played in the devastation, or they will offer "free" food with a barb in it. Food will be used as a tool to ensure obedience, to create a class of slave laborers who work at grueling tasks in the hopes of a single bowl of soup. The house servants of the upper class might live somewhat more comfortably. Of course, personal responsibility *does* play some role in survival, as those who are prudent and responsible enough to take action against future famine will come out better than those who are taken by surprise.

Do you have a belief in the basic kindness of our leaders, or the will of the CEOs of mega-corporations to see to the well-being of citizens that buy their goods? Even in the absolute best cases it's probably safe to say that many of the ultra-rich are out of touch with reality. In 1992, George Bush Sr. was completely baffled by grocery store scanners and credit card readers, simply because he had not had to set foot into the common man's grocery for so very long [9]. In another case of the ultra-rich either being completely callous or completely clueless about those who work to uphold their organizations, one might consider Wal-Mart's CEO Michael Duke, who earns more in one hour than his workers will make in a single year [10]. Wal-Mart's callous response to the pay gap is not to raise wages to something a bit more fair (which could be done simply by lowering Duke's wage, a dent he'd barely feel, keeping prices and profits exactly the same), but to drain taxpayer money by placing welfare forms in the break rooms [11]. It does not take a conspiracy theorist to suspect that relying on the largesse, intelligence, or care of those who would be least harmed by the famine is a zero-sum proposition.

The most sobering levels of desperation arrive when humans begin to feed on one another, another horrific phenomenon dutifully recorded in the Bible. Cannibalism has occurred in every famine throughout the centuries. Children are especially vulnerable, being unable to defend themselves, and sometimes *parents* are the culprits. The Bible is *not* engaging in clever symbolism or vast hyperbole when Leviticus 26:29 reports: *"and ye shall eat the flesh of your sons, and the flesh of your daughters ye shall eat."*

The desperate mindset of the starving man begins erasing natural love, morality, or even sense. Hunger literally drives suffering people to madness. To really understand this madness, you should turn your full imagination upon the picture that's presented in 2 Kings 6:28-29. The image is heart sickening:

> *And the King said unto her, "What aileth thee?" And she answered, "This woman said unto me, 'Give thy son, that we may eat him today, and we will eat my son tomorrow.' So we boiled my son and did eat him: and I said to her on the next day, 'Give thy son, that we may eat him.' And she hath hid her son.'"*

There is no evidence of grief for the woman's lost child; there is simply anger and desperation that she has been tricked and deprived of her expected meal for the day. There is no compassion for the other woman's child either, and absolutely no remorse for admitting to the highest authority in the land that the woman boiled her own son to live another day.

If you think we've grown any more civilized than the woman of 2 Kings 6:28-29, you would be incorrect. In his essay *Count Our Holiday Blessings: At Least We're Not Starving* C.J. Maloney offers these chilling facts:

> *During the time of Stalin's terror famine upon Ukraine (when at least six million perished) it was dangerous for children to walk around*

alone—they were prone to be snatched, strangled, and cooked. In the town of Poltara an entire operation for the processing of children's meat was discovered by the Soviet Secret Police. But the consumption of a child didn't necessarily need to be done by strangers. When Mao's famine was raging through China from 1958-1861 a couple in Anhui province, driven mad by hunger, murdered, then ate, their eight year old son. [12]

Humanity *doesn't change*. We are the same in 2010 as we were in 600 B.C. Technologies change; societies change, but even those changes come in cycles, now rising, now disappearing. We are no better, no smarter, no kinder and no stronger than anyone who was alive before Christ was born. Madness is also beyond anyone's control. It's sobering to wonder if you, or someone you love, might ever stoop to such tragic depths as a result of a terrible famine.

1.2 Famine in Ancient Times

ℰᴑ•ᴄℛ

Famine and food shortages were ever-present threats in the ancient world. Food-related problems were common enough to become a major shaper of the political, technological, and military landscape to a degree which we can scarcely imagine today. Monitoring famine, planning for famine, and adjusting to famine and shortages took center stage as major issues of the day. This stands in direct contrast to our modern-day society, in which the possibility of food shortage outside of a third-world country isn't even acknowledged.

There are three instructive case studies of the ways in which food issues and shortages shaped the ancient world. Egypt and Athens developed strategies that were specifically aimed at keeping their people fed. The Romans also had strategies, but they were more destructive and eventually contributed to the ruination of the Empire.

The crops of ancient Egypt depended largely on "good" flooding from the Nile—flooding that was neither destructively high nor disappointingly low. The floods watered the fields and brought nutritious silt that aided the performance of the crops. This had a direct impact on Egyptian technology, as even a very small drop in the Nile's flood level could leave vast portions of farmland unable to produce a satisfactory yield [13]. Necessity leads to innovation, and the Egyptians built a system of stairs and staff gauges along the banks of the Nile, allowing the ancient Egyptians to measure the water levels of the Nile. This was a feat of ancient meteorology that helped Egypt stay prepared for times of trouble—these "nilometers" allowed the Egyptians to predict the coming high mark for the coming year's flood with a reasonable degree of accuracy [14]. Irrigation was also developed in Egypt as a means of keeping the grain producing even in low-flood years [15].

Fekri Hassan, Professor in the Department of Egyptology in the University of London, also offers these insights on the way food shortage issues might have even shaped the authority structure that eventually arose in ancient Egypt.

> *From the earliest times, boats were used to transport people between villages…ferry across the channel and haul cattle, grain, and other substances from one place to another. They were also used in military campaigns. Boats thus played a major role in unifying the country. Besides the donkey, which was used for overland transportation, boats made possible the economic integration of the country. Food from one district's central granary could be used to secure the welfare of people in another region. The emergence of kingship in Egypt might have been linked with coordinating the collection of grain and relief activities as the most viable strategy to cope with unpredictable crop failures in any of the districts.* [16]

We have touched on Egypt once already, of course, by covering its Biblical role in the Genesis famine. It's worth noting that kingship was *already* in place by the time Abram or Joseph appeared on the scene, and both times the Egyptians were able to serve as a sort of "bread basket" in times of hardship. Their ability to do so in the second famine was aided by God and Joseph alike, but the Pharaoh's instant response and the ability to provide grain to many other countries speaks of an infrastructure that was already well in place.

"Well, wait," you may be thinking. "The United States government does that. They've been stockpiling excess food for a really long time, right? In case of food shortages?"

Those stockpiles began drying up in the year 2008. Above and beyond the question of whether or not you want to rely on your government to provide for you in the event of a food shortage, there is the fact that they just don't have the means. An article ran in *USA Today* on May 2, 2008, with this sobering news:

> *U.S. government food surpluses have evaporated because, with record high prices, farmers are selling their crops on the open market, not handing them over to the government through traditional price-support programs that make up for deficiencies in market price. Because of the current economics of food, and changes in federal farm subsidy programs designed to make farmers rely more on the markets, large U.S. reserves may be gone a long time.* [17]

The fact also remains that our own government, politics, technology and society are *not* focused on farms, food-shortages, or potential famine, but on active *urbanization*. Any time you have a large urban-based society, you put more pressure on the rural areas to produce and supply foodstuffs for the urban population, who are always engaged in some other sort of work. We haven't been preponderantly agricultural since the 1890s. Dan P. Van Gorder, in his chilling 1966 narrative of what he called "planned famine" for America, offered a stark picture when he said, "Unaware of the consequences, our forebears made a choice between remaining a preponderantly rural, agricultural nation and turning to urban industrialization, relegating farming to a secondary place in the economy" [18]. According to the USDA, fewer than 2% of Americans farm for a living today, and 83% of us are crammed into non-food producing urban areas [19]. Much of this trend can be traced back to pushes by Big Government and Big Business to get people into factories. While our booming manufacturing industry was wonderful for a while, much of that trade has since dried up. Big Media is culpable for this trend as well, presenting farms and farmers as boring, ignorant, overworked, and poor—and yet they herald and laud the power of technology to somehow feed everyone while "freeing" American citizens from the drudgery of farming. No, it is clear that we cannot lay claim to keeping food production at the front and center of our national and social consciousness as the Egyptians did, nor can we claim to have anything like the infrastructure that managed to help Egypt serve as an international bread basket during a 7 year famine.

The ancient Athenians faced a constant food shortage problem simply because of their circumstances: a heavily populated island without enough farmland, causing them to rely heavily on imports. George M. Calhoun, author of *The Business Life of Ancient Athens*, drew an analogy between World War I and the situation of ancient Greece in order to help his 1920s readers understand how Athenians viewed the problem of grain and why they dedicated so much of their time and attention to it.

> *In order to realize how serious this problem appeared to the ancient Athenians we have but to recall the somewhat analogous situation in which Great Britain was placed during the recent war. Like Great Britain, Athens had known, during the later years of the Peloponnesian War, what it meant to be entirely dependent upon importations and constantly faced by the possibility of having them cut off by a naval defeat. In the case of Athens this actually occurred, and the city was finally forced by starvation to surrender to the Peloponnesians after courageously enduring several months of famine.* "[20]

Just as the Egyptians developed "nilometers" in response to the need to monitor the Nile for satisfactory flood activities, the Athenians developed their massive navy in order to get their grain. This need pushed their colonial activity far and wide.

But the navy and importation activities alone cannot fully demonstrate the extent to which the Athenians focused on the need to keep the grain flowing into their city. So prepared for trouble were the Athenians that they kept the state of the food supply under constant review, to the point where the standing agenda of the main assembly meeting of each prytany included a discussion on the food supply [21].

The loss of Athens' navy in 322 BC brought on the expected famine, demonstrating its weakness as an independent strategy. For all of their focus, the Athenians were ultimately unsuccessful at keeping famine out of their streets. This case study shows us that even careful attention to the food supply and the development of coping measures to handle it can result in upheavals that lead to citizens starving in the streets.

In contrast to Egypt and Athens, tracking the famines of the early Roman Empire has proven to be a particularly difficult task for scholars, as there is less evidence of food shortages and famine actively shaping society to such a degree as the cases listed above. Part of the problem is that ancient Roman writers had a propensity to use the word "famine" as a rhetorical tool as often as they used it to accurately describe a real event as we would understand it [22]. We have more information on the various ways the Empire coped with food shortages. It's also worth noting that the Empire covered such a vast area of land that it was conceivable to find food-based problems in certain *regions* of the Empire without necessarily indicating a broad, sweeping famine raging across the length of the Empire itself. There were, for example, a series of local famines during the reign of Claudius [23].

As to the various coping mechanisms, we know that the Roman Empire took several measures. Provincial grain taxes, magistrates who sent for emergency grain supplies so they could sell them below-price [24], and imports were all part of the strategy of keeping all of the citizens fed. During times of famine or shortage you'd also see prohibitions against hoarding. Private individuals and politicians would also court popularity by supplying grain to the citizenry at low cost, or for free [25]. This is distinguished from the later welfare state that was set up during times of plenty, in which poorer Roman citizens were allotted a share of free grain (the "bread" part of the famous "bread and circuses" line) in order to avoid riots or uprisings.

The waters get less murky as one reaches the period known as Late Antiquity, as records got better and with more sources to choose from. This is the result of a number of factors. First, Christianity rose and ultimately became the dominant religion of the region. Second, the capitol of the Roman Empire was moved from Rome to Constantinople. A split between east and west occurred, enough to leave the Byzantine Empire—the Eastern Empire—in place after the Roman Empire fell to Alaric I. Christian writers were especially concerned with recording famines, wars, earthquakes, and other disasters as part of looking for the signs of the End of Days. To the early Christian writers, apocalyptic events were immanent. The three prevailing world eras marked the 6000th year since the creation of the world as falling between 492 and 508, and Jesus spoke of these events as if they could expect them very soon [26]. Every generation since has tried to mark the end of days, using catastrophes as evidence to back them up, but from a historical perspective it does give scholars much more reliable material to work with when it comes to tracking the incidence of famine. For example, we know that the city of Rome experienced 12 famines between 284-750, including the great famine that came about as a result of the fall of Rome. We also know that the city of Constantinople suffered seven famines during those same years [27]. That's roughly one famine every 38 years for the city of Rome and one every 66 years for the city of Constantinople.

Alaric I's sack of Rome and the fall of the Roman Empire produced a famine which swept across the remains of the empire as surely as the barbarians swept across the remaining western territories. This chaos rocked the Western world from 400 to 800 AD, and trade was hampered on every side. The upshot for the city of Rome was a 90% reduction in the population over the 400 year period [28]. So vivid was the memory of citizen starvation during the initial siege that a legend rose up about a wealthy woman who, moved by pity for the citizens who had already fallen to cannibalism, finally ordered her slaves to open the gates to the Visigoths [29]. There's no particular historical evidence to back up the claim, and there are other stories about how those gates got opened, but the sheer scope of human misery and hunger must have been telling to create such a story.

Comparisons between Rome and the United States, particularly as it relates to the fall of Rome, are nothing particularly new, but there are some important take-aways for modern readers. The Romans didn't just get unlucky in battle; they were facing problems long before Alaric began his march. The Roman government spent more than it could afford. The military was over-extended. Money was being spent both to support the "bread and circuses" welfare state and to import luxuries to support the upper class lifestyle. With no "Federal Reserve" to print money out of thin air, Rome actually ran out of gold to produce coins [30]. Weak and corrupt leaders were unable, unsuited, or simply apathetic to the situation: when Alaric's army began marching, Theodosius I took off for Ravenna. We can arch our eyebrows and make a comparison here as well. George Bush played guitar and vacationed at Camp David while Hurricane Katrina raged and made landfall [31]; Barak Obama played golf and made time for concerts during the BP Oil Spill. Fiddling while Rome burns? [32]

Rome was also plagued by constant infighting, and America, with its red states and blue states, is not much different. The last three presidential elections have been described as divisive and rancorous. Bush v. Gore in 2000 was marked by the entire "hanging chads" election debacle. Bush's re-election vs. Kerry in 2004 carried shadows: accusations of election fraud on the voting machines in Ohio were the tip of the iceberg for a year in which the nation's popular vote was split almost in half, 50.73% to Kerry's 48.27% [33]. The 2008 presidential election was so rancorous that McCain went so far as to put out a commercial that made un-subtle comparisons between Barak Obama and the anti-Christ. Yet underlying all of this is the shadow of a suspicion that the parties are two sides of the same coin; both basically in the pocket of Big Corporate, who in turn owns Big Media—a spectacle to keep the child-like citizenry distracted while the grown-ups go off to talk. Under such circumstances, it is extremely difficult to create unity, sensible policy, or a strong defense against disaster.

Then, of course, there were the people that Rome angered: enemies on every side, brought out by its constant push into every corner of the known world. The United States is more subtle about its empire, choosing to frame foreign incursions as a defense of our "business interests" or as part of the "War on Terror," but it's well known that the United States isn't making too many friends these days. Many of the countries we are angering are either those whom we import from or allied to those whom we import from. An extended war could easily break out at any point, cutting off those imports, straining our own military, and forcing the government to admit its own bankruptcy at last.

One can make another comparison as well—in its latter days, Rome became heavily urban. In every other case you can make a good argument for over-simplification. Yet it is in the urbanization of America—with, as you'll recall, just 2% of the population working the land—that you find an eerie comparison which ever-so-inevitably demonstrates the truth of the old wisdom: those who don't study history are doomed to repeat it. The excerpt below comes from historian Guglielmo Ferrero's *Ancient Rome and Modern America, a Comparative Study of Morals and Manners*, written in 1914, and it adequately sums up the plight of both ancient Rome and the United States of America.

> *In the first and second centuries, every rich family spent part of its possessions on the embellishment of the cities. They built palaces, theaters, temples, baths, and aqueducts. They distributed grain, oil, amusements and money. They endowed public services and assumed the role of pious founders.*

The Empire covered itself with cities great and small, rivaling each other in splendor and wealth; and into these cities, at the expense of depopulating the countryside where nobody was willing to live, it attracted the peasantry, the village artisans and the yeomanry. In these cities, schools were opened in which the youth of the middle class were taught eloquence, literature, and philosophy, and trained for official posts and for liberal professions."

Little by little, the expenditures of urban civilization, the cities, and their increasing luxuries, outdistanced the fertility of the countryside and from that moment the latter began to be depopulated and sterilized by the cities. With each succeeding generation the impulse towards the cities became stronger. The numbers and requirements of modern populations increased. The state and wealthy classes were inundated with requests, prayers, and threats, urging them to satisfy these requirements, to adorn and enrich ever more the cities, which were the glory and splendor of the Empire.

In order to feed, amuse, and clothe crowded city populations, to carry through the construction of magnificent monuments, to provide work for the industries and arts of the cities—agriculture was little by little ground down by ever-increasing burdens. The position of the peasant in the solitude of the countryside became ever more sad and gloomy, just as the cities became fairer, bigger, fuller of amusements and festivals. The impulse toward the cities increased, and one day the Empire awoke to find its cities were swarming with beggars, idlers, vagabonds, masons, singers—in fact, the whole tribe of the artisans of pleasure and luxury. But in the fields, which were expected to feed all these men who crowded into the city to work or to idle, there was a dearth of peasants to cultivate the land. [XX]

Dan P. Van Gorder, author of *Ill Fares the Land*, quoted this passage as well in his 1966 book. We can note the ever deteriorating situation just by monitoring the dates. In 1914, 33% of the population farmed the land. In 1966, when Van Gorder authored *Ill Fares the Land*, only 6% of the population farmed the land. Now we are down to 2011, and only 2% of the population, a population much larger than the populations of either 1914 or 1966, farms the land. No amount of high-tech factory farming techniques is going to bridge that gap, especially when you factor in that we are engaged in feeding the citizenries of other countries as well. One might start to wonder how we've done as well as we have for as long as we have. One might also start to wonder why, then, we continue **to pay farmers not to farm**. In point of fact, we pay people who aren't even farmers not to farm. Here's a 2006 report from the *Washington Post*.

> *Even though Donald R. Matthews put his sprawling new residence in the heart of rice country, he is no farmer. He is a 67-year-old asphalt contractor who wanted to build a dream house for his wife of 40 years. Yet under a federal agriculture program approved by Congress, his 18-acre suburban lot receives about $1300 in annual 'direct payments' because **years ago** the land was used to grow rice. Matthews is not alone. Nationwide, the federal government has paid at least $1.3 billion in subsidies for rice and other crops since 2000 to individuals who do no farming at all.* [34]

So we've spent an average of $1.6 million per year in making sure we don't have enough to eat out of our own soil. Either our leaders are completely asleep at the wheel, or there's something deeper going on. In either case, the situation is as unsustainable as the Roman Empire. We would be better served to allow food and food policy in defense of famine and shortage to take center stage, to shape *our* society, culture, and political decisions.

1.3 Famine in the Middle Ages

ℰᏅ • ᏅᏅ

There is much more to say about famine in the Middle Ages than in ancient or Biblical times simply because we have much more information about occurrences all over the globe. In fact, from 800 AD to 1599 AD there were so many famines in so *many* places that it would be impossible to address them all without creating an entire book devoted to them. This means cherry-picking famine case studies, choosing those which were serious and well-documented enough to better help us learn the lessons within.

Europe

Food security would have been a laughable notion to the Europeans of the Middle Ages. In England alone there were 28 famines—not counting general food shortages, only outright famines—recorded between 793 AD and 1400 AD. In France, there were 10 famines during the 1300s alone. There were plenty of wars, uprisings, plagues and bad harvest years to guarantee a series of food problems, and, in many cases, history was changed because a lack of food inspired the populace to rise up in rebellion. A fury of millennial fever gripped the medieval populace in the 1300s, with preachers declaring the year 1400 to be the definitive date of the end of the world.

One famine overshadowed them all, however: the Great Famine of 1315-1317. This famine struck throughout Europe. Millions died of starvation, and society began experiencing upheavals that would echo throughout the century as a result. This famine would have a similar impact on the people of the 14th century that the World Wars had on the people of the 20th: a re-evaluation of values and a loss of trust for the leaders of the day, which would in turn prompt reforms in both the churches and the governments of Western Europe. Try to imagine it—a famine so devastating that it loomed as large in the minds of those who faced it as "The War to End All Wars" loomed over the 20th century—and even into the 21st.

The cause of this famine was twofold—population shifts and climate change. The population of Europe grew between 800 and 1300, and eventually reached the point where "only the best of conditions" would allow the land to provide for the people. When there's no margin for error it doesn't take long for Murphy's law to kick in, and a climate change that caused cooler, wetter summers created less-than-the-best conditions. A too-wet spring in the year 1315 and in 1316 meant that many fields went unplowed and seed rotted before it could germinate. By 1317 people of every class were suffering. The food supply did not return to normal until 1325, in spite of the return of normal weather patterns, because starving people had eaten up the seed grain and draft animals and were often too sick and weak to work the fields [35].

It's always problematic to begin discussing population problems in the modern political climate. Too often, the idea of "overpopulation" is used by those who want to forward an agenda of forced sterilization, involuntary limits on childbirth, abortion, death counseling for the elderly, and other dark programs. Addressing issues of population by no means implies support of these programs. Human life is valuable and precious, and stating that there could be a problem of population does not reduce this fact. Our advocacy would be to *increase* food supply, not *decrease* human life. We could, for example, begin shifting the balance of population to production more favorably by fostering programs which bring farmers back to America; curtail sprawl by the cities and transportation networks; and explore new ways to solve the food problem, such as fostering urban farms cared for by local neighborhoods or exploring Dickson Despommier's ingenius vertical farm project, something that we'll explore later. With that distinction made, we can speak about the population vs. production problem far more intelligently, sanely, and humanely than those who would kill the many for the comfort of the few, or destroy freedom out of fear.

These caveats offered, there is a population-to-production problem in America. Simply put, the population of America is projected to grow to 520 million by 2050. The projections show that only 0.6 acres of farmland will be available to grow food for each American at that point, when at least 1.2 acres per person is required in order to maintain a diet consistent with American standards of living. Soil erosion, urbanization, and problems with the water supply are aggravating the problem. The current depletion rates of land and water, as well as the dearth of farmers to work the land, suggest that U.S. agriculture may already be unsustainable—we just haven't begun to feel it yet. Or, at least, the middle-to-upper classes don't feel it yet. There are 44 million people living in poverty in America and many of them are "food insecure," meaning at any given time they might not have sufficient food to sustain their families [36]. It would be safe to say that America relies on the "best of circumstances" as well, and that those circumstances involve a much more complex web of domestic farming and imports. This is before we even address any weather problems our farmers might be facing. This is *also* prior to addressing any worldwide ripple effect that a loss of those "best circumstances" could cause.

The number of food-insecure in America is an important number. The U.S. Department of Agriculture reports that 50 million people in America are "food insecure." This means that even some people who are technically over the "poverty line" are having trouble feeding their families [37]. It echoes the AGRICULTURAL CIRCULAR NO. 296 debacle of the 1930s. Authors Steibling and Ward put out a document which stated, among other things, that "under consumption is our problem – if our people were eating all the food they need and the food required to keep them at a safe nutritional level, we would be facing a serious under production problem." AGRICULTURAL CIRCULAR NO. 296 came out, however, at a time when politicians were declaring an *overproduction* problem as a justification for farm control, food destruction programs and farm subsidy programs. 15,500 copies of this document slipped out in December of 1933 before it was subject to a sudden recall. It was re-issued as a far more innocuous document, FARMER'S BULLETIN 1757, better known as the pamphlet *Diets At Four Levels of Nutritive Content and Cost*. This pamphlet had absolutely no mention of under consumption in America [38]. All of this suggests that we never had those "best circumstances," or had long since lost it by the early 20th century. What we had, instead, was a carefully constructed illusion of prosperity for all. The people of the Middle Ages, of course, had no such illusions.

There were indications of trouble before 1316. Long before the food issue reached epic proportions, the prices began to rise. The *Oxford Journal* published a paper noting that the prices of livestock, dairy produce, and most other foodstuffs had risen considerably as early as 1305, due to the falling value of the currency. An influx of foreign currency was re-coined into sterling. The last re-coinage had been in 1299; prices rose 25% in the 6 year period. Grain harvests were poor enough between 1308 and 1310 to bring price increases of the staple crop. This meant near-famine conditions for many long before the "official" famine years. Scotland reached the level of famine as early as 1310, thanks to warfare. By 1315 the *Journal* describes the price situation as "serious" [39]. Though rising food costs *can* be the result of a "blip" in the marketplace, they can sometimes be symptomatic of far worse things on the horizon.

So how are we stacking up in light of this information? How close is our price situation to the price situation of the early 1300s? Pretty close, if *USA Today's* November 30th, 2010 article and the U.S. Department of Agriculture are to be believed.

The increase is nothing astronomical when you look at food prices as a whole. The U.S. Department of Agriculture is predicting that food prices this year will rise 0.5% to 1.5%. Next year, the forecast is for an increase of 2% to 3%...it's not as reasonable when you look at some individual items or categories, such as **meat and dairy***, where the jump is significant. Pork, for example, is up 13% from a year ago;* **butter is up 25%***; and milk has risen 6%, according to the USDA. To consumers, many of whom are still struggling financially, the increase can seem unbearable.* [40]

Now, obviously, an eerie parallel between the early 14th century and the early 21st century does not mean that we will see famine conditions in America, or the Western World. It does, however, demonstrate that conditions are favorable. A warm front doesn't necessitate a thunderstorm either, but a meteorologist will still take a look at it and forecast a chance of rain. It certainly helps demonstrate a vital point: conditions are dangerous *now*. This isn't some fanciful doom and gloom scenario. The dark clouds are swirling overhead, and the fact that they might move on is no reason to avoid reaching for an umbrella.

Speaking of thunderstorms, the 2010 Food and Agriculture Organization of the United Nations *Food Outlook* reports "unexpected production shortfalls driven by weather events negatively influenced the outlook for the global cereal supply in the early months of the 2010/11 marketing season from July to October." In other words, we had some lousy weather, which led to some lousy harvests, which put even more pressure on a difficult market. Again, conditions are eerily reflective of those seen in the 14th century [41].

The Black Plague in 1348 reduced the population, which reduced pressure on the food supply, though this is scant consolation considering both events took their toll in millions of lives. The trouble sweeping across Europe was far from over.

1337 would bring The Hundred Years War between England and France, a conflict that would last all the way to 1453. The war brought economic ruin to France as well as great instability. Unemployed mercenaries roamed the countryside, turning to banditry in the absence of a war to fight. This would happen every time there was a lull in the war as well as after the war. Farms had been burned during the war—by both sides—and trade was disrupted, causing food shortages across France, if not actual famine. England was spared many of these consequences simply because the entirety of The Hundred Years War was fought on French soil [42].

However, by the end of the Black Plague, England was suffering from labor shortages which put pressure on the entire economy. Noble landowners wanted the same amount of revenue from their lands as they'd enjoyed before. This desire was only aggravated because they had a war to fight, which cost them money and made their revenue priorities high. They had fewer people to pay rents, and so they raised them. In turn, the serfs demanded higher wages so they could feed their families. The lords responded like any day corporation might when the bottom line starts falling—they froze wages. But while a corporation can simply declare a wage freeze, a feudal lord had to have a law passed. Thus, Parliament passed the Statute of Laborers in 1351. Wages were frozen, now by law, at those paid in 1346. Abruptly, peasants were again facing a food shortage, this one of government make, as the rents either remained high or increased. The common man could not adequately feed his family, and the nobles demanded more work than ever out of their peasants. When the government's next move was to impose new, higher taxes to pay for their war, thus all but insuring the inability to pay for food, the peasants rebelled [43]. The rebellion eventually failed, but would pave the way for 15th century reforms, as did the failed Jacquerie in France.

Whether you call it a food riot, a rebellion, a civil war, or a War for Independence, people will ultimately rise up when their ability to feed themselves is threatened, especially if the government or big businesses have any hand in the problem. The outcomes of such resistances can result in anything from heads on pikes and a crackdown by the state to a new era of freedom and prosperity. But along the way, many more people lose their lives, adding to the butcher's bill that gets rung up when food grows scarce.

Asia

The Middle Ages did not spare Asia their share of hunger either, and China and Japan both provide interesting case studies. A famine led China into an uprising of its own in 875–884, and Japan faced what was potentially the harshest famine in their history, the Kangi Famine, which occurred from 1229–1232. Both of these famines provide a different sort of case study from those we've seen before. In the discussion of these famines, you will see the worst of what humans have to offer from those who seek to exploit misery for their own gains, the best of what humans have to offer from surprisingly noble and noteworthy leadership, and the grim decisions that good people sometimes make in an attempt to spare human lives, decisions that have ramifications for decades after.

The most significant feature of the Chinese famine of 875–884 is less the famine itself (other than to mark the presence of yet another period of starvation in human history) and more the opportunities the famine offered to one ruthless individual, a man known as Huang Chao. The son of a wealthy salt merchant, Huang Chao came dangerously close to becoming the new Emperor of China, weakened the Tang dynasty to the point of collapse 50 years later, and changed the course of Chinese history [44].

The famine itself was a weather famine, caused by droughts. Yet it also drained the capability of the government to handle other forms of crisis. Poverty created numerous bandit gangs. The weak government and the ranks of the bandits provided Huang with the chance he needed to strike. He gathered the bandit gangs into an army of his own, if a particularly undisciplined and rapacious one. As Harold Miles Tanner would report in his *China: a History*, Huang had, in fact, tried to take the civil service examinations several times, ultimately failing. Tanner marked this as a significant departure from many other rebellions and uprisings in times of food shortage and economic trouble in that Huang "was not a poor peasant, but rather a man who had sought fame and power through legitimate channels before rising in rebellion" [45]. This time, it was the frustrated ambitions of one man, rather than the hungry bellies of the many, that brought about rebellion. Hungry bellies just gave Huang all the tools he needed.

The point of famine's indirect butcher's bill remains, however. In Guangzhou, Huang ultimately turned his troops loose to slaughter 120,000 of the city's 200,000 residents. The reason was petty. Huang demanded a governor's post from the imperial government. They offered a lesser position. If they were in for the penny of negotiating with Huang, they might as well have gone for the whole pound and let him have his wishes; his sights were certainly lower than "Emperor" at that point and the entire affair might have stopped there. Instead, they enraged him and spurred him to continue his bloody campaign.

Huang Chao took his army north to Chang'an, the capital city. The Emperor fled, and he occupied the city. At that point, he was very close to founding his own dynasty, and had God, fate, chance, or just plain human nature not intervened, the Huang Dynasty might well have followed the Tang. But he lost control of his forces, who looted and destroyed the city. He lost any legitimacy he might have been able to claim, both with the common man and the officials and administrators, that he would have needed to set up his imperial government. A capital city without the support of the provinces does not an Emperor make, and soon Huang would face the very situation he'd taken such advantage of: grain shortages [46]. In time, he was driven out of Chang'an, hunted down, and killed. But he'd done his damage [5]. Decades later the Tang dynasty failed entirely, China split, and the Five Dynasties and Ten Kingdoms period began.

Famines often open the way for coups. The Russian Famine of 1916-1917, for example, brought on two of them, one for the parliamentarian provisional government and one for the Bolsheviks who took control just eight months later [47]. This example is offered not to deviate from the time period or geographical region at hand, but merely to point out that this is not some ancient, Middle Ages phenomena or Chinese phenomena that could never happen again. A significant enough famine or food shortage in America could, in fact, end the United States as we know it, and the dominos could fall in any number of directions.

If Huang Chao's rebellion demonstrates what famine and poor leadership can do to a country, the Kangi Famine in Japan demonstrates how good reason can rise to the occasion. Though the aristocracy of Japan was unable to keep 30% of the population from falling to the worst famine in Japan's history, they nevertheless performed admirably under the pressure, with a care and concern for their people that is a wonderful example for leaders everywhere. Though they made a particularly grim decision in their attempts to save lives, it will be clear that they did so with feeding the hungry in mind, rather than taking advantage of a desperate people.

In the 1200s, heavy winds, heavy rains, hail, frost, and drought often led to crop failures and regional famines. In 1225, these turned particularly bad. Heavy rains hammered the countryside for three more years, and in 1228 a typhoon destroyed most of the homes in Kamakura. Another drought in 1229 brought on full scale famine. The weather at one point turned so sour and atypical that the Japanese experienced snow in summer [48].

The crop failures were massive enough that entire estates were producing nothing at all. Nobleman and poet Fujiwara Taika began pulling up his decorative gardens to plant wheat for the poor, writing, "Even though it is only a little bit, its purpose is to support the hungry during this awful year. One shouldn't insult the poor. Is there something else I can do?" [49]. Indeed, the question of whether or not more could be done seems, by the actions of the nobility of the period, to have weighed heavily on the minds of most of the ruling class.

Hojo Yasutoki, the leader of the Kamakura Shogunate, began immediately pressuring the wealthy to lend money to the poor in order to keep them alive as early as 1229. Many of the nobles began conferring over possible action, but, in spite of their best efforts, the streets were still littered with the dead by 1231, and typhoons and rain continued to beat away any hope of recovery. Civil chaos began to rear its ugly head. The farming class began asking for tax relief or simply allowed their taxes to slide into arrears. Overzealous tax collectors in the warrior class at times abused their privileges to the point where entire estates worth of cultivators would wind up fleeing from their blades. Mobs began breaking into the homes of the wealthy, and, after eating their fill, walked away with any rice or cash they could find [50]. In direct contrast to how matters normally go, the nobility, the wealthiest and most powerful of the people, continued to display concern and fairness for all of their people even as they tried to keep order. As William Wayne Farris would report in his *Japan's Medieval Population: Famine, Fertility and Warfare in a Transitional Age*:

> *The shogunate wrote more laws trying to ensure order in 1232...it issued a directly to newly established land stewards exhorting them to take only their due from peasants, whether it was rice, labor, or other items...the warrior council ordered its men to strengthen their enforcement of provisions against robbery and night attacks... Members of the chief decision making body, the hyojo shu, signed an oath swearing to conduct administrative matters without taking personal advantage of the crisis...In Kyoto [the court] attempted to place a ceiling on the price of rice. The court also doled out grain relief*

(shingo)...in 1232 aristocrats demanded...that wheat no longer be provided to horses and cattle for foder...Kyoto re-issued an older law limiting the interest on loans (suiko) to the amount of the principal.

If Kyoto provided more frequent economic aid to the hungry, Kamakura made the most spectacular gesture. In fact, the first act taken by Yasutoki, the de facto head of the bafuku, was to issue a call to "virtuous rule," (tokuse rei). On the nineteenth of the third month in 1231 he had wealthier persons in charge of the warehouses in his home provinces... open their doors and lend rice to the peasantry. He guaranteed the wealthy repayment with his own resources if his beneficiaries died or fled. Eventually, the Hojo leader enacted similar legislation. [51]

It's also worth noting that, in direct contrast to English or French peasants, Japanese peasants basically had legal freedom of movement so long as their taxes were paid up. So if the local samurai were harsh or unfair, workers who weren't in arrears could just move on, a phenomenon which acted as a check against the power of the feudal lords.

So in this regard, the Kangi Famine provides an object lesson for those who are in positions of power. It is possible for power to be wielded in a virtuous manner, with care taken for and towards the value of human life. The impetus is on us to choose such leaders, or, if we ourselves are in a position of leadership, to take the concept of "tokuse rei" to heart. Note that this is not a call to socialism or a welfare state. Even the benevolent aristocrats in Japan issued loans, which the beneficiaries had an obligation to repay, under fair terms, once the crisis had passed. There were, however, loans issued without regard for ability to repay and without resorting to exploitation of the needy and the desperate. Responsible citizens who survived the famine would repay when things got better. The rulers were prepared to absorb the results of those who did not or could not repay. Work, however, was still expected of the able-bodied in every strata of society, and while there was no upward mobility, there was at least enough lateral mobility to stave off the kinds of abuses seen in European feudalism.

Yet even the best of leaders have hard choices to make during times of darkness, and not all of the countermeasures taken by the nobility were quite so positive.

This period of time also saw the legalization of the sale of human beings. A family faced with starvation might choose to sell children or other kin into servitude; both the seller and the sold would then get enough to eat as a result. This sort of behavior had been going on illegally for centuries, but the Kangi famine was serious enough for the nobility to legitimize it in the hopes of saving more lives by spreading starving victims around to those who could take care of them. They intended to abrogate the laws after the famine, and indeed tried to, but they were unsuccessful in doing so [52].

This negative outcome stayed with the Japanese for centuries after the famine, and it provides yet another object lesson. Slavery has often arisen from circumstances where people were unable to feed themselves, and so they sacrificed their rights and freedoms to work, be fed, housed, and clothed in a wealthy household. Though this *can* be a perfectly benevolent arrangement, no more abusive than an employer to an employee (as expressed by some of the Biblical households with slaves), the potential for abuse and the eventual widespread increase of human misery is inherent to such a system. A crisis of this magnitude brings an increase of human trafficking due to lawlessness and desperation alike, and some arrangements amount to slavery without ever being *called* slavery. Thus it is imperative for freedom loving people to watch the signs and prepare, if they wish, to avoid this potential fate for themselves and their children: legal or illegal, named or unnamed, initially willing or coerced.

The Americas

Famine was no less a determinant of history in the Americas of the Middle Ages than anywhere else in the world. In the time between 800 AD and 1500 AD famine would spark the fall of two civilizations, spark the migration of another, and influence the expansion and warfare of a third.

Two of these will get only brief mention. A famine in 800 AD to 1000 AD triggered a series of events that ultimately led to the fall of the Mayan civilization [53]. There's more to say about them, of course, but the scope of events was rather complex, enough to make it unsuitable for this brief overview. The second case, the migration of the Toltecs, only gets brief mention because there's so little information. We know famine is what drove the Toltecs into central Mexico, but not much more [54].

The longer case studies begin with the Anasazi people. The Anasazi were the first pueblo builders, and they had a society that was almost analogous to the ancient Greeks. They were spread out across Utah, Arizona, New Mexico and Colorado in an area known as the Four Corners, and had been spread out long enough to begin developing individualized groups, each with a local cultural flavor, cultures that the local people were much more attached to than the idea of the Anasazi as a whole. In the same way that one would view ancient Greeks as being more properly from Athens or Sparta than from anything called "Greece," you could view the Anasazi as being the people from the Chaco Canyon or the people from Mesa Verde. In point of fact, "Anasazi" is a Navajo word, and there's no evidence whatsoever that the Anasazi themselves ever used it to refer to themselves [55]. Still, they were affiliated enough to be considered a single group in the same manner that we mean all of the ancient Greek cities when we say "ancient Greece."

Drought swept through the Four Corners region as early as 1130, but the advent of the 1200s and the years just before had amounted to what archaeologists call a "mega drought" [56]. This sparked a wide scale famine across the region that was complicated by a number of other factors, as Eric Skopec mentions in his *The Anasazi Guide*:

> *Worse yet, the years prior to the drought had been uncommonly Productive, and the Anasazi population had grown substantially. Wild plants and animals were no longer sufficient to support the people, even under the best of circumstances. And circumstances were far from good during the drought. Plants died or ceased producing seeds, and animals fell victim as well, or escaped to areas less affected.* [57]

This famine was severe enough that archaeologist found evidence of the old specter of famine-based cannibalism. A paleoanthropologist named Tim White proved this after an exhaustive forensic analysis of 2,106 bone fragments from an obscure Anasazi pueblo. He even discovered evidence of some of those remains having been cooked [58].

Yet it was not the starvation or even the cannibalism which led to the eventual, total downfall of the Anasazi as a people. As famine conditions grew worse, large groups of Anasazi began trying to move to better areas, which meant they ended up in the territory of other Anasazi. They were not welcomed. Open warfare broke out between groups. By the time it was all over, 75% of the population had simply disappeared, falling victim to starvation, pestilence, or warfare. The other 25% abandoned the area, settling elsewhere, and becoming known by other names [59].

Many people assume that modern Americans are not particularly vulnerable to drought conditions. There's a tendency to believe we are far too advanced to face any problem that might have plagued people of other times. But a casual glance at some headlines disputes the notion.

December 18, 2010 Shreveport Times
Drought Hurts Crops, Cattle

January 3, 2011 Bloomberg
Wheat Advances as Dry Weather in U.S.
Threatens to Hurt Crops

January 5, 2011 KOAA Colorado Springs
Local Grocery Stores will Weather Florida Freeze,
Texas Drought

Though it's hard to imagine the population of Los Angeles turning on the population of Phoenix because the people from Phoenix tried to cram into Los Angeles for food, one must remember that chaos is quite capable of breaking out and the dominos could indeed fall in any direction. Again and again, history teaches us that we have every reason to take famines and things which can lead to famine very seriously indeed.

The Aztecs provide another interesting case study in their famine of 1450-1454. In spite of the fact that the wealthy generally fare better in a drought than the common people, there have been famines in the world where even the elite class have been among the starving. The Aztec famine of 1450 is one such case. The government was forced to make some major changes just to maintain the respect of the people. Aztec historian David Carrasco describes the social impacts of this famine in his book, *Quetzalcoatal and the Irony of Empire: Myths and Prophecies in the Aztec Tradition.*

Accustomed to living in a state of high luxury, the royal elite and the meritoriously elite faced the humiliating necessity of changing their lifestyles. The famine was a tremendous blow to the entire society, which had been deeply involved for decades in preventing such a shortage of food and goods. Now, at the supposed apex of Aztec history the entire population was looking starvation and disaster in the face—for the upper class a radical reversal of their access to quality goods seemed necessary. In this situation, a crisis of confidence developed in parts of the population, and more oppressive measures were employed against tributary communities.

As an antidote to the crisis, the office of tlatoani and the person of Monctezuma were elevated to the new, more inaccessible rung on the ladder, the rung of full divinity. Previously the temporary successor to the king-god Quetzalcoatl of Tollan, Monctezuma now became a king-god in his own right. The accounts of Diaz de Castillo and Cortes both contain descriptions of the protocol around Monctezuma in which people were not allowed to gaze on him or eat with the divine ruler. [60]

Rulers have declared themselves to be gods before; it was a strategy adopted by Roman Emporers and Egyptian Pharoahs alike. However, simply declaring a thing would not make the people accept it. The element of fear has to be added to such a bold claim; increasing the level of oppression on the common people was not, ultimately, enough. The Aztec elite needed some other leverage to quiet the loss of confidence. They'd find their answers in the superstitions and fears of their people.

The Aztecs are known for their human sacrifice, but what are less well known are the reasons why. The Aztecs believed that human life energy was required to make the cosmos continue in its perfect working order: without doing so, the sun would not rise, the stars would misalign, and monsters whose coming would bring about the end of the world would pour out of a hole in the sky. The victims were thought to be rewarded with places in paradises designed by the gods they were sacrificed to [61]. So they spread the story—which in truth they may even have believed themselves—that the famine had come because the gods had not had enough blood. More sacrifices were necessary to restore the cosmic order.

Having effectively declared himself a mouthpiece for the gods, Monctezuma now accomplished a shift in the blame. It was not the leaders who had failed, but the people as a whole who had displeased the gods. He offered a remedy, and as fearful people so often do, the Aztecs leaped on it. Having such a remedy restored a sense of control to the people. This was followed in turn by direct action:

> *The sovereigns of Mexico, Texcoco and Tlaqpan, and the lords of Tlaxcalen, Vexotzinco and Cholula mutually agreed that, there being no war, they would arrange combats, so the captives might be sacrificed to the gods...Fighting was primarily a means of taking prisoners, on the battlefield the warriors did their utmost to kill as few men as possible. War was not merely a political instrument, it was above all a religious rite, a war of holiness.* [62]

Such a series of events leads one to believe how our own government might respond if their own power was threatened by such a famine—or what opportunity the famine might cause for them. Though we no longer believe monsters will leap out of the sky and eat us, we have an entire priest class of scientists and media people who are willing to spill out a multitude of data. Much of that data is contradictory, and the data that is accepted by the people and on which policy rests often amounts to the data that has received the best P.R., simply because few people have the skills to critically evaluate exactly what they are seeing or being told. Global climate change, for example, whether warming or cooling, may very well be a fact. After all, climate changes across the globe caused many of the crop failures and famines we've looked at so far. However, the cause – in this case, that man is a pollutant and a cancer on the earth – has been attractively packaged and mass produced by the media, to the point where some people are literally calling for the sacrifice of lives to lower the population and "save the planet," just as if the planet will stop turning or suddenly crumble if we don't voluntarily cull our own numbers. While many modern people would be quick to shudder in revulsion at the thought of an Aztec priest plunging his knife into the heart of a victim, there are entire voting blocks of people who really don't think terribly differently. They simply *think* they think differently. What one-two punch of Science as God Priesthood and Government Control could result? Martial law? Forced abortions?

The murder of our grandparents for the crime of getting sick? Mass sterilization of any population deemed to be "undesirable?" Think well.

1.4 Famine in the 17th and 18th Century

ℵ○ • ℭℜ

Though there were plenty of famines in the 16th century, they were relatively small by comparison. More major famines picked up again in the 17th century. For many of them, the stories of misery are much the same as you've seen in other famines: stories of people dead in the street, of people eating people, of wars and revolutions sparked. There are some interesting case studies to share, but there is one other facet of history as it relates to famines that is of extreme noteworthiness, because we continue to feel its effects all over the world today. This is the rise of Malthusian thought in the 18th and, through Malthus' continued work, on into the 19th century. Two other philosophies would rise up to combat it, philosophies that were far more reasonable and humane, but sadly the words of Thomas Robert Malthus continues to guide many of our leaders in government, business, and the media even today, and thus, in turn, public policies. As important as it is to trace the historical effects or blunders of famines and search for parallels to our own current state, it is equally important to understand how these tragedies impacted conversations that are still being held today, and which, in some regard, are at war for the hearts and minds of the men and women who will act on them.

Noteworthy Famines of the Period

A famine in Russia in 1601–1603 would spark the Time of Troubles, a 12 year period of civil war that swept across the nation. One of the most interesting facets of this case study is not the famine itself, but the spotted picture that it paints of Emperor Boris Godunov. On one hand you see great acts of generosity; on the other, you see him blocking actions that could have saved many more of his people. The picture that gets put together when three different accounts are compared is a picture of a ruler with very little support acting almost desperately to receive it, but fearful of anything that might have weakened him, painting a striking picture of the lives of a populace used as pawns of a usurper who was rapidly losing his grip.

Boris defeated rival aristocrats in order to become tsar, but many questioned the legitimacy of his claims. Among other things, Emperor Boris was accused of killing Ivan the Terrible's son, Dimitrii, in order to end the ancient dynasty and clear his own path to the throne. The famine only served to make Boris look less and less legitimate [63]. There's evidence to suggest that at least some of the population looked at the famine as a Biblical style punishment of the people for their ruler's sins and refusal to repent or humble himself before God.

In an attempt to either stave the tide of death or to save his reputation in the eyes of the people, Boris began distributing alms to the poor of Moscow and sending vast amounts of money and relief to Russian villages, to the point of draining his own treasury by the time the three year period had ended. This strategy backfired, however. People from the countryside came pouring into the capital in the hopes of receiving money. Some who had been able to support themselves in the countryside came anyway, and found that they could not support themselves in the city after all. This led to 120,000 dead in the streets of Moscow, each of them being carted off to special burials, a bill which also came out of the treasury. Boris stopped this when it became abundantly clear that he was depopulating the countryside only for people to come and die in the cities. A French soldier in the employ of the Russian Army named Jacques Margeret remarked, "besides the disbursement that was made in Moscow, there was not a town in all of Russia to which Boris did not contribute something for the poor" [64].

Boris also made cheap grain available. Unfortunately, this, too, backfired. In *The Disturbed State of the Russian Realm*, Conrad Bussow and George Edward Orchard wrote:

> *But even though all this was done, the devil of avarice, through the will of God, so prompted the Muscovite grain speculators to take advantage of the situation that they persuaded poor people to buy up cheap grain for them from the tsar, boyars, and monasteries, which afterwards they resold at greatly inflated prices.* [65]

It's said that God sees the heart, and as similar as these strategies may, on the surface, appear to the Japanese rulers of the Kangi famine, they were an abject failure. One interpretation is simply Boris' lack of support—the Japanese aristocracy had all pulled together on their famine, but Boris appeared to be more or less acting alone, with, perhaps, the help of the monasteries. Another interpretation is that God truly did see the heart, and noted that Boris was not, in particular, really out for the welfare of his people. The clue is in this passage from Bussow and Orchard:

> *And even though God in his mercy saw to it that some ships came from the coastal cities to Russian Narva...which could have fed some hundreds of thousands of people, Boris could not countenance such a disgrace, that grain from foreign countries should be bought and sold in this country, so rich in grain, and so ships turned around and put out to sea without selling their grain. Nobody was permitted to buy a single ton of grain, on pain of corporal punishment.* [66]

Whatever the reasons behind Boris' actions, however, he was not to continue for long. After three years of depleting the treasury he had little to help him when, in 1604, a small army marched on the capital. At its head was a man claiming to be Tsarevich Dimitrii, somehow saved from Boris Godunov's alleged plot to kill him. Many towns, fortresses and soldiers happily threw in their lot with this army, and the first popular uprising against a tsar began [67].

Other famines of the period are notable primarily for their horrifying death tolls. In India, the Deccan Famine of 1630–1631 would wipe out 2 million people. Between 1708–1711 a famine in East Prussia would take down 41% of that population. Between 1738–1756, one half of the population of Timbuktu fell prey to catastrophic hunger, as well [68]. Large numbers don't help anyone understand human costs, however, so in order to do so simply imagine your neighborhood right this moment, then imagine half of the houses standing empty because everyone who used to live in them is dead.

The other famine case study has a famous noblewoman's words attached to it. The French famine of 1788 sparked the French revolution, and is often casually associated with Marie Antoinette's careless or ignorant famous last words: "Let them eat cake."

The famine of 1788 began as many do: with crop failures and rising prices. Riots for bread weren't even an uncommon sight before 1788; therefore, the government of France requisitioned grain from the countryside and regulated the sale of bread. The system was elaborate—so elaborate, in fact, that the slightest disruption caused shortages. A real shortage, caused by massive crop failure, couldn't help but cause a famine. This problem was exacerbated by just how much of the average worker's wage was spent on bread alone. Any worker could expect to spend 50% of his wages on food. In 1788 this figure rose to 58%. By 1789, workers were spending a staggering 88% of their wages on food alone. The economy failed and entire industries closed down simply because nobody could afford to buy anything else. Free trade with England had exacerbated this because the British provided textiles at prices significantly lower than any French company could match, leading to even more unemployment [69].

It's tough to imagine, isn't it? We spend about 10%-15% of our wages on food right now, on average [70]. Try to imagine half of your income going to nothing but your groceries. Then 75%. Then nearly everything you make. Imagine the sense of desperation as you find yourself unable to provide anything else for your family. Clothing? Shelter? Shoes? Impossible. That said, we can all identify with jobs going overseas due to cheaper prices, to people in India offering services at prices we could not possibly compete with. We're seeing our own economic downturn as a result right now. Meanwhile, the elite seem to be doing just fine, even profiting from the misery. It is dry straw waiting for someone to drop a match.

The French Revolution is important as a case study for more than the ways it changed the French political structure and as more than a triumph of democracy. It gives us hints, for example, as to how a global food crisis might fall out. In many ways, we study the French Revolution and the famine that sparked it as an individual food event that created a class war, particularly when grain speculators got wealthy off of the rise in prices. But there's some interesting global data from 1788 that is worth paying attention to:

William Roxburgh and Alexander Beatson, Scottish scientists who lived at the time of the French Revolution, compiled environmental data collected by ship captains and the East India Company clerks.

Their reports show disorderly weather and starvation across the globe. In Egypt, three successive years of low floods plunged the Middle East into famine. In Mexico, a prolonged drought dried up much of Lake Patzcuaro that farmers squabbled over the rich land unmatched by the receding waters. Off the coast of Peru, the surge in the El Nino current devastated fish stocks and parched coastal farms. [71]

In other words, had the world been in the same state of global inter-dependent economy that our world is in today, the violence of the Revolution could have swept across the world. What touched off the revolution was as much a rumor about the reasons for the high price of bread and grain as it was the fact that the nobility continued to eat well while the working class starved. In short, people came to believe that the famine was planned by the elite, by design, so that they could continue to profit off of artificial scarcity [72]. In this day and age, a rumor like that could spread around the world at the speed of light, carrying the capacity to touch off violence across the globe.

Does this seem far-fetched? You might be surprised to realize that we nearly saw this very scenario play out worldwide back in 2008. Evan D.G. Fraiser and Andrew Rimas spun a vivid picture of this close call in their 2010 book *Empires of Food: Feast, Famine, and the Rise and Fall of Civilization*:

None of the world's developed countries took fright during the food riots of 2008. In the West, we don't normally empty our pockets when we buy groceries. A typical household spends about 10% of its income on foodstuffs, so a rise in prices by 50% means we would only be committed to spending 15% of our weekly budget on daily provender. But in poorer countries, where families may spend half their income to keep body and soul together, the same price hike of 50% would be disproportionate, costing the family 50% of their money. The most troubling fact in the 2008 crisis was that the year's harvest was one of the best since the agricultural revolution, with record crops of American maize, Asian rice, and African cassava. Supply was not a problem. So when fuel prices subsided towards the end of 2008 and economic recession cooled the markets, food prices floated down to less

painful levels and the rioting stopped...What would have happened
if the 2008 harvest had failed? Prices wouldn't have subsided, nor
would the rioter's fury. [73]

The complex social and political factors that govern the distribution and sale of
food around the world guarantee that even an increase in food supply does not
guarantee that people will not go hungry. And much as we might cheer on those
who resist oppressors, fight for their freedom, and press for accountability from
their leaders, the flipside is a bloody, chaotic, dangerous time that would create a
frightening world to raise a family in, and in which there are no guarantees.

The Philosophies of Hunger

Against the backdrop of famines and social chaos around the world, it is natural
enough that the learned men of the 18th century would start attempting to
deconstruct the problems in the hopes of preventing more. Though several
philosophers were egalitarian and freedom loving in their interpretation of the
ways that famines could be reduced or eliminated, it's undeniable that some
very dark philosophies made their way into popular consciousness, where they
remain even today. Primarily, these ideas began with Thomas Robert Malthus,
author of *An Essay on the Principle of Population as it Affects the Future*
Improvement on Society, with Remarks on the Speculation of Mr. Godwin,
Mr. Condercet, and other Writers, written in 1798. His arguments should be
familiar to any 21st century reader as they've been passed down, repeated, and
forged into policy across the globe. In short, Malthus believed that populations
would always increase to a breaking point where it would overcome the available
resources. At that point, famines, wars, pestilences and disaster would bring the
population back down to manageable levels in a never-ending cycle.

Had Malthus stopped there his paper would not have been either surprising
or terrible. A brief study of history such as the one we've conducted here does
indeed suggest that things run in cycles for nations and people; there are good
times and there are bad times, times when the weather brings good harvests and
times when it does not, times of famine and times of plenty. There is nothing
inherently sinister about stating the fact, nor is there anything inherently sinister

in admitting that, at times, different nations have faced a population-to-production problem. The question is "what shall we do about it," and it is in the "what shall we do about it" portion that Malthus created a dark monster.

First, he suggested that there was a point that all of humanity would be destroyed if the population was not brought down to more "manageable" levels. He predicted, without any evidence whatsoever, that in 300 more years—somewhere around 2098—the world ratio of people to food would be roughly 4,000 to 13. This inspired a rather panicked picture of an entire world swallowed up in darkness and chaos, where nobody at all would enjoy any kind of plenty or peace—basically, an apocalyptic scenario far out of scope to the actual famines that have come upon the earth, which often last as little as one year or as much as seven or ten years, but which do eventually end. Often, the longer famines are perpetuated by human problems, not issues with the soil, production, or weather.

So in order to keep his fictional destruction from swooping down upon the human race, Malthus suggested that the poor and laboring class people should be prevented from having children. Furthermore, certain disasters should be *deliberately engineered* to get rid of the poor, the needy, the week, and the "undesirable." For example, he openly spoke of cultivating plague as the good, right, and moral thing to do. "Instead of recommending cleanliness to the poor," he wrote, "we should encourage contrary habits. In our towns, we should make the streets narrower, crowd more people into the houses, and court the return of plague. In the country, we should build our villages near stagnant pools, and particularly encourage settlements in all marshy and unwholesome situations" [74]. He also advocated the killing of illegitimate newborns.

In a saner world, Malthus' theories and recommendations would have been dismissed as the cruel ravings of a deranged madman. But they began receiving support, instead. In part, this was a result of the French Revolution, and a certain amount of fear that the "elite classes" were beginning to feel towards the poor. This was also because his theories relieved them of all responsibility towards the poor. A number of movements rest on Malthusian principles, so the fact that there is no scientific basis for them whatsoever makes his work all the more tragic. For example, at the time Malthus wrote there was no data regarding population increases at his disposal. The first national census in Great Britain was carried out in 1801, *three years after* Malthus wrote his *Essay*. In any case, in order for Malthus to calculate *growth* he would have needed statistics for years *prior* to 1801, as well. Malthus also had no data whatsoever to actually calculate the growth of any food resources. At the time, there·was no way of calculating how much land was under cultivation nor how many crops produced [75].

Fortunately, there were other, saner philosophers during the day, and if all of them had begun to worry about population, they did not all come to the same conclusions. In point of fact, Godwin and Condercet, mentioned in the title of Malthus' essay, were opponents of the Malthusian philosophy and offered much different interpretations to the problem of hunger.

Malthus and other writers of the day acknowledged a fairly simple fact—a single acre of land can produce more food if put to the growing of vegetables than the growth of meat. William Godwin then concluded that the proper response to a growing population would be to voluntarily give up beef in order to feed more people, and not to limit the population as he believed that more people led to more happiness. Godwin had his own share of followers just as Malthus, who was not willing to even consider giving up his beef, and those followers adopted his strategy of willingly abandoning meat in favor of a vegetarian diet. The Marquis de Condercet, by contrast, believed that nobody had to give up anything—neither human lives nor meat—but that technology would surely mean that there was plenty of everything for all in the end [76].

All three of these philosophies survive into this day, and have impacted people's opinions, policies, and beliefs. China follows extremely Malthusian policies, for example, with its one child limits and the fact that the Chinese will ruthlessly kill babies born to parents who have already met their quotas [77]. Godwin's argument is echoed by vegetarians as a reason to turn to a vegetarian or vegan diet—often much to the fury of dedicated carnivores who believe that a failure to eat meat can actually lead one to be weak and sick. And for many, faith in technology reigns supreme. However one feels about the feasibility or desirability of a vegetarian diet, or a faith in technology, one can be thankful that there were at least some restraining, compassionate voices among Malthus' peers. And in a time of famine, food shortage, or rising prices, meat and dairy are often the first substances to end up out of reach for the average person.

1.5 Famine in the 19th Century

$\mathcal{EO} \bullet \mathcal{CR}$

Debate over the proper way to handle a crowded population and food shortages raged clear into the 19th century. Charles Darwin, for example, was influenced by Malthus to an alarming degree. His theories, too, received support even into the 21st century and still influence human thought today. A fusing of Malthusianism and Darwinism formed the philosophy of Social Darwinism—the idea that the "survival of the fittest" could be applied to human society as a rationale for any sort of cruelty or neglect towards fellow human beings unable to prevent it through wealth, power, or strength [78]. The cruel philosophy of eugenics—the idea that we should actively breed out "undesirable" people by forced sterilization or mass murder—followed. Normally associated with the Nazi movement, eugenics made its way into the United States and was even actively supported by churches and courts for a time. We would need another entire book to cover the abuses, atrocities, and murderous practices of people who would espouse such a philosophy, believing that they are somehow better, more human, or more worthy than others. All it takes to reject such an unfeeling philosophy is some basic modicum of human compassion and empathy.

In the meantime, in spite of all theories, the course of famine marched on. Nothing Malthus or Darwin had to say stopped it, in spite of an increase in human misery and death that reverberating down the centuries. The only difference was, now, powerful people who espoused such philosophies looked on such occurrences with glee, believing that the race was getting stronger, and a future of steak and wine awaited those left.

Two case studies are worth paying attention to from this century. First, the Irish Potato Famine of 1845–1852, which led to a large influx of Irish immigrants to the United States, greatly impacting our history. There is also the Bihar Famine of India in 1873-1874, a famine which represents a rare relief success story and offers a bit of hope after discussing such grim subjects as Malthusianism and eugenics.

The Irish Potato Famine

The Irish Potato Famine makes a good case study due to the massive influx of immigrants that fled to America. It also helps to show the folly of the "one crop farm," a folly our own agricultural system has been following for some time. It's also interesting because laws and policies directly impacted the famine—from the English imposed Irish property law that set the conditions of the Irish lifestyle, to an oppressive government that continued to exploit a populace while profiting off their misery. It also shows the direct influence of Malthus and his Social Darwinist cronies in terms of the death and misery of millions of people, an unacknowledged Malthusian genocidal holocaust of epic proportions. Everybody knows about Hitler. Few people know about the British Minister of Famine Relief that coldly asserted, in essence, that Ireland should be left to starve "for its own good," in order to assure its eventual "quiet" and "prosperity" [79]. An *Economist* writer named Nassau Senior lamented that the famine would "only" kill about a million people, too few to "do any good" [80].

Though there is some debate about the legal and social causes for the Irish Potato famine, the physical causes are well-documented and well-understood. The potato crops were struck by the prolific fungus *P. Infestans* during a year of fungus-favoring hot, humid weather, which in turn caused potatoes to rot quickly [81]. The effects were immediate, stark, and grim:

> *Potatoes rotted in the fields and in the storehouses. In 1845, the potato harvest was reduced by about a third because of this pathogen, and the following years were even worse. The poor, so completely dependent on one species, were devastated. Many tried to eat what appeared to be the less damaged parts of the potatoes, and got sick. Many tried to separate the rotten parts and make flour or porridge out of the other parts, and got sick. Many resorted to wild herbs and seaweed as alternative food sources, and starved.* [82]

With such a variety of foods on the supermarket shelves, it's extremely difficult for the 21st century reader to understand why this problem was so pervasive. When this famine is called the "Potato Famine," one may have images of there simply being no potatoes, of a people who just had to go out and buy some other kind of food. The key to understanding this is to understand there was no other food. In part, this was a result of the way the British Empire had been managing the country, creating a severe legal issue that caught up to the Irish at last.

In feudal Britain, the eldest son inherited the family farm. Younger sons went to cities, joined the army, or entered the clergy; daughters were married off. Although this practice had high social costs, there were also benefits: British farms were kept together as they passed the generations. With larger tracts, British farmers could safely diversify their crops and experiment with new ones.

*The British applied a different law in Ireland. Small farms were physically subdivided among all male heirs. Average farm size thus shrank from generation to generation. By the early nineteenth century, many Irish farms were so small they could barely support a family, and then **only if they grew potatoes**, the crop that provided the maximum nutritional payoff per acre. With just one viable crop, Irish farmers were particularly vulnerable to environmental shocks and disease.* [83]

The problem would have been solvable with a few changes in legislation. In truth, that problem needed to have been solved before *P. Infestans* arrived and rendered most people's farms useless tracts of dirt.

Crop diversification is a major issue for us, as well. Most of our farms only produce one crop at a time, in a direct break from older farming traditions. There are multiple reasons why one-crop farming is a concern and a potential factor that could play into the overall famine soup that's threatening our world and nation.

Not only does this practice exhaust a particular group of soil nutrients, but it invariably leads to more reliance on chemical fertilizers and an eventual semi-sterilization of the land. Then, too, it causes the famer to "put all his eggs in one basket," with the certainty that he must throw himself on the charity of taxpayers and rely on the government getting him loans from the federal treasury to continue in his ill-conceived folly.

Seldom do one-crop farmers grow vegetable gardens, maintain fruit trees, or raise chickens and hogs to supplement the family food supply. [84]

The Irish Potato Famine provides us with an excellent picture of how a government can cause a famine through oppression and indifference. The British ruling class opted to blame the Irish themselves for the famine, saying they were "slovenly" and painted a picture of unintelligent savages too stupid to prevent this from happening, people who were less than animals and did not deserve to be saved. The effects on the population of Ireland were stunning and long lasting; "approximately one third of the country's people died or moved away. Afterward, Ireland's population continued to drop until as recently as the 1990s. Today, more than 150 years later, Ireland's population is approximately half of what it was before the Great Famine" [85]. Meanwhile, the survivors who chose to flee the country flooded into America, permanently bringing a touch of Ireland to our culture. And if their arrival sparked acts of racism and contempt, they too sparked the creation of new charities and agencies set up to deal with the sudden influx.

The Bihar Famine of 1873–1874

If the twisted legacy of Malthus won the day during the potato famine, the same British Empire created an impressive new version of the famine story in the provinces of Bihar (also spelled Behar) and Bengal in India. However, the success of this story is that there were no famine related deaths during this time whatsoever. Cynically, this might merely have been the result of an Empire's attempts to win over a native population, or there might have been genuine feeling for the people. The results are what matter.

The central character in this case study is a man by the name of Sir Richard Temple, who served as the Lieutenant-Governor of Bengal as the famine began to unfold [86]. He was an extremely careful record keeper and recorded all of his experiences in an autobiography titled *Men and Events of My Time in India* in 1882. He is somewhat dry and matter-of-fact about the entire affair, reducing much of it down to numbers and as an explanation for a budget deficit. Of this famine, he writes:

I had to produce in March 1873 the budget for 1873-4 without an income-tax. The estimates, however, still showed a surplus for the year of a quarter of a million. The surplus would, in this year, as in preceding years, have become a large one, had not a calamity beyond human control supervened. But as the autumn approached it became evident that famine was impending over Bengal and Behar. The Government was obliged to make preparations on a most extensive scale for the relief of the anticipated distress and for preserving the lives of the people from danger. Before the end of the year operations for the prevention of famine were begun throughout a large area. The charges on account of famine relief during the year amounted to £3,864,707, which caused a deficit in the finances of £1,807,668. Had there not been this famine no deficit would have occurred, but on the contrary there would have been a surplus of more than 2 ½ millions...

It may indeed be conceded to the critics that the relief given to the distressed was liberal and unstinted, that the object was to secure effectively the preservation of life, and that for the complete attainment of their object neither expense nor labor was spared. This was the policy which, to the best of our understanding, we were ordered to pursue, and which we unhesitatingly pursued. The object, then, was absolutely attained, a contest with famine was undertaken and was won conclusively. Whether any lesser resistance to so dread an enemy as famine would have sufficed is doubtful... Whether may be the merits or demerits of particular measures, it must be acknowledged that in some instances, large expenditure has been allowed by the State and yet there has been a loss of life. In this instance, the money was liberally spent indeed, but then all the lives were saved. If there are to be great expenses, it is well to be sure of success for the sake not only of the material results but also of the moral advantages. [87]

In the face of these two very different famine stories, we must seek out the "take-aways." That is, we must deduce the lessons that history is teaching us. First, it is clear that governments are fickle. The same government that fed Bihar allowed Ireland to starve. While that presents a case for acknowledging that governmental action is not universally evil or suspect, it also goes to show that governments will tend towards helping those in which they see political or economic advantage. The

Malthusian movement was still very much in full swing. There was, however, a need and a desire to earn the loyalty and trust of the native people of India; in Ireland, with its widespread poverty, there was no such need. But even if we would be led to believe that England learned from its mistakes in 1845, enough to make sweeping changes in policy that saved the lives of the Indian people in 1874, this Tale of Two Famines still demonstrates an important point. In all of the histories we have compiled thus far, there have been two cases in which compassion and competence ruled the day and alleviated suffering: the Kangi Famine and the Bihar Famine. We have seen one famine where reckless, on-the-surface attempts to alleviate suffering simply led to greater deaths. It is telling that only one led to the salvation of all of the people in the affected region. In short, the odds aren't on your side if you're still waiting for the government to open its hands and heart in the event of a dearth.

Given our government's track record, it would be safe to say that even if the Malthusian elements in our own government could be defeated long enough to stop musings about famine-afflicted people dying and reducing the carbon footprint (all for the greater good, of course), the odds are good that at best they'd achieve a Kangi, and at most likely achieve an Emporer Boris, exacerbating the situation still further as they did in their sluggish and fool-hardy responses to Hurricane Katrina in 2005.

The second take-away is this: "forewarned is forearmed." The success at Bihar stems, in part, from the fact that enough people watched the signs and acted on them. Where other famine relief efforts jumped into the fray when the crisis had already begun, in Bihar they began the moment it became evident that one was threatening. And if you cannot inspire your government to such action you must at least inspire yourself.

1.6 Famine in the 20th Century

෨෮ • ෨෮

The increased technological acumen of the Western World, the higher standard of living, and the secret belief that we've moved well past our ancestor's mistakes has led any number of people to declaring that famines are a thing of the past.

Unfortunately, huge, sweeping famines are no more put to rest by the presence of a large one than wars are put to rest by the presence of two World Wars. As we move into our own generations it's difficult to remember that the century we just left not so very long ago saw famines somewhere in every single decade.

There are three, however, that must get special attention. The oppressive regimes of Stalin in Russia and Mao in China provide a wealth of information, as well as spooky echoes of rhetoric even now being repeated by pundits who broadcast from major news outlets. There is also the Great Depression, an unacknowledged famine. While we claim that famine has never touched our shores, millions of people experienced death by starvation during the Depression, a time when big corporate interests actively and unconscionably destroyed food sources for their own economic gain. Here, in all three cases, are specters which cast shadows over America as it moves into the 21st century, shadows that point to rising prices and empty shelves somewhere in our future.

The Great Depression

A large part of our sense of security as modern day Americans comes from the idea that we have *never* seen a famine in our nation. We have a variety of reasons for this: we believe we are unique, we believe our democracy protects us from such things, and we believe that God has and always will bless us more than any other nation. This Chosen One mentality easily falls prey to pretty words and propaganda. When the truth gets swept under the rug, we're happy to see it go. We stubbornly cling to the idea that we are safe. Big Media politely helps us out by putting together movies which show a rather romanticized view of the Great Depression, so that the picture we have of this time in our recent history is one of people having "not much money" but "getting along somehow." Even the poignant, disturbing picture presented by the end of *The Grapes of Wrath*, the quintessential novel of the Great Depression, fails to sink into our consciousness: where a mother who has recently lost her baby leans over to feed, with her own milk, a weak and starving man who is too sick to eat solid food. It's an image that produces a shudder of revulsion for most, and the desire to stop thinking about it as quickly as possible. Yet it also demonstrates courage and altruism between people who are not, in fact, "getting by somehow."

Our high school history books list the October 19, 1929 stock market crash as the reason for the Great Depression. But it cannot be the reason, as stock markets do not simply crash out of the blue, independent of any other reason. The crash was a catalytic event, but not a causal one. Instead, you have to look back through the 20s. A decade of prosperity? People were living large in the 20s, after all. Except that they were living large on *debt* more often than income. The banks and the Federal Reserve created a "massive, credit induced spending binge." Federal Reserve Governor Benjamin Strong called issuing cheap debt to the masses a "little coup de whiskey to the stock market." Any credit bubble like this shall eventually pop, and the banks begin calling in their loans as a result [88]. Spending was down, companies were closing their doors, farms, already suffering due to a drop in food prices, were repossessed. The resulting failure of the banks and the "bank runs" are famous enough images.

Does it sound familiar? Does it sound a bit like the 2008 sub-prime mortgage crash? That's because it's the same old story. One also has to be aware of the fact that sub-prime mortgages weren't the only notes in default. There were sub-prime car loans and all sorts of easily obtained credit cards and personal loans, too. Plenty of banks failed in 2008 as well, but this time the government, fearing another Great Depression, supposedly "bailed out" the biggest banks on behalf of the people. The people were not at all amused when the three trillion dollars went to little more than paying bonuses to bankers, but by the time it became clear that almost none of the bailout money would benefit Main Street, the damage had already been done. Much effort has been spent on trying to make matters appear as if we are nowhere near a Great Depression, including pundits who assure us that recovery is on the way, happening, right around the corner. In the meantime America as a whole is suffering a 9.4% unemployment rate as of January 2011, and the figures do not count those who are under-employed; the working poor who may have jobs but are still unable to support themselves. States that depended on the automobile industry, such as Michigan, are suffering a staggering 15% unemployment. Agencies struggle to keep up with an increased demand for unemployment payments and food stamps. CNN reports that 43 million Americans are now relying on food stamps to put dinner on the table [89]. Charity food pantries remain overwhelmed—largely with the working poor [90].

Tent cities are on the rise, and while some sarcastically call them "Obamavilles," we must be fair in our criticism - the tents were already being pitched before Barak Obama reached office. A truly honest account would be aware of the fact that everyone shoulders some of the responsibility. There were, and still are, abuses of the system by both the rich and the poor, by politicians, bankers, corporations and the common man alike. Yet there are also honest people in all categories who live responsibly and try to make a difference. Finger pointing happens a little too often and doesn't change the facts: though it's well hidden from those of us still fortunate enough to afford shelter, transportation, and food, the parallels between the Great Depression and today are staggering. The question is not so much "who is to blame" as it is "how then, should we live?"

Glossing over tragedy isn't anything new, however. The government and the media went to staggering lengths to downplay the extent of the tragedy involved in the Great Depression, which is why most of us believe that America has never seen a famine. It is, however, possible to uncover the truth. There are several compelling and telling case studies.

In 1931, a man died on a park bench in Detroit, murmuring all the while that he was hungry. The city denied the incident, but 16 eye witnesses gave sworn testimony in order to get the story out to the public. In the spring of 1932, New York's Welfare Council decided to test the city's claim that only 2 people had starved to death in 1931. A quick survey of just 4 hospitals turned up 95 more cases, as well as many other cases listed by the diseases that the starving are so vulnerable to. In Albany, New York, a ten year old child simply fell over at her desk, dead from starvation. The *San Fransisco Chronicle* ran a December 15, 1932 headline which read, "Starvation Hits 14000" [91]. Estimates, primarily born of census data, vary about the number who starved on American soil, ranging from 6 million all the way up to 10 million; 7 million is the most agreed-upon figure.

The food rhetoric being lobbied about in 1933 borders on the farcical; the government would have had us believe (and many did) that the reason everyone was having so much trouble is that we just had **too much** gosh darn food! Clearly, killing 12,377,434 pigs would put ham in every belly. *Of course* reducing the supply in relation to the demand, as opposed to the other way around, lowers prices [92]! The fact that such nonsense doesn't even jive with basic high school economics didn't seem to occur to Washington politicians, who charged ahead on their own agenda. In the past, you see a whole lot of starvation because of crop failures and climate problems. In our very own history, the famine we supposedly never had stands out as one of the great famines caused by sheer indifference, incompetence, repressive government and greedy corporate!

> *Oscar Emeringer, testifying before a congressional sub-committee in 1932, described the paradox of "appalling overconsumption on one side and staggering under-consumption on the other side..." and described wheat in Montana left unharvested because of low prices, thousands of bushels of apples rotting beside the road in Oregon, an Illinois farmer who killed 3,000 of his own sheep and threw their bodies into a canyon because the cost of shipping the sheep was greater than the cost of sale. In Chicago, men picked through garbage cans for rotting meat scraps.* [93]

One has to wonder, if these people were going to wastefully rid themselves of their food anyway, why would it have been so difficult to simply call up the Red Cross, for example, and tell them to come get 3,000 sheep's worth of meat to feed to all those people in Chicago. Or why selling it at a lowered price to those in their own localities would have been so onerous. In California, the cost of transportation surely couldn't have been the issue. There were thousands of starving fruit pickers, former farmers of the Dust Bowl, standing right there in the orchards, picking fruit that would either be bought up by the rich or dumped into ditches. But it was never, ever simply given or even sold to the poor at reduced cost, because that would be too much like doing the right thing. Economists can justify this all they want to, but there's nothing complicated about this equation. People were starving and the rich and fortunate were wasting food to line their own pockets. It's very, very vital to note that most of the people who suffered during the depression were *not* simply lazy, they were *not* looking for handouts. They were former farmers, former store-owners, and former businessmen whose desires were simple: honest work, and food at affordable prices so they could feed their families.

A number of reasons have been floated for this shameful behavior, everything from Communist infiltrators in Washington to simple greed on the part of Big

Business. It has its defenders, people who insist that raising the cost of food by destroying the supply in order to save the economy just made good sense, because the large farms—the ones who hadn't already gone bankrupt and been repossessed—needed to make enough profit to keep their operations going, which would lead to more jobs. The excuses just don't ring true on a human level, any more than the assurance that a three trillion dollar payout to the banks and the salvation of CEO bonuses would lead, somehow, someway, to economic "stimulus" and the "creation of jobs." Whether due to stupidity, greed, indifference, maliciousness or Malthusianism, few people in power seemed willing to stretch for humane, creative solutions that, again, might have been as simple as a call to the nearest branch of the Red Cross. In Birmingham, Alabama, for example, the Red Cross bore almost the entire burden of trying to get relief to the poor, serving nearly 21,000 families on about $1000 a month from the municipal government, whatever they could scrape up in donations, and nothing from the state [94]. How different might the picture have been if private farms with surpluses had stepped up to the plate to funnel some of those resources to relief organizations? Here, yet again, we see still more proof that looking to the government for salvation in the midst of a crisis amounts to sheer folly. Instead, a policy of personal preparedness and the fostering of strong communities who will help one another must become the focus of our actions.

Utopia Gone Wrong

You could attempt—and many do—to boil the 7 million people that Stalin's policy murdered in the Ukraine to a simple war of genocide, or an attempt to put down a rebellion against a resistant satellite nation. You'd be vastly oversimplifying if you did. In fact, Stalin's Famine—for it was Stalin's famine, a forced famine, an artificial famine, was the result of utopian fever turned into zealotry turned into madness. The story is a wonderful example of the reasons why, if anyone tells you they're about to build an earthly paradise, it's probably time to run the other way.

Well, wait, you might say. Didn't the founding fathers attempt a utopian vision in America? The answer would be, "not really." The founding fathers viewed the government as a necessary evil; the system they built was built with an air of "this is as good as it gets." The checks and balances they put into place were built out of the philosophy that every government, sooner or later, is likely to slide into corruption, so the best one could hope to achieve was to build a government which caught itself and which largely left people alone (and the ways in which Washington's been fouling that one up for over a century would fill another book). As James Madison said, "if men were angels, we wouldn't need government."

Communism, by contrast, starts out with the notion that people can be angels— if one gets rid of all that nasty individualism, a system of money, and provides food and housing for all if they do their part and go to work in collective production points (factories, farms, etc.). Inevitably, of course, there are those who don't want to play along, and there is no room in communism for people who want to do their own thing. There is no room for compromise, and even among communists there grows a snarling desire to wipe out and suppress those who don't follow the "correct" vision of communism. The result is a kind of madness; the very people who wished so desperately to create a heaven on earth wind up twisted with frustration and hate until they are only capable of creating hells. Communism begins with a premise of "wouldn't it be so great if everybody had food and shelter and medical care and education and nobody exploited anybody else ever." And it would. It's just not at all possible, and it puts a burden on government, backed by men with very large guns, that government was never meant to take. Taking care of the less fortunate is a wonderful goal. It should be left to private charities. Putting a check on Big Business by requiring them to have clean, humane, and safe working conditions is little more than acknowledging that Big Business can come to acquire nearly as much power as government and needs its own set of checks and balances.

And if you're wondering why the government can't do as good of a job at helping the poor as private charities, the answers are pretty simple. Your local Salvation Army or church doesn't have an armed force of soldiers and police officers, nor the ability or right to throw you into prison if you don't pay up. Your contributions to either are 100% voluntary (yes, they can use a variety of rhetoric to solicit said donation, but so can your average used car salesman. Buying that car or making that donation is still voluntary). The Salvation Army can't reach into your paycheck and legally take money out of it; the government has worked it around so that they can. A private charity can also tell someone who is abusing the system that they won't receive any more help because of said abuses. The government, however, cannot carry off such a program without applying the rules of the masses. There are too many people to regularly look into individual cases. Everybody who meets certain criteria on paper gets help without regard to the larger picture, and thus you create a permanent underclass of folks who are better off on the dole than they are working for minimum wage.

We can make that determination without making any judgment on the people themselves; numbers alone create this situation. Can you really blame the mother who goes to work for $300 a week and loses all of her benefits as a result, then discovers the option to receive $1200 a month? The average rent is $600 a month, the average daycare is $800 a month, and that's before taking care of transportation, utilities, and food—can we blame her for deciding that staying on the dole means housing, food, utilities and the ability to stay home with her children? Even married parents often find that the jobs they qualify for present a similar situation (before we try to simplify it *again* to those "immoral single parents", especially considering that there are far more reasons than simple licentiousness that might leave a woman or a man alone to care for children).

The government's very attempts to help have thrown the system so out of whack that rents and other necessities have become more expensive as a result; there's no market-incentive to keep rents low and affordable in order to ensure that your housing offering gets purchased at all. Thus the cycle continues. There is a give-and-take of responsibility and despair between the welfare recipient and the government who supports said recipient that was set into motion the *day* welfare was offered in the first place.

For those who would like to see a "day in the life" of people who do attempt to work minimum wage without welfare, read Barbara Ehrenreich's *Nickled and Dimed*. Though she's accused of many things, her account of working people living in vans and the conditions they're forced to deal with is fairly straightforward. Most would prefer to oversimplify and be content to blame only one set of people (It's those welfare people! Wait, no, it's exploitation by Big Business! No, it's our socialist trending government!), but at the end of the day it boils down to the pavement on the road to Hell, and a set of impossible conditions that has been created as a result. We're always going to want to pay *someone* to pour our coffee, so blaming the people who are educated for little else is *also* useless, as we will never, in fact, pay very much for the service of getting that coffee poured. However, there was a time where a person who poured coffee for a living could, if they were careful and frugal, meet all of his or her basic life necessities. *Now*, however, we face a situation where re-setting the system to sanity would result in widespread disorientation and misery.

It is another case of a "perfect storm" scenario—multiple conditions creating big trouble, rather than a single, isolated condition. We've all been unsuccessful in thinking our way back out of the situation we've created precisely because it seems so difficult for people to stop fixating on *one* condition of the storm's formation. Just remember: a storm is formed by low pressure meeting high pressure; not by either factor alone.

This same principle applies to corporate welfare programs—again, let us spread the critical thinking process evenly. Emperor Gudonov of Russia demonstrated all of this for us back in 160—he gave out free money to the masses. Even people who didn't strictly need the help came to get that free money. Thus the treasury was emptied, the "system," such as it was, ended up strained, and far more people died than would have died otherwise. I would venture a guess that at least a portion of those on, say, food stamps are the same—they probably don't strictly need the help, but as long as it's there they feel they might as well take it so they can make their money go farther. It takes a certain type of honor and restraint to ask oneself how much one really needs of said help before applying for it.

We're taking this digression into discussing the very nature of communism and Utopian vision because America has been, much as Ben Franklin grimly predicted, sliding away from its status as a republic for a long, long time. That same vision of Utopia seems to be gripping our own people today, and what began as a system of kindly safety nets is expanding into a many-tentacled beast of policies, regulation, and control. You need to understand this because you cannot, must not, feel tempted to skip over Stalin and Mao's famines with the idea that it "could never happen here." Of course it could. Men do not have to call themselves communists or socialists to try to put together Utopia-at-Gunpoint. They don't have to call themselves anything at all. They don't have to follow the philosophies of Karl Marx to the letter. The basic mistake is the idea that anybody short of God can build a perfect world.

With all of this in mind, let us look at the various factors that played into the deliberate starvation of 7 million individuals.

The struggle between Russia and the Ukraine was as much a struggle to destroy the nationalism of the people of the Ukraine as it was to bring them under Soviet rule. The elimination of ethnic and national consciousness was one of Lenin's stated goals, to the point of forging a one-world system. He wrote: "The aim of Socialism is not only to abolish the present division of mankind into small states and all-national isolation, not only to bring the nations closer to each other, but to merge them." To this effort the Soviets devoted time and energy to suppressing the schools, cultural institutions, art, and especially language of the Ukranian people during Lenin's rule, shooting anyone who dared to speak their own tongue [95]. This method of conquerors is certainly nothing new.

Stalin's famine to come was not the only purposeful famine that the people of the Ukraine would suffer. Lenin caused one of his own in 1918-21. He had made no decision to starve the people of Ukraine per se; rather, Lenin demanded the requisition of grain far out of proportion to what the people could produce and enacted a policy which bluntly stated that the needs of the peasant were not at all to be taken into account. As it stands, 1/10th of the population died under a man considered far more "lax" and "tolerant" than his successor [96].

Through the course of these events, and on into Stalin's rule, it became fairly clear that communism and collectivization was much harder to enact in rural areas. Marx's philosophy was a philosophy of factories, and it truly had no frame of reference for the mindset or way of life of the peasantry. It was because of these difficulties that the term "kulak" entered the Soviet National consciousness. At its most basic form, the word "kulak" means "enemy." It was meant, at first, to apply to hard-line capitalists, particularly among farmers. As time went on, however, you begin to see the term entering literal national debate. Who was a kulak? Who wasn't? Did having a horse make you a kulak? Did employing a farmhand or two to help during the busiest months make you a kulak? There were repeated struggles, early on, to come up with an "accurate" description of these "enemies of the state." They were *serious* in these debates, as serious as any earnest believer debating any issue relating to their beliefs (that is where the fanaticism and the Danger of Utopia grows). There were real political gains to be had from the naming of an enemy. Naming an "enemy" always brings the "allies" closer together as well as provides an excuse for all manner of atrocities deemed 'necessary' by those who named the enemy in the first place. As the philosophies got even more convoluted, the paranoia began to rise, as did the dangers associated with the term.

> *Pravda also warned that 'even the best activists often cannot spot the kulak' because they failed to realize that given a good harvest sale, certain 'middle-peasant' households are rapidly transformed into kulak households. The perennial problem which had all along stultified the scheme for class war in the countryside.*

> *Thus, by strange logic, the middle peasant could become a kulak by gaining property, but a kulak could not become a middle peasant by losing his. In fact, the kulak had no escape. He was 'essentially' a class enemy, a sub-human. Yet the naming of the kulak enemy satisfied the Marxist pre-conceptions of the Party activist. It presented a flesh-and-blood foe accursed by history; and such a target made for a far more satisfactory campaign than mere abstract organizational change. And it provided a means of destroying the leadership of the villagers, which might have greatly strengthened the resistance, strong enough in all conscience, which they offered to collectivization.* [97]

What followed can only be described as "frenzied." Denial of jobs and services to kulaks rapidly descended into confiscating everything they owned, mass arrests, and deportation to work camps. Those who remained to work on collective farms had it little better, forced to work on very small rations. Some were shipped, at gunpoint, to labor in mines. This was not even the worst of what was to come, in part because the spirit of the Ukrainian people would not be broken. They burned their houses rather than allow them to be taken; when their property was stolen from them they stole it back, assassinated Soviet authorities, and left oats and grain to rot in the field rather than be forced into the "collective farming machine" [98].

The response was deadly. Stalin set out on a policy of deliberate starvation. First, he increased the grain quotas on the collectivized farms, which represented about 75% of the remaining farms in the Ukraine, until there was just no food to feed the people. He then rushed in over 100,000 soldiers. These soldiers sealed up the borders in order to prevent any food from entering, "...in effect turning the country into a gigantic concentration camp." The troops then went house to house, confiscating every scrap of food they found. It was claimed that all food was the property of the State and hoarded food represented "stolen property;" violators were either shot or sentenced to 10 years in prison [99].

To stem the potential consequences of international outrage, the Soviet Union denied any famine or policy of forced hunger. Those who tried to speak the truth were accused of spreading anti-Soviet propaganda; those within the country who dared to so much as breathe the words "famine," "hunger," or "starvation" were arrested. The Soviets arranged careful tours for international celebrities in order to further maintain the illusion [100].

Those who agreed to work on the *kolkhoz* (collective farms) were at least fed rations (though in many, many cases not enough rations to prevent them, too, from starvation or near-starvation), and so it became inevitable that the survivors succumbed to obedience.

In April 1933 a memorandum sent to Stalin and Molotov from the Dnepropetrovsk region reported that, 'the attitude of the collective farmers this year (in the sense of their readiness to struggle for the harvest) is incomparably better not only than last year but also than in proceeding years. The causes of this are...an understanding that... bad work in the kolkhoz leads to hunger. [101]

The Soviet leadership coolly and proudly lauded the famine as having had a "positive educational role" in "teaching the peasants to work well on collective farms." As far as the Soviet leadership was concerned, the famine was not a result of the authorities taking the grain away, but a result of peasants who gave poor work or pilfered from the collective farm. Hunger was "a stick that would teach the peasants a need for conscientious work in the collective farm fields" [102]. Feeling his intentions met, Stalin resumed the normal distribution of food inside the Ukraine at the end of 1933, ending the famine, but not before millions of people (estimates as low as 3 million or as high as 13 million, with 6–7 million appearing to be the favored number based on limited information) perished as a direct result of coercive action.

China's Great Leap Forward

If Stalin's Famine of Terror gives the impression of a zealot's warfare, the famine Mao caused in his Great Leap Forward is characterized by the results of putting a hyper-enthusiastic madman into power. Most of what Mao had to say was ignorant yet often seemed to be earnestly said. Most people around Mao slowly but surely came to understand the depth of the catastrophe and foolishness they were facing, but, by that point, the top officials of the Chinese communists had a problem—they had to mollify the madman or be hunted down and killed. Only the enthusiastic sycophants survived. Thus false reports that further exacerbated the growing tragedy of China poured out of various provinces in a giant surge of what, in the vernacular, would be referred to as "cover your ass." In spite of the difference in attitudes, the dead were no less dead, and another deadly example of the wages of collectivization, grain quotas, and socialist-communist regimes passed into history as an offering to the world of all of the reasons why it might be a good idea to avoid such things.

Stalin's famine was deliberate warfare. Mao's famine was not. Mao had extremely unrealistic expectations and a too-healthy dose of ambition. The entire "Great Leap Forward" in 1958–1962 came about as a result of Mao's desperate desire to "catch up with and overtake Britain [in terms of production] in less than fifteen years. By unleashing China's greatest asset, a labor force that was counted in the hundreds of millions, Mao thought he could catapult his country past his competitors" [103]. In point of fact, Mao wanted to develop industry and farming on an equal basis *because* he knew that a poorly fed populace could not achieve very much at all.

Indeed, at first Mao thought things were going extremely well. "With so much grain," Mao mused, "in future you should plant less, work half time and spend the rest of your time on culture and leisurely pursuits, open schools and a university, don't you think? You should eat more. Even five meals a day is fine!" This misperception on Mao's part came from the increasing pressure he put on each of the provinces and their leaders to meet ever more unrealistic targets, pressures which resulted in falsified reports and boasts. Any detected lack of enthusiasm or failure to "meet targets" could result in trouble for any official in the party. "In informal exchanges [Mao] needled and goaded local bosses to commit to ever higher production targets." Eventually, anybody who expressed reservations about the Great Leap Forward was hunted down. In 1960, Mao eventually came to hear and understand the reports of mass starvation, and in fact took to his bed in a state of depression, "seemingly incapable of confronting adverse news" [104]. Not that his lack of *desire* to starve his population exculpates him from the fact that he *did* starve his population.

The entire Great Leap Forward was an ill-conceived disaster. While he was busy raising production quotas, Mao pulled farmers out of the fields to produce steel—by instructing them to build furnaces in their back yards and melt down anything they could find. Of course, most of what they produced was worthless material. While half the farmers were producing sub-standard iron, the crops weren't being harvested [105].

In addition, overseers and party members didn't spend a lot of time listening to the peasants who'd been farming for years. They demanded that the peasants engage in a great many "new, improved" techniques that were ultimately worthless, thinking those techniques would produce greater yields [106].

We in the Western World aren't yet over this fallacy, ourselves. We are constantly following in the footsteps of Condorcet, adopting new technologies as the method to create enough food. Some of those new technologies have proven themselves, some have been dismal, and some have had unforeseen consequences. Right now the political pundits are praising GMO crops as the "new, improved" technique that will feed us all—"wisdom" that runs counter to growing techniques that we've known for centuries work with no unpleasant side effects. A January 15, 2011 *London Telegraph* article ran with the headline, GM Crops Can Save Us From Food Shortages.

The past decade and a half of scientific discovery has opened up a vista of even greater improvements, yet our reaction has been to reject them all. I refer to genetic science and the ability to modify a plant to make it resistant to pests, to need less fertiliser, as well as many more innovations.

It is sensible to be cautious about science when it comes to our food. But we have rejected GM foods almost entirely. That rejection has been shared with the European Union, but it cannot be blamed solely on the EU: scares about "Frankenfoods" and the antics of Lord Melchett and Greenpeace are just as responsible. [107]

True, the parallels aren't 100%. Mao was hardly splicing genes. But the cadres in charge of farm policy still flung themselves into the heart of experimentation:

Increasing the yield encouraged a scramble for fertilizer. Every conceivable kind of nutrient was thrown on the fields, from weed dragged from the sea and garbage salvaged from refuse heaps to soot scraped from chimneys. Animal and human waste was carried to the fields by endless rows of people, sometimes deep into the night...Human waste extended to hair, and in some Guangdong villages women were forced to shave their heads to contribute fertilizer or face a ban from the canteen.

Deep plowing was another revolutionary recipe meant to free the farmers from the capricious soil. The deeper the planting, the stronger the roots and The stalk, or so ran the logic behind this experiment... Goaded by cadres eager to achieve a coveted red flag, villagers now and then burrowed through the earth to the bedrock, destroying the topsoil...This was followed by heavy concentrations of seed in the search for higher yields...Close cropping [was also used]...Villagers, of course,, knew better: they had tilled the land for generations. Many were incredulous, some trying to reason with the cadres...but their advice was ignored. 'It's a new technique, you don't understand!' [108]

While the Chinese crowded seeds and suffocated the soil with human hair and the detritus of houses, we began (and continue) to suffocate our own fields with chemical fertilizers. We don't even have to get into GMOs to see the disturbing, hellish optimism at play. Research in the *1960s* indicated that these fertilizers eventually sterilize the soil, kill off the birds which eat the insects, requiring chemical pesticide as well, and create weaker and weaker plants [109]. Here we are in 2011 *still* spraying our fields with poisonous substances. That doesn't even begin to cover the effects of the chemicals on the humans who consume these products of "new, improved agriculture."

Here's another parallel—national debt. The increased production targets were in part a result of the debt that China owed the Soviet Union. China only had so much in the way of currency and gold reserves, so they paid their debt in exports, specifically foodstuffs, to pay the bill [110]. The Chinese were starving as all of their grain went to Russia. And even in the midst of famine and debt, the Chinese went right on shelling out foreign aid, unwilling to "lose face" to the international community.

That's what happened when China owed *one* country. So what happens when the United States, with a falling dollar, owes *twenty-five* countries, plus assorted oil exporters and Caribbean banks [111]? It's certainly something to think about.

Even if China had managed to produce plenty of food, keep it in their borders, and report on it correctly, there's still one more fact worth paying attention to. Just like Stalin's regime, Mao's regime used food as a weapon to force people to work collectively. And just as in Stalin's regime, Mao's regime eventually invaded private homes to search for food, punishing those who "hoarded" so they could export even this grain. Think it can't happen here? Pay close attention to two relevant executive orders, remembering that executive orders are essentially the law of the land, in spite of being decided upon by one man's "stroke of the pen."

Executive Order 10998, signed by John F. Kennedy and never repealed, gives the government the authority to seize all food sources, farms, and farm equipment. It also gives the government the authority to ration food [112]. Should any American president ever activate this order, it would mean the government would have full authority to knock on your door, search your cupboards, and take any and all food found.

Executive Order 11000, also signed by Kennedy, says that all citizens can be seized for work under Federal Supervision [113].

As to the end of the Great Leap Forward story, it was over in 1961. This man-made famine managed to take center stage as the *worst* famine in world history. Estimates on the death toll don't go any lower than 16.5 million and rise as high as 60 million. As is often the case, the suffering that men can produce in their arrogance outstripped the suffering caused by the cycles of nature.

It's so important to pay attention to the *lack* of malice that caused starvation. Mao was sure the entire affair was the result of "counter-revolutionaries," surely not his own policies. The fact that the men at the very top never intended for anybody to starve is demonstrated when a committed party man named Liu Shaoqi went back to his home village. After seeing the devastation, he said, "I haven't returned home for nearly forty years. I really wanted to come home for a visit. Now, I have seen how bitter your lives are. We have not done our jobs well, and we beg for your pardon." He then ordered the canteen dissolved [114].

Why is noting the lack of malice so important? It is because Americans base much of their safety on the idea that our fellow Americans are good, kind people. We may know that there are executive orders out there that could be enacted against us at any time, but we're pretty sure it's "only in the event of a nuclear war or something." We're content that we would never seek this kind of power for no reason other than to have it, so it is very difficult for us to imagine our leaders doing so either. Americans are unique. We are special. We're nice people. And it may be true. It could be true that most of our government is full of nice people. Most of us don't have the benefit of knowing them personally; we can only see their actions, usually through the lenses of media bias. It's entirely possible that our leaders could be *nice but clueless*, have too much power, and still *starve millions of American citizens* as a result of hare-brained policies that only make sense to people who don't live and work on the ground. If you've ever worked on the bottom of a company's totem pole and listened to management produce a new policy that seems completely out of touch with reality, you know this phenomenon for yourself. The American system isn't just there to defend against evil people—it was supposed to do a pretty fair number on stopping plain old stupidity, too. Unfortunately, little by little, those safeguards have been stripped away and left meaningless. Ultimately, the lack of evil motive is no comfort at all in the face of the dead; of entire villages wiped out and widespread misery. This doesn't even cover all of the millions that Mao's regime had imprisoned and shot for speaking against the system, earnestly and insanely believing them to be the enemies of the "little guy."

1.7 And in the 21st Century?

ഇ•ൽ

If you want to know about the state of hunger in the 21st century you need only note that as of this writing, we have had 11 years of this century and there has been a food crisis or famine situation every single year. Many of them, such as the Darfur crisis, are just as man-made as Mao and Stalin's famines. So far, these have been in Africa, Afghanistan, and North Korea; sadly, we are so accustomed to associating some of these places with food crisis that we've become numb to them.

Yet what is the food outlook for the early 21st century, both nationally and globally? We can answer the question by combing through the headlines and news stories. Put together, each of these stories paints a picture. Trouble isn't on the way, it's already here. The only question is how long it will take Americans to feel the effects.

Weather Problems

Freak weather has encircled the globe. These storms have had a negative impact on food production world-wide. Remember that we are now in an extremely globalized economy and that our country relies, in part, on imports to feed its people. Prices are already on the rise. CBS News ran the headline, "Nowhere to Hide from Rising Food Prices" on January 15, 2011.

"Corn is a big one" in the higher prices department, Bloomberg Businessweek Assistant Managing Editor Sheelah Kolhatkar told "Early Show on Saturday Morning" co-anchor Betty Nguyen. "The Agriculture Department released a report a couple of days ago about crop forecasts for the year and predicted corn production is going to go down very significantly, which led to a spike in prices."

Why corn's rise?

"There are a lot of reasons," Kolhatkar replied. "Weather is cited as a big one. There's been sort of freak weather in different parts of the world. Russia experienced a drought. There are floods in Australia. There's been sort of freezing weather in Florida. Our own Midwest experienced flooding earlier this year." [115]

AccuWeather.com notes some of the extreme weather that's been affecting the harvests, including what they call "history-making" heat waves and droughts in Russia, unusual cold in the United States and Europe, flooding in Pakistan, flooding in Australia, excessive heat in Latin America, and the bee colony collapse. Among all of that and the resulting crop failures, they also mention the rising costs of oil [116].

Food riots have already broken out in Algeirs, Tunisia, Haiti, and Mexico. Food protests have begun in Egypt.

The factors that are being cited as reasons for the food crisis are myriad, like shots coming from every side: rising fuel prices, bio-fuel which cuts into the corn supply, bad weather. But most of all, the demand has exceeded the supply, worldwide. *National Geographic* reports:

> *Between 2005 and the summer of 2008, the price of wheat and corn tripled, the price of rice climbed fivefold, spurring food riots in nearly two dozen countries, and pushing 75 million more people into poverty. But unlike previous shocks driven by short-term food shortages, this price spike came in a year when the world's farmers reaped a record grain crop. This time, the high prices were a symptom of a larger problem tugging at the strands of our worldwide food web, one that's not going away anytime soon. Simply put: for most of the past decade, the world has been consuming more food than it's been producing. After years of drawing down stockpiles, in 2007 the world saw global carryover stocks fall to 61 days of global consumption, the second lowest on record.* [117]

Now, with such poor harvests, the presence of a global food crisis seems inevitable. And the poor soil, water, and weather conditions are likely to continue for some time. Scientists are concerned about what they call a "perpetual" global food crisis. *Foreign Policy* reports:

> *While the annual demand growth for grain was doubling, new constraints were emerging on the supply side, even as longstanding ones such as soil erosion intensified. An estimated 1/3 of the world's cropland is losing topsoil faster than new soil is forming through natural processes—and this is losing its inherent productivity. Two huge dustbowls are forming, one across northwest China, western Mongolia, and central Asia; the other in central Africa. Each of these dwarfs the U.S. dustbowl of the 1930s.*
>
> *Satellite images show a steady flow of dust storms leaving these regions, each one typically carrying millions of tons of precious topsoil. In*

North China, some 2400 rural villages have been abandoned or partly depopulated as grasslands have been destroyed by overgrazing and as croplands have been inundated by migrating sand dunes...

Meanwhile, aquifer depletion is fast shrinking the amount of irrigated area in many parts of the world; this relatively recent phenomenon is driven by the large-scale use of mechanical pumps to exploit underground water. Today, half the world's people live in countries where water tables are falling as over-pumping depletes aquifers. Once an aquifer is depleted, pumping is necessarily reduced to the rate of recharge unless it is a fossil...aquifer, in which case pumping ends altogether. But sooner or later, falling water tables translate into rising food prices. [118]

This is not to say that we're all doomed to die, that these problems can never be solved, or that there's no hope at all. It's just a note that things are going to get bad, and they're going to get worse before they get better. These factors don't even take into account the complex web of dark political factions and movements growing across the United States and the world. All of this adds up to a turbulent 21st century on the way, one which smart, freedom loving people are going to have to prepare for in order to survive.

PART 2

ॐ•ॐ

THE CAUSES OF FAMINE

Though a study of history helps to provide one with a fair understanding of the causes behind famine and the events that come into play when a famine occurs, it is useful to look at each one of the causes of famine on an individual basis. A historical perspective demonstrates patterns, but those patterns can sometimes be lost in a broader perception of the individual events—and to an extent, the question of how much those circumstances were unique to that time and place. A factors-based analysis, by contrast, helps you conclusively identify warning signs as you work your way through your morning newspaper.

Doing such an analysis by necessity will touch on some very controversial subjects. At some point, we'll have to take a hard look at current climate change. We're not going to try to decide who or what is causing the changes in climate. The truth is this: climate has always changed. The medieval Little Ice Age caused many, many deaths by famine, and, whatever the cause, the end result was the same. Where environmental factors come into play, this review is not going to focus on greenhouse gasses and carbon footprints, which are being used as a political war drum by socialists, communists, and eugenicists all over the world. That does not mean we can't address topics like sustainable farming, toxic chemical pollution, soil and water conservation issues, and a host of other resource management questions. We can also take a look at solutions to various resource problems that are forwarded by man-made global warming enthusiasts, not because we agree with the assessments or political rhetoric behind climate change, but because they are decent innovations for other reasons.

Take the electric car. A truly electric car with a viable battery would reduce our dependence on oil, removing oil and gas from the food production equation entirely. The end result? The price of food falls. If it makes the man-made global warming people feel more confident about our future too, that only means that continuing to get funding and consumers behind such research is easier. It is possible to agree that our treatment of the environment has caused severe problems (it's almost impossible to deny in the face of overwhelming evidence on, say, aquifers alone) without leaping immediately to Malthusian conclusions and "solutions," and without leaping to the idea that a tightly controlled, global dictatorship is the only way to save us. In point of fact, a more free, more agrarian, less regulated, less taxed society with smaller farms and a stable republic would do more to reduce food and pollution problems than any sort of cap and trade scheme. There's nothing wrong with getting more for your money with energy efficient light bulbs, either (which also ultimately can reduce pressure on the food supply by reducing pressure on the energy supply), or with conserving water. There are those who will weaken their discourse considerably by rejecting *all* conservation and management measures simply because the political philosophy of the ones pushing them the loudest is flawed.

Further, there are points where the numbers are difficult to escape. It is, for example, difficult to dismiss the true numbers that drive meat centered diets vs. the production capacities of vegetarian ones. It is entirely possible for a freedom loving person to say that it would be desirable for each compassionate person to limit or even avoid meat simply by virtue of these numbers *without* resorting to a stance that anyone should be *forced* to go without meat. The problem-solving methods must be individual decisions made without coercion in order to be valid solutions. Otherwise, we run the risk of devolving into the very sorts of tyrannies that starve their own people in the course of a quest to "save" them. But indeed, just as Victory Gardens were a vital part of our freedom-preservation strategies during World War II, the *100 Mile Diet* or a vegetarian lifestyle might become our own, freely embraced, expressions of patriotism.

It is one thing to simply say, "Stock up for your own survival." And we'll certainly cover that. That, too, is a conscious, patriotic choice: the choice to be prepared in the event of an emergency. In part, we do this so that we can take care of ourselves and our families. But one can recognize a more civic-minded reason for doing so: so that we will not be a burden and a drain on those who are less fortunate, less far-sighted, or more burdened than we are when trouble comes, as trouble always must.

Many times, when people begin addressing the reasons behind famines, there is a tendency to want to retreat back to the Left-Right paradigm. Yet as we've already mentioned, this Two-View paradigm is unrealistic, serves only the establishment, and creates a false circus of politicians who, at the end of the day, really aren't so different. Abuses of power and foolish decisions have come from Republicans *and* Democrats. Barak Obama made us more socialist when he passed his health package, but George W. Bush signed our national sovereignty off to Mexico in 2005 and gave us the Patriot Act. We don't have this luxury any longer. We cannot divide ourselves solely into "people who do things as they always did," and "people who want to try something new." All who support the constitution and who believe in freedom, as well as all of those who would want to avert food tragedies, *must* find common ground. If you read a "conservative's" book and a "liberal's" book on the same problem, and that person is a common citizen rather than a government or U.N. power-monger, you will find many of the same observations and concerns, and much room for common ground. Our tendency, though, is to reject everything that doesn't fit in our pre-arranged, comfortable worldview. And so, more often than not, the statements that people make are predictable and expected rather than offering insight.

But if any solutions or analysis forwarded are **just, loving, moral, voluntary, constitutional, and feasible**, then there is no reason not to examine them just because one problem solver uses the language of ecology and another problem solver uses the language of the Bible. Therefore, absolutely no attempt has been made to censor or filter the sources of information about famine or the discourse on solution, so long as those solutions and conversations fit the above criteria. Whole heartedly rejecting a strategy of eugenics and murder is absolutely essential. Rejecting, say, a thinker's attempt to discover whether there are ways to improve our concept of constitutional freedoms, citizenship, and problem-solving simply cuts off at the knees our abilities to think clearly.

Of course, we're not even to Part 4, where the solutions, vis. a vis. what the individual can do, today and in the future, are to both prepare himself in the event of a famine and to perhaps live a life which helps to fend off tyranny, consume more responsibly and produce sustainably. But discussion of the problems, in and of themselves, grows controversial. Those who are heavily focused on tyranny sometimes don't want to discuss topsoil and aquifers. Yet a balanced, objective view *must* discuss *both* topsoil *and* tyranny if any useful conclusions are to be reached.

2.1 Oppression, and How Food is used as a Weapon

ഓ•ൠ

In Stalin we have an excellent example of how food can literally be used as a weapon. All Stalin or any would-be oppressor has to do is cut any of the strands in a delicate food web. An oppressor can close borders (denying food entry into any area), ramp up exports (sending as much food as possible out of an area), engage in a campaign of confiscation (meaning even those with their own, self-sufficient gardens are in danger of losing their food) and use food as a means to force people to work on government programs, as in the kolkhuz's and Mao's communal farming canteens.

Yet using food as a weapon doesn't even depend on these factors. Richer nations can extend or deny food aid as a method of control over the actions of poorer nations. Debt can be used as a tool or a stick to strip people of everything they own, simply by taking over more and more of a country's available income. Often, the debt is backed by a threat of force—pay, or we'll come in and take our due.

Sadly, we have plenty of examples of food-as-a-weapon in our modern day society, and no small number of them are coming out of American policies. However, from the high halls of the IMF and World Bank, to the halls of Washington D.C., to the camps of regional warlords, all are terribly conscious of the fact that resistance happens only on a full belly. Therefore, seek to restrict those full bellies wherever possible.

How the Existence of a True Republic Defends Against Famine

Though many people misname it as simple "democracy," it is widely recognized that the structure of a free Republic as envisioned and carried out by the Founding Fathers creates real safeguards against famines and food shortages caused by oppression. In order to understand this, you must first have a good understanding of the differences between a "democracy" and a "republic," and why the distinction is both extremely important and widely misunderstood. In most of the quotes that follow, it's important to understand that too many people these days use the words interchangeably; however, we can understand this and still understand the basic intent behind the points that are being made.

A democracy is actually an inferior form of a republic; a devolution, if you will, of a much stronger structure. There are really only two types of government—those that govern by rule of law or those that govern by the whims of the people. Republics, like the United States, are ruled by law. Each person has inherent rights that exist which are considered God-given and not at the mercy of whatever political faction is in power at any given moment.

*Democracies, on the other hand, are the **rule of the mob**. These types of Government quickly deteriorate into tyrannies as groups of people try to attain power through whatever means they deem necessary. What usually arises through the ashes of these power struggles is the "benevolent" dictator, one who justifies his totalitarian take-over with the belief that only he can provide a more effective means of governing the masses.*

...The Founding Fathers viewed democracies as unstable and dangerous. "Democracies have been spectacles of turbulence and contention; have ever been found incompatible with personal security or the rights of property, and have in general been very short in their lives as they have been violent in their deaths," said James Madison. [119]

American military historian Mackubin T. Owens put it another way. He pointed out that major thinkers, from Plato to the founding fathers, all understood that democracies had a way of becoming what he called a "soft despotism," taking the public's freedoms in exchange for fulfillment of the people's needs and whims. This sort of populace winds up "happily abiding the tyrant's pursuit of limitless desire so long as the tyrant's government fulfills their own." This might even sound like a decent enough place to live at first (especially since that is the state we find our own country in today). The problem is this: a soft despotism has all the weapons and tools of a hard despotism at its disposal. The first "crisis" will put even the kindest of tyrants into "crisis mode," in which all manner of tragedies are enacted and countenanced in the name of the "public safety" or the "maintenance of the current political and social order." Once the government has succeeded in going this far, the tyrant and his successor have little need or desire to revert back to even the soft despotism. It's a very, very slippery slope. It happened in ancient Greece; it happened in ancient Rome.

Alexis de Toqueville, author of *Democracy in America*, observed the seeds of this very phenomenon back in 1831. His famous quote sums it up in a nutshell:

"The American Republic will endure until the day Congress discovers it can bribe the public with the public's money."

Every schoolchild hears about the checks and balances of the legislative, executive, and judicial branch at the federal level. What we've forgotten to teach our children is the true role of the states. Most people these days think of the states as convenient regional designations. Any variations in laws or practices between the states are dismissed as being the laws too un-important for the federal government to bother with. But the rights of states, and their abilities as independent lawmaking bodies, is another vital portion of the fabric of the republic. It is in fact locked up in our Tenth Amendment rights: The powers not delegated to the United States by the Constitution, nor prohibited by it to the states, are reserved to the states respectively, or to the people.

More and more, our federal government has sought to ignore, marginalize, and circumvent the powers of the states until the states hardly seem to matter. States, in turn, have begun trying to flex their Tenth Amendment rights to overturn Obamacare, the Food Patriot Act, and other pernicious pieces of legislation that move us ever closer to the kind of nightmare scenario that most Americans believe is absolutely impossible within these shores. In fact, it has gotten to the point that Chuck Baldwin, 2008 Constitutional Party nominee for the Presidency of the United States, has stated that Washington is a "lost cause." Instead, he calls to freedom-lovers to look to their state and local governments. If those who respect the Constitution are brought into power in their states, there may be hope for peacefully resisting a federal government that has gotten far too big for its britches.

We've set up thousands of banana-boat "democracies" where the people go out and vote, and yet they still basically live under a miserable, oppressive regime. It happens *because* we no longer understand or accept the fundamental differences between republics and democracies.

We also, on the whole, have trouble understanding the responsibilities of citizenship. In *Diet for a Small Planet*, food researcher Francis Moore Lappé asserted that we had missed the mark entirely with every attempt at government, including our own.

No current concept of the social order legitimates the central role of ***citizens****—their responsibilities, their capacities for common problem* *solving. All inherited models share the mechanistic assumptions. In the now-discredited state-socialist model, the producer is central—and who makes the decisions? The Party. In the capitalist system, the consumer is all important—and who makes decisions? Owners of capital. In welfare capitalism a new role is added: the client—and who makes decisions? The professional, the "expert," service provider. In other words, there is no vision of public life that puts citizen responsibility at its center. Thus, none of our inherent models take seriously the task of creating capable citizens.*

...Most of us have learned to submerge our common sense, even our own values and tastes, and turn to "experts"—whether in child rearing, making workplace decisions, or even in decorating our homes...we learn at every turn to defer to others "better qualified. [120]

It is true that our current citizenship has no such belief, nor is taught to. We are indeed led to believe the experts, from the government on down, should make our decisions. And while the capitalist free market system is the best we have to interact with a republic, Lappé is not the first person to observe the tensions between a free republic and capitalism gone out of control. In *Dynamics of International Relations: Conflict and Mutual Gain*, Walter C. Clemens observed:

Democracies value the individual; markets treat individuals as tools to make money. Democracies value equality, markets foster inequality. Democracies depend on compromise, markets encourage competition. Democracies need a stable, settled electorate; markets and modern technologies promote a nomadic lifestyle. Democracies require majority rule with respect for minorities; markets reward self-seeking. Markets and modern technology praise the ephemeral—today's fashion, the price differential, sensation. Television and sound bites and expensive advertising, paid for by lobbies seeking favors. Market elites win out over democratic elites. [121]

Indeed, a sort of Corporate Tyranny has become interwoven with the deteriorating democracy in which we find ourselves. Big Corporate owns Big Media and tells them what to say with an iron hand that neatly circumvents the Constitution. They then use millions of dollars to influence the course of our government and to keep making money—more and more money—usually at the expense of the average citizen, who is mollified in turn with a "bread and circus" mentality. Our Congress is not in charge anymore, our judges make crazy decisions like mini-dictators, and our president is a figurehead who can now make laws with the "stroke of a pen," all at the direction of bankers and moguls in the shadows, each seeking to forward their own private interest.

It is the Corporate Tyranny and the deterioration to democracy that makes Lappé's ideas seem like something new. Throughout her book she puts out a call for ordinary people to "step up" and make a difference. It seems like a brand new idea, but it *isn't*. The founding fathers named such activities as *vital* to a functioning republic! We've come so far afield of their original intentions or from being taught anything about those intentions! Thomas Jefferson, in a letter to a friend written in 1787, said, "Cherish, therefore, the spirit of our people, and keep alive their attention. If once they become inattentive to the public affairs, you and I, Congress and Assemblies, judges and governors, shall all become wolves. It seems to be the law of our general nature."

Perhaps more eloquently, James Wilson in his July 4, 1788 address gave us this wisdom: "Need I infer that it is the duty of every citizen to use the best and most unremitting endeavors for preserving it [the Constitution], pure, healthful, and vigorous. For the accomplishment of this great purpose, the exertions of no one citizen are unimportant. Let no one, therefore, harbor the mean idea that he is and can be of no value to his country. Let the contrary manly impression animate his soul."

The Founding Fathers never meant for rule by the corporations, either. Corporations are treated, in our modern "democracy," as if they themselves were people. They are given "rights", they essentially have votes, and they are the recipients of corporate welfare packages that are further eroding our freedoms. "All the perplexities, confusion and distress in America arise not from defects in the Constitution or Confederation, not from a want of honor or virtue so much as from downright ignorance of the nature of coin, credit and circulation," said John Adams in 1787, speaking at the Constitutional Convention.

But here's the biggie. Back in the early days of the nation, most states had rules on the books making any political contribution by a corporation a criminal offense. Indeed, so restrictive was the corporate entity that many of America's greatest entities were set up to avoid the corporate restrictions. Andrew Carnegie formed his steel operation as a limited partnership and John D. Rockefeller set up Standard Oil as a trust.

Not surprisingly, as corporations grew larger and their shareholders wealthier, they began to influence the rule-making process that governed corporations. Using the money they had accumulated, they began to chip away at corporate restrictions. Eventually, corporations were permitted to go on forever. Where shareholders had once been personally responsible for the actions of the corporation, modern corporations shield them from liability. And as more money became involved, the politicians who regulated them grew increasingly seduced by what the wealthy corporations could do for them. [122]

It is necessary to point this out because the "free market" is often used to relieve anyone of responsibility for what it does; it's simply "the market" that does this, and "the free market" is a cornerstone of our "democracy." And laissez-faire economics is a cornerstone of the republic. It was just never meant to provide corporations the kind of power that those corporations wield today. Corporations are as powerful as any ruler; in some cases their power is greater than any elected official. Going to work for some corporations means signing off on your rights at the door. You have to understand that, because, throughout this section, you will see the ways in which the "free market" has been twisted to circumvent freedom, to create a state of oppression, and even to forward the unnamed American Empire throughout the world, with all of the abuses that Empire implies. You have to be aware of all of this *before* you understand how and why a republic structure (commonly called a democracy) defends against famine. The fact that most of those protections have now been twisted or downright thrown out of a window will become fairly obvious. The reasons why we have to step up and once again take our citizen responsibilities seriously, rather than waiting for expert decisions, will become abundantly clear—and perhaps give you a sense of empowerment by the time you make your way into Part 4. So with all of that said, what are the mechanisms of a free society that help it to prevent deliberate, oppressive famines?

One, of course, is that in a functioning republic we hold our leaders 100% accountable for their actions. We know what they are doing. We wield the right to pull them down and replace them should they take actions which are widely detrimental to the people (such as starving large numbers of them to their own gain). That accountability keeps public officials wary; even if they had the inclination to do such a thing, they are hesitant to do so. In addition, there are always different political parties and groups; if one party is allowing the wholesale starvation of the populace, another party will immediately rise up to bring that abuse to light, if for no other reason than it will help them gain power to discuss the abuse and bring it to an end [123].

But it is, perhaps, the existence of a free press, defended in America by the rapidly diminishing First Amendment, which helps to prevent famine in a free society. Politicians who would do evil are in fact more afraid of a free press than any other medium. A free press speaks directly to the people. Governments are typically afraid of their people; they do not like opposition and they do not like dissent. In a functioning republic, our leaders have to live with it. In many countries, massive amounts of open bribe money have been spent on controlling the press—more so than say, controlling judges or other entities of state. Governments like to own the press, and there is a direct correlation between their being allowed to do so and the increase of hunger and misery.

Government ownership of the press is associated with (statistically significantly) lower levels of political rights, civil liberties, security of property, and quality of regulation and higher levels of corruption or risk of confiscation...these results support the public choice view that government ownership of the press restricts information flows to the public, which reduces the quality of government. [124]

In addition, democratic governments, due to the fact that they are held accountable by the people, tend to develop contingency plans to cope with food shortages.

They will typically pay whatever is required to purchase food at market prices in order to feed their people. Under British rule, India experienced many famines; they have rarely done so after achieving independence [125].

All of this culminates into a series of instructive "take-aways."

- The restoration of a constitutional republic over a mob-rule democracy caught between the twin corruptions of socialist sentiment and corporate abuse is absolutely vital towards any broader efforts we might make to prevent famine or hunger in our own shores.

- The restoration of an empowered citizen-responsible mindset with the rights and duties of citizenship, coupled with the restoration of the belief that we the people, not they, the experts, are capable of great things and can creatively address solutions as families and communities without having to appeal to the government to solve them for us. It does not, for example, take the whim of a federal government welfare state to decide for a community that the time has come to begin an urban community garden that will lower the grocery bills for all involved citizens while taking just a little bit more pressure off of the global food production machine. This would include, as well, the need for citizens to reclaim their entrepreneurial and independent heritage, gradually weaning *ourselves* off of the welfare state. We cannot count on the state to do it for us, nor can we count on Big Corporate to provide jobs. We can, perhaps, count on ourselves, and each other, to restore industry through cooperation, local opportunity, and the judicious use of new technology, such as the internet, to regain some independence from the state and corporate created societal machine. This means restoring a sense of confidence in ourselves and our fellow citizens, recognizing that we are smart enough, creative enough, and "expert" enough to do anything we need to do. It also requires us to care about each other, our fellow human beings, the way God asked us to do.

- A hard look at the way our current corporate media is controlled and disseminated. While many "alternative" and "indie" media outlets have risen up in the wake of corporate-controlled media, it remains that few people trust Amy Goodman's Democracy Now! or Alex Jones' Prison Planet to the extent that they trust CBS, Fox News, CNN and NBC. In addition, some independent media outlets have allowed passion to steer them in the direction of bias, have relied on swift internet searches to fact-check over more intensive methods, and have taken on a slightly more hysterical tone than their counterparts, leading them to be further discredited in the eyes of citizens who truly need to listen.

- A reform of the system that allows Corporate Tyranny and which uses laissez-faire economics as an excuse to justify any and all corporate abuses. Primarily, corporations treat the many as "objects" for the gain of the few shareholders in moves that the Founding Fathers never intended. In addition, it can easily be noted that the interest of most American Corporations is not, in fact, American; they have shipped jobs overseas so they can pay sweatshop workers $2.30 a day for shoes they will sell in America for $100. This hurts both the worker in America and the worker in the overseas sweatshop and is contrary to the way that a loving God would wish to see people treat one another.

We also need the recognition that America has been acting as an Imperial power for a very long time, leading to wide-scale hunger outside of our own borders. This international, foreign hunger has not mattered on a physical level (though to many it has on a moral level) to any American citizen—until, possibly, now, with a global food crisis on the horizon. As you will soon see, our own policies, as well as the policies of the IMF and World Bank, have created a scenario where massive amounts of productive land in many, many countries has gone unused, underused, or inefficiently exploited to serve the interests of the rich and powerful. Had that land been used as it should have been by a series of sovereign nations able to steer their own destinies, one might submit that there would either be no population-to-production problem now, or, if there was, the problem would be far less severe than the one which we currently face. Read on.

The American Empire—
Starvation through Food Aid

You'll not hear people talking about The American Empire on CNN or Fox News, but the Empire nevertheless exists. We started our imperial journey at the end of the 19th century when we seized the Philippines and Puerto Rico at the end of the Spanish-American War. We simply managed to couch our invasion in terms of "teaching" these two countries how to be self-governing democracies; spreading the ideals of government by the people, for the people, and of the people [126]. The paradox inherent in having someone *force* government by and for the people onto a country did not, apparently, occur to the supporters of this move, nor has it in any successive move where we have gone into a country and taken control under the guise of helping to spread the twin virtues of democracy and human rights.

An empire can be defined by a number of characteristics. First, an empire must exercise political control or influence over territories beyond its natural or original borders. The empire will typically meddle, politically, in the affairs of foreign nation, as well as maintain military posts or bases throughout the world. Empires also typically conduct wars of aggression, rather than defensive wars, on foreign soil. Empires are happy to play the role of "world policeman" in order to maintain their own stability and interests. Empires self-assign interest in the political, economic, or educational welfare of smaller, lesser nations. You can also identify empires by their citizens, who eventually, typically, grow rich, lazy, and fat, concerned only with the entertainments, diversions, and luxuries the empire has to offer. The government becomes top-heavy and corrupt. Other nations approach the empire and attempt to gain influence there in order to influence that empire's foreign policy or to have favors granted it. Empires usually become replete with so many laws that the average citizen hardly knows what's legal or illegal anymore, all in the name of keeping the citizenry under control. In the meantime, taxes on the citizenry tend to spiral ever higher to keep imperial expansion and projects going. Empires also try to maintain vast highway and transportation systems, the better to move their armies quickly to anywhere they might wish to be [127].

Is America an Empire? Yes, it is. An empire is a state that surpasses all others in capabilities and sense of mission. An empire usually exceeds others in capabilities like the size of its territory and material resources. Its capabilities are much greater than the average or norm prevailing in the international system.

...Second, an empire has worldwide interests. Its interests are coterminous With boundaries of the system itself, and the interests are defended directly by the imperial states or by client states. There is almost nothing that does not concern the United States; from Paraguay to Nepal, or Sweden to New Zealand...You know you are

*an empire when other States cannot ignore you and must acquiesce
to your interests, but you do not have to satisfy theirs.*

*While almost the entire world agrees that the United States is an empire,
it is not according to American leaders. They almost never use the "E"
word...They prefer to speak of American "leadership," or "direction,"
the "key role of the United States in the Western "community" or
"civilization."*

*...While American leaders may not use the "E" word, plenty of others
do— from all around the world, in fact. In 1998, French foreign
minister Hubert Vedrine found that "superpower" was too weak a
word to describe the United States, so he created a word "hyperpower"
to describe its formidable capabilities...worldwide media such as the
BBC and al Jazeera television lament the unpleasantness of living in
a world dominated by Uncle Sam's Empire.* [128]

Why is it important to make it very clear that America is, and has been for a
long time, an Empire? First, because the existence of America as an Empire runs
counter to the republic that our Founding Fathers were trying to create (though
there are those who would disagree with that interpretation). If we can go so far
as to create an Empire, we can go farther still towards despotism. Empires are
rarely very nice neighbors, and though our Empire has been very good for its own
citizens, we have already caused starvation through oppression throughout the
world. In the grand double-speak tradition of our Empire, we label this starvation
through oppression with the ironic name, "food aid."

From the very beginning, our willingness to extend food and aid to other
countries has not been altruistic whatsoever. While the average American citizen
believes that we generously give food to those who are incapable of producing
food for themselves, this is far from the truth.

We can begin tracking down inklings of the real truth by examining the 1974
Kissinger report NSSM 200, *Implications of Worldwide Population Growth for
U.S. Security and Overseas Interests.* Typically, alarmists all over the Internet
refer to this document as "the Genocide memo." They claim, among other things,
that within the memo, Kissinger refers to 80% of the world as "useless feeders" (he

never does), that he advocates abortion (he in fact stipulates that no aid money should go to any abortion program at all), and that he implies that other countries should be starved and left to pestilence in order to reduce world population. This is, again, not true. All he says is that controlling population growth is a long term project because other nations would have to enact "draconian measures" to reduce or even stabilize its population in the short term. At no point did he put forth "draconian measures" as desirable.

Kissinger's main points are that an increasing world population represents a national security problem, and that better education, better access to birth control, and a better economy in other countries will help alleviate the problem; it would therefore be within the United States' best interest to foster these things.

That does not mean everything in the memo is benevolent, however. In point of fact, there are some truly malevolent ideas in NSSM 200. It's simply important to debunk what isn't true in favor of taking our arguments to what is true. Otherwise we're giving into hysteria, and that's useless. It devalues our arguments to anyone who takes the time to read all 230 pages of the declassified memo.

Here's what the memo *does* say. The memo suggests that United States food aid should be extended or withheld in direct proportion to what the leaders of each country, especially "LDCs," or "less developed countries," are doing to control their own population. It also says that LDCs that don't control their population are bad for American interests because it makes it harder for us to go in and exploit those country's national resources.

And so food is used as a weapon to steer the policy of other nations, not just because of a Malthusian theory about population, but also for the direct purpose of allowing our empire to swoop into those countries and get our hands, one way or another, on the resources within. Kissinger, ever the diplomat, made it clear that they would have to "spin" this action so it was taken in a different light. "In these sensitive relationships, however, it is important in style as well as substance to avoid the appearance of coercion" [129].

All of this would be bad enough, but the actual work of "food aid" has the opposite effect. The style and substance of American food aid actually serves to impoverish the people of the countries who receive it, while actively benefitting elite interests within those nations.

Reason number one has to do with livestock. Most of our agricultural exports actually go to livestock instead of hitting the market as grain. The hungry abroad can't afford meat, so they certainly are not benefitting from "food aid" [130]. In the meantime, the presence of that livestock is taking up space in fields that could be used to grow domestic grain—grain which would feed far more people than the cows ever could.

In addition, two-thirds of U.S. food aid has gone under Title I of Public Law 480; that is, as long-term loans from the United States, not as charity aid given gratis. The bulk of what we call "food aid" is simply loaned out to foreign governments who go on to do whatever they want with it. Generally, that food is sold on the open market—meaning that those who can pay for it get it. And those governments sell that food at prices that immediately undercut the local farmers, who are then forced out of business and off of their land, placing them squarely in bread lines. As farmers disappear from the land, unable to compete with cheaply acquired foreign grain, the country's production then plummets. Thus, the world food shortage situation grows even worse through our welfare mentality. Yet in many cases, the only form of "food aid" that countries would need is the donation of *transportation* during short-term food crisis, transportation that can help governments move resources from their existing agricultural areas on to emergency sites [131].

Far too often that aid never makes it to the people who really need it, even if they had the money to buy the grain. It becomes subject to corruption, graft, and the activities of local warlords and corrupt governments. Ethiopia provides a prime example:

> *During the final two years (1973-1975) of the U.S. Supported Haile Selassie regime, some 100,000 Ethiopians died of starvation due to drought. At least half the amount of grain needed to keep those people alive was held in commercial storage facilities within the country. Emperor Salassie's National Grain Corporation itself held in storage 17,000 tons of Australian wheat which it refused to distribute, while commercial interests thrived by selling hundreds of tons of Ethiopian grains, beans, and even milk to Western Europe and Saudi Arabia. The Ethiopian government received 150,000 tons of free food from aid donors. Government officials at all levels withheld stored food from*

the market, awaiting higher prices even as "peasants could be seen
starving within a few kilometers of grain storage." At one point, the
Ethiopian officials offered to sell 4000 tons of stored grain to the United
States **with the idea that the United States could then donate it**
back for relief inside the country." [132]

More recently, we've seen some of the same scenario in Darfur. We could ship over every grocery we had in the hopes of feeding desperate refugees, but we'd never reach them. Instead, they'd be eaten up by the very warlords who are starving, raping, and killing those refugees in the first place.

If we truly wanted to "aid" other countries, we'd get out of them and stop sending grain that will undercut the local farmers in order to increase the profits for our own shippers, agribusiness partners, and processors. We aren't "aiding" these countries out of the goodness of our own hearts, though it's sold to the American people that way. The only thing we're really aiding is the nests of executives and managers in the food industry; we practically hand them the feathers while they laugh. These countries could recover if we'd simply support the grassroots efforts of local people to change the way food is grown, distributed, and consumed inside of their own countries [133].

So we need to turn and face the facts square: our government is already an oppressive regime; our government already starves people on purpose - they just do it with the benefit of a good public relations campaign. They know how to sell it. And they know exactly what they are doing. They then turn around and further compound the misery by their involvement in the IMF and World Bank, who takes the exploitation and the starvation to even higher levels of iniquity.

Oppressors in Nice Suits:
The IMF and World Bank

According to the IMF and World Bank, they exist to help out those poor struggling nations when they reach a point of crisis poverty. Isn't that nice of them? They do this out of the goodness of their own heart, of course. That's why we filter trillions and trillions of dollars of taxpayer money into these institutions every year. Because we're "helping."

When an "underdeveloped" or "disadvantaged" nation needs money, they'll first go to the World Bank and take out a loan. Supposedly, the purpose of these loans is to help the countries "build schools and health centers, provide water and electricity, fight disease, and protect the environment" [134]. With this oh-so-wonderful agency pouring money into all of these poor countries, why is the Third World as poor and miserable as ever? Because the terms of the loan repayment take up such a significant part of the country's budget that any improvements able to be made fall into disarray shortly thereafter. Usually, countries wind up defaulting on these loans, which means they have to refinance...through the IMF.

When the IMF comes in, they put together a re-payment schedule that eats up 40%-60% of the country's wealth, usually in the form of exports, not actual money. Like a stern father who is "helping out" his teenaged daughter with her finances, they also come in and demand that the country, in order to receive the fund, enact what they call structural adjustment or "austerity measures." That's code for turning their country into a miserable pit of despair by:

- Massive cutbacks in government spending, especially social spending, which usually includes most of the things the government was trying to achieve through their World Bank loan in the first place.

- Cutbacks or containment of wages for government employees. When a massive number of employees in a country start receiving wage cuts, the economy is necessarily impacted. There are fewer people to buy products which means more businesses close or cut wages, which means more people can't buy products, which means the cycle of misery continues until it hits rock bottom.

- Privatization of state enterprises and de-regulation of the economy. Translation: rich private companies from overseas are going to sweep in to take care of whatever few services the government can still offer, sucking up the rest of the government's wealth. They will tell that government that they are "saving them money" by privatization, when in fact it has been well documented that privatization often only saves money on paper—in the initial estimates. The actual execution of services nearly always costs more money than the public run services did. Because the economy is "de-regulated," these large corporations can also sweep in to undercut the local small businesspeople, just like Wal-Mart has done for thousands of Mom and Pop shops across America.

The result? More poverty, more people unable to get by, more homelessness and hunger.

- Elimination of protection for the domestic market and fewer restrictions on the operation of foreign investors. On paper, of course, this sounds a lot like encouraging new businesses to come in and provide good jobs. But this isn't what happens. Instead, foreign investors come in and either build de-regulated, unsafe factories where they pay women and children sweat shop wages to work 12-15 hour days in conditions you wouldn't make your dog suffer, or they simply come in and buy up land so that they can exploit natural resources directly, without doing anything so crass as helping one of those native people make money.

- Devaluation of the currency, which is mostly a result of everything else that has taken place, but is now done on purpose because supposedly, this will help the country pay back the debt. Of course, it won't. It's simply that the IMF *doesn't want their currency*. They want the natural resources—including grain, shipped out by the ton, keeping it out of reach for the citizens of that nation and putting it back into the hands of greedy businessmen who will then go on to sell it in richer Western countries in order to make even more money.

Since Americans, on the whole, are fairly decent people and have been shown time and time again to not really approve of our country sweeping in like the Evil Empire to do these things to other countries (witness the number of anti-war demonstrations for Vietnam and Iraq), the government, the IMF, and the World Bank have to *sell us* on why these countries are poor. Otherwise, we might start asking questions, and they can't have that. So what do they tell us?

They tell us that these countries are hopeless "basket cases." They tell us that they don't have enough natural resources to produce food. They lie and say that the *other governments* are *so corrupt* that they are keeping their people down. There's never any mention of the IMF and World Bank waltzing in there with a massive, contrived vacuum cleaner to literally suck away the wealth of a country until there's nothing at all left. In the countries themselves, only the very wealthy elite survive, and they often throw in their lot with the IMF and World Bank. Why? Because *they benefit*, of course.

Think about the 2008 housing crisis. While your Average Joe was losing his house to foreclosure, rich investors went in and bought $100,000 houses for $24,000 *or less*. Since they couldn't really "flip them" in this economy, they made money off of them the other way—by renting them out, often to the very people who had just lost a home to the housing crisis they benefited from. Get 10 homes to rent out at even as little as $500 a month and you've just pulled down $60,000 a year for as long as you own the home…meaning your little investment portfolio has paid for itself and is generating little but pure profit (minus maintenance, property management, advertisement, tax and vacant unit charges to be sure) in just four years. And, of course, most landlords raise the rent a little bit every single year to "keep up with the market," often by $15-$20; so in 4 years that same family is either now paying a $600 rent or they've had to move on to even worse accommodations. In the Third World, as it applies to farming, a few "mega farmers" go in and buy up all the land that the middle-class farmer or the peasant-subsistence farmer just ultimately lost because they couldn't make enough money selling their small yields to make up for the costs of creating those yields in the first place. The mega-farmer then proceeds to farm it, perhaps hiring back some of those displaced farmers at slave wages, and proceeds to make a fortune selling them off to the exporters (because, after all, nobody in their own country can afford to buy it; which was one of the very problems that threw the smaller farmers out of business in the first place).

*Bangladesh is one of the countries marketed to the average United States citizen as being an absolutely hopeless case, incapable of feeding itself. Here's what people who have actually visited the country have to say to that: Bangladesh isn't a hopeless basket case: there are indeed **enough resources** in that country to provide for all. The media-generated image of an entire people condemned to perpetual hunger is now being challenged. The truth is more hopeful, if paradoxical: despite its current low productivity, Bangladesh may already produce enough grain for all its people. Moreover, it has barely tapped its agricultural potential—among the greatest in the world. But this abundance has been siphoned off for centuries: first to British colonial rulers who 'underdeveloped' the country and* *eliminated the peasant's right to till the soil, and since independence to rich landowners and merchants who control the lands and agricultural markets. The wealth of the countryside is controlled in a few hands, with poor peasants and landless workers suffering from chronic poverty, and, periodically, massive famines.* [135]

Bangladesh pays $1070 million in debt servicing each year, primarily to the IMF and World Bank, for loans taken out by a dictatorial regime in the 1990s, a regime that is no longer in power. While several individual countries have forgiven their share of the debt entirely, the IMF and World Bank continue to impose theirs— and some of those same individual countries are members of the IMF and World Bank, meaning they continue to carry culpability for the plight of this "HIDC" (heavily indebted country). This is the Corporate Tyranny, the oppressive banker-created "government" that starves a staggering 24,000 a day all over the world.

It's bad when you can say that even the *King of Babylon* from 2250 BC, the undisputed bad guy nation of the Bible, can be said to be kinder than the IMF. That is, the Code of Hammurabi stipulated that someone who owed any kind of a debt was to be allowed to restructure that debt and pay nothing in the years where the "storm god" or a lack of water wiped out his crops through no fault of his own. "If the Babylonian farmer who had lost his crop had been forced to pay back his creditor anyway, he would soon have sold off his possessions, his animals, and his land. Instead of living as a more or less prosperous and independent farmer, he would have joined the ranks of the landless poor, surviving on casual labor from hand to mouth. A wealthy neighbor or merchant would have bought the farmer's property on the cheap and grown richer exploiting it…the IMF does not see natural disasters as mitigating circumstances. A few days after the Mexico City Earthquake of September 1985, the Fund's flying squads were back in town, demanding their due" [136].

Countries can always refuse to pay the debt—but if they do, all of the member nations of the IMF and World Bank, as well as the funders themselves, will refuse to lend to them in the future. This is a fear that keeps many nations marching in lockstep with the IMF's demands. Increasing the taxes on the people, even those barely earning enough to live, is usually the only way the governments can ultimately keep up with ever increasing demands from hungry bank barons. For countries already in trouble, already relying heavily on debt just to function, the threat of being expelled from the lending network is usually enough. Just imagine how well the United States would function if all of the other nations stopped agreeing to lend to us?

Who else benefits from the activities of the IMF? Why, Wall Street does, of course. In 1995, for example, the IMF contributed almost $18 billion to a Clinton administration bailout of the Wall Street interests which stood to lose billions with Mexico's peso devaluation [137].

So to put the entire picture together for you, let's look at how oppression destroys lives every single day...

The American Empire begins by offering "food aid" to "distressed countries" which put local farmers out of business. Sometimes this plan also goes by the name "Food for Peace," implying that these countries will be so grateful that they'll never attack us. In point of fact, we're simply going to bankrupt them to the point where their military could never compete with ours. In doing all of this, we line the pockets of the biggest of the big Agribusinesses concerns.

As the economy continues to decline, the country itself gets into financial trouble and finds itself unable to offer essential services. So they go to the World Bank and take out a loan. Servicing the debt takes the wind out of the sails of their economy even more, until the economy tanks and the country is forced to refinance its debt. Until this happens, the bankers profit.

The IMF refinances the debt and adopts "structural measures" which force the country to open the gates wide to elitist business concerns who can now waltz into the country and do whatever they want. The IMF destroys the currency and demands exports of real goods, usually in the form of food, to service the debt. The country is plunged down into a poverty from which it can't escape. A few elites within the country are glad to jump into bed with the IMF as they can now buy up most of the country at rock bottom prices and profit. The bankers profit, Big Business profits.

Occasionally, something goes wrong on Wall Street, and out of the heart that bleeds for people that will only make a billion or so this year, the IMF steps in to finance bailouts.

Are you angry yet?

And because they feel they don't yet have enough power, the IMF bankers are at the bleeding edge, beating the drums for world currency and world government. From the *London Telegraph*, April 3 2009:

A single clause in Point 19 of the communiqué issued by the G20 leaders amounts to revolution in the global financial order.

"We have agreed to support a general SDR allocation which will inject $250bn (£170bn) into the world economy and increase global liquidity," it said. SDRs are Special Drawing Rights, a synthetic paper currency issued by the International Monetary Fund that has lain dormant for half a century.

*In effect, the G20 leaders have **activated the IMF's power to create money** and begin global "quantitative easing". **In doing so, they are putting a de facto world currency into play.** It is outside the control of any sovereign body.* [138]

The Business Insider ran the following headline on February 26, 2010: **Head of IMF Calls on Member States to Give Him Global Oversight of the Financial System.**

But even if you're not disturbed by these obviously unscrupulous individuals gaining even more power, you ought to be disturbed by this. Those actions really do directly influence your pocketbook. What would happen to global food prices if we got out of these Third World nations, if we cancelled their debts, if we stopped sending "food aid," and stopped demanding most of their exports? What if, if we must give out loans, we focused on individual Kiva style loans to entrepreneurs who wished to begin buying back pieces of their country? What would happen to global food prices if, for example, Bangladesh fed itself and began using the full production capacity of its own country?

All of this information pokes even more holes into the "overpopulation" theory. Wouldn't the gap close if we'd just get out of the way and let people produce and keep their own food? Even with resource management problems, climate problems, and all of the other problems, it seems that food prices would have to go down if more people were producing food, even if they were only subsistence farming and feeding themselves rather than putting pressure on the markets to feed them. It's just basic math. Simple math. The bankers would love to tell you it's all more complicated than that, because they are served by that complication, but are they telling us the truth? Is it *really* that complicated at all?

2.2 Poor Resource Management
ℰↄ•ℭঽ

Resource management happens on several levels. Countries and corporations set policies which impact the use of resources; individuals with control over any given resource also make choices. Often these choices exist in a very fragile web. For example, an individual trucker controls one portion of the transportation resources that gets food to tables. By choosing to engage in a sit-down strike, that trucker can contribute to famine. An individual farmer can choose farming techniques which exhaust the water and soil, or he can choose careful, slower techniques which may produce fewer short-term yields but will ultimately allow the land to continue to produce for a long time. Urban planners can choose whether to put up yet another shopping center or subdivision, or can decide whether that land has, ultimately, better uses for the production of food.

At given times in history, resource management has either directly impacted or adversely affected the course of a famine. But during the 20th – 21st century, we've seen resource management hit crisis proportions across the board. The resources we can immediately look to are land use, water availability, soil quality, the transportation infrastructure including the cost of energy and the way we produce that energy, and the spread of urbanization vs. an encouragement through whatever means are available to raise that 2% number to a higher, more sustainable number of farmers.

Land Use

To an extent, any use of the land we make represents a zero-sum proposition. That is, the earth is not getting any larger. The amount of land we have is finite.

When we use land for any one purpose, we necessarily remove the ability to use that land for any other purpose. Unless we eventually make it into space or start terra-forming planets to support ourselves, this problem will always be with us.

It's about more than urbanization vs. rural population, though this issue makes its way into the scope of the problem as well. It's also about arguments over how to use the land and who should benefit from it. It touches on meat production vs. vegetable production, on environmental regulations that shut down a farmer's ability to farm, and on a host of other issues.

Urbanization

We've already discussed urbanization somewhat—we drew parallels between the over-urbanization of Rome and the urbanization of the United States. Urban sprawl takes up quite a bit of farmland, and beyond that, so many people are leaving the countryside. In short, it does no good to have acres and acres of farmland if there's *nobody there to work it*. One of the resources being mismanaged in the case of urbanization is people.

> *Civic and business leaders in the places most affected by hollowing out will tell anyone willing to listen how it is their young people, not iron, steel, beef, corn, or soybeans that is their most valuable export commodity...in a post-industrial economy that places such a high premium on education and credentials, the flight of so many young people is transforming rural communities throughout the nation into impoverished ghost towns. A new birth simply cannot replace the loss that results every time a college-educated twenty-something on the verge of becoming a worker, taxpayer, homeowner or parent leaves... hollowing out has repercussions far beyond the boundaries of the small town it affects...this is the place where our food comes from.* [139]

In addition, the proliferation of "urban sprawl" has led to the active gobbling of farmland. Those farms are becoming new highways, fringe industrial houses, strip malls, and sprawled housing developments, all the while reducing our ability to grow food. In many areas, the problem is exacerbated by the trend towards development because the development raises property taxes, which in turn forces many farmers to sell—often to the very developers who began the process in the first place [140].

The increase in city-space is also an active factor in taking money out of the pockets of farmers. The larger the city, the farther the food has to be transported, putting demands on energy and increasing the amount of transportation vulnerability. A chain of wholesalers and retailers grows up between the farmer and the consumer, which means that the farmer has to get higher yields to make a living. This leads to unsustainable farming practices which quickly exhaust the land [141].

According to the American Farmland Trust, we're literally losing an acre of farmland every minute, amounting to a poorly managed resource if one were ever seen.

Combating land-use problems in America would therefore mean the following:

- Farming would need to be an attractive option for workers once more. This is about more than the amount of money they could make—it's also about the level of respect that they could enjoy. Respect and prestige can drive many more decisions than money. Expanding college agricultural programs and advertisement of farming as a viable life option may help get people working the land once more. As *actual farming* needs to be the focus, let's save $1.3 trillion every year and stop paying people to *not* farm. Property tax and income tax incentives to farm might also be helpful. The American Farmland Trust notes that there are often "insurmountable obstacles" to young people who wish to own or rent a farm unless they are already related to current farm owners [142].

- Increase attention to the problem of urban sprawl and get policy behind combating it. Strike a balance between the needs of developers and the needs of farmers by actually testing the viability of each slice of land as farmland. Land which is not good for farming due to poor soil or water access could be zoned in for these projects without eating up more farmland. The American Farmland Trust suggests that "State governments should enable, and local authorities should operate, effective programs for purchasing development rights to farmland, thereby either adding to the base that agricultural zoning supports, or achieving what zoning fails to realize. Local government should apply zoning policies which help maintain an adequate land base for farming" [143].

- Increase our personal patronage of vehicles which get farmers directly in touch with consumers, such as the local farmer's market. Encourage our local retailers and restaurateurs to buy from local farmers as much as possible in order to decrease the pocket-book distance between the farmer and the city the farmer ultimately supplies.

Many of these solutions require that we ourselves become active citizens who pay attention to land-use issues in our own communities and who act to see the right things done. It also requires us to eat locally whenever possible; to spread the simple message that we need farms to have food; that the food is in jeopardy because the farms are in jeopardy.

To our current land use resource management problems we can add the practice of creating biofuels. In theory, biofuels sounded like a great idea: grow our fuel, a renewable resource, and lose our dependence on foreign oil. And thus a quarter of our corn crop was sent to the pump instead of to the table. In light of the food crisis, it might be time to re-think that strategy, especially given the costs most of us don't see. "In practice [biofuels] sacrifice the food needs of the poor to the transportation needs of the relatively well-to-do. As Robin Maynard of the U.K. Soil Association points out, the same amount of grain needed to fill the tank of a sports utility vehicle could be used to feed a person *for an entire year.* This is not a fair or sustainable trade-off" [144]. This is especially true in light of the fact that bio-fuels can be made out of waste oil, rather than fresh corn. Fresh corn, however, seems to be the favored method.

Production Prevention on Cultivatable Land

In spite of the fact that land-use issues are making their impact on the amount of arable farmland available for use worldwide, there's some startling facts about how much farmland remains. One might expect that cultivatable land is disappearing at an alarming rate, but that has not, in fact, proven to be the case. Instead, more often, some other factor is preventing that production from happening.

In *Human Adaptation and Population Growth: a Non-Malthusian Perspective* author David S. Kleinman shares some of these important facts.

The eminent agricultural economist Colin Clark estimated In 1967 that the earth could feed 47 billion at an American Standard of consumption and 157 billion at a Japanese standard without recourse to what he called science fiction technologies. Other observers, though not as sanguine as Clark about the carrying capacity of the earth, are nonetheless cautiously optimistic. Even the United Nations Food and Agriculture organization, which in 1952 was described in **The Economist** *as a "permanent institution devoted to proving there is not enough food in the world to go around" sees hopeful prospects, though with various caveats and qualifications.*

A number of studies indicate that less than half of the land which could be used for crop production under current conditions is cultivated worldwide; only one-third of the potentially arable land is cultivated at any one time. These studies include such considerations as topography, water availability, the absence of serious problems such as alkalinity, types of crops and forages, transportation, location, possibilities for multiple cropping, and costs of bringing land into production." [145]

We saw this very phenomenon in action when we examined Bangladesh in section 2.1. Again we must ask ourselves, what might change about the food situation if we began giving serious attention to actually making use of the available land? One also wonders who continues to benefit from the insistence that there are just "too many people," as well as arguments that it's all going downhill from here and the world will never produce enough food again.

The reasons for this lack of production are varied. Environmental regulations can join the debt-related reasons seen in section 2.1. So can a simple lack of people, as we explored in urbanization. An inability to purchase farmland due to a lack of availability of credit and a high degree of expense also contributes here in the United States; it is not easy to "get back to the land," even for people who would like to do it. However, this fact provides a very handy rebuttal to those who wish to embark on a campaign of "population reduction" in order to make sure there's enough food for everyone. The answer remains: increase production. Creation is always a bit more challenging than destruction, which might account for the reasons why many more people want to embrace overpopulation theories instead. Or it could just be that you have to dig very deeply to understand the amount of land that actually is available, even in the face of topsoil problems and brand new dustbowls. The corporate-controlled media would rather focus on overpopulation because to focus on anything else would be to bring the activities of the IMF, the World Bank, the Agribusiness elite and the wealthy developers into clear focus.

The Problem of One-Crop Cultivation and Other Poor Farming Practices

Monoculture, the practice of cultivating a single sort of crop, has become widely embraced simply because it creates a much larger yield for a much smaller area of land. Unfortunately, the problems of monoculture have been repeatedly shown to outweigh the benefits. Many of our current agricultural ills can be laid at the feet of this practice, and we've been aware of this since the 1960s. Unfortunately, the complex web of policies that continues to make this a profitable avenue for farmers around the world continues.

Yet even the farmers who feel forced into such practices must be aware of the dangers. The Irish Potato Famine amply demonstrated how vulnerable monocultures are to any one incidence of disease, pests, or fungal invasions. On a global scale, we depend largely on just five plants: wheat, corn, soybeans, rice, and barley. "It may not be until one of two monocultures fail on a massive scale," writes Michael Shuman, author of *Going Local, Creating Self-Reliant Communities in a Global Age*, "causing millions to die from famine, that markets will sharpen the resolve of governments and entrepreneurs to revive community farming. Localities mindful of their own survival, and smart entrepreneurs living within them, must act sooner. The goal of every community needs to be to collect, plant, and develop, through new community businesses, seeds uniquely suited to its bioregion" [146].

Monocultures also provide a fertile ground for pests and diseases. They are simply less resistant to trouble, even as the things which attack them grow more resistant to any resistance the single-crop field has to offer. Meanwhile, the single crop structure has the effect of stripping nutrients from the soil, rendering the soil inert and largely useless. The only way to combat the problem is to exacerbate it, through ever-expanding quantities of chemical weed killers, pesticides, and fertilizers. That's not to say monoculture is a hopelessly unsustainable practice. Indeed, some ingenious farmers have simply begun planting species rich "islands" at intervals throughout their fields, islands containing hundreds of indigenous plant species. They've found the practice to contribute to pest and disease control as well as in restoring fertility to over-taxed soils [147]. To combat resource mismanagement, it would be wise to increase awareness of the practice so that it can spread, alleviating some of the tragic problems of monoculture while allowing farmers (and the consumers who eat the food!) to continue to benefit from high yields and fast crops.

Disease alone has led to some staggering numbers about our food supplies:

Our food supply is about as secure as a Florida trailer park in a hurricane. According to Cornell University ecologist David Pimentel, approximately 70,000 pests and plant diseases now consume half the world's crop yield every year, despite the use of $35 billion worth of pesticides. [148]

Monoculture has also been linked to colony collapse syndrome, which wiped out nearly a quarter of the world's honeybees in 2007. The theory is that the immune system of the bee needs a variety of different pollens and nectars to choose from; a single diet of one crop makes them more susceptible to illness and death [149].

Organic farmers have turned away from the monoculture practice, relying on a polyculture practice to help them resist pests, disease, and fungi without having to rely on chemicals. An effort to eat local foods farmed in this manner is one way that the average, everyday person can encourage farmers in this practice. Though organic foods are extremely expensive at your average supermarket, a visit to your local farmer's market can usually prove to be quite economical.

The Problem of Meat

Meat consumption is tied to deep cultural roots, practices, and assumptions. Many people get angry or defensive when one starts addressing the issues behind meat, especially as it pertains to use of the land. Yet it's difficult to deny that plant-based foods can feed more people per acre than animal-based foods can. Yet people have been known to get infuriated at any suggestion that eating as much meat as we Americans do isn't a good idea. The defensiveness has some surprising sources at times. The resistance to reducing meet has ranged from racism and cultural superiority issues (a meat based diet is considered to demonstrate affluence and civilization over a grain based diet), gender issues (i.e., meat is considered manly, salads are considered feminine), habits, availability of good vegetable-based alternatives, and cultural teachings which have made vegetables the red-headed stepchild of the meal, that thing which must be choked down before one can get to the desert. Meat tastes good, and most of our cookbooks and beloved holiday meals feature meat in one form or fashion. Expensive meat can be seen as a status symbol, a proclamation of wealth and prosperity. Biblically, there's certainly no prohibition against eating meat. Yet Christian compassion, as well as concern for achieving enough food to go around, may require us to at least reduce our meat consumptions, if not give it up altogether.

The methods for feeding livestock have changed since the 1950s, and as the methods changed, so too did the ethics. We've made a shift from cows grazing primarily on grass, hogs eating primarily slops, and chickens eating worms and kitchen scraps to huge factory farms where grain, hormones, and antibiotics are the order of the day. Each animal thus consumes almost two and a half tons of grain, soy, and other feeds each year. And of course, all this conversion of grain to animal protein doesn't just go to making steaks: the animals have to make a lot of bones, hair, and other parts that we don't typically eat. Beef is the worst: for every 16 pounds of grain and soy we feed to cattle we get back exactly one pound of meat on the plate [150].

It's not just the amount of grain needed to produce meat, but the very fact that we lose meat in the course of production. "John McFarlane, Executive Director of the Council for Livestock Protection, has calculated that 'the amount of meat lost each year through careless handling and brutality would be enough to feed a million Americans a year.'...If everyone in the developed world became a vegetarian, it would be possible to give four tons of edible grain to every starving person" [151].

We also simply consume more meat per person than we did in the 1950s. The USDA reports:

Now more than ever, America is a Nation of meat eaters. In 2000, total meat consumption (red meat, poultry, and fish) reached 195 pounds (boneless, trimmed-weight equivalent) per person, 57 pounds above average annual consumption in the 1950s. Each American consumed an average of 7 pounds more red meat than in the 1950s, 46 pounds more poultry, and 4 pounds more fish and shellfish. [152]

When you do the math you come to realize that yearly, each American is now consuming 3,120 pounds of grain per year in meat, which does not count the consumption of every other type of food matter. We have to ask ourselves whether this amounts to our "fair share." What is our Christian duty in a world where babies go to bed with swollen bellies and emaciated frames, not because their countries can't produce food, but because our appetite for the taste of meat has had such a dramatic impact on the global food production picture? If we would avoid or ameliorate famine, how then should we live?

Most people can live quite happily and healthily on a vegetarian diet. It does not make the majority of the populace sick or weak. It doesn't suddenly reduce a male's testosterone to the point where they become effeminate wimps. Most who try it find their waistlines slimmer, their energy levels higher, and their bodies healthier.

There are some people who experience what's called a "failure to thrive" on vegetarian diets, either because they don't take the time to put together a proper vegetarian diet offering a good mix of proteins (some, for example, go vegetarian and then proceed to eat nothing but Doritos), or because they have a metabolism which demands a heavy use of proteins.

Thankfully, there are actually several options short of full scale vegetarianism. As it stands, in the event of a global food crisis, most people are going to end up on vegetarian diets anyway, because that is what they will be capable of producing in their own yards, and that is what is going to be affordable as prices spiral ever-higher.

But you don't have to go all out to make a positive difference. You could do a world of good simply by reducing your consumption to 1950s levels. Reducing portion sizes to recommended levels (above common levels) and making meat a bit more of a garnish and a bit less of a main course would also have a positive impact. You can also steer clear of any meat that is produced on feed lots, opting instead for free-range meat by local farmers who are fed in the old fashioned manner. If you have the capability, you could raise your own cows, chickens, or hogs without impacting the global food picture in a negative way, especially if you also opt to feed them in the old fashioned way. If shifting your portion size or cooking style does not appeal, perhaps it would be possible to reduce meat consumption to 2-4 dinners a week, instead of 7 dinners a week. In addition, you could avoid, as much as possible, fast food meals that use the cheapest meat (thus the meat produced by the most destructive practices).

This is an individual, personal, free decision. But God did command us to look after the needs of the hungry, so it seems as though each of us ought to choose to do *something* positive in light of this information.

Water

Water is one of those life basics we in the Western World take for granted. We walk to the tap and, so long as we've paid our water bill and nothing's wrong with the plumbing, water reliably comes out of the faucet each and every time. Farmers, fishermen, and analysts might spend a lot of time worrying about the use and abuse of water as a resource, but the average person does not, except perhaps to be vaguely aware that some people say it's a good idea to turn off the water while brushing your teeth.

But water is absolutely vital to life, not just for itself, but as a critical element in food production. Mismanagement of water has as many terrifying potential consequences as mismanagement of the land. Without water, we can't grow crops at all. Without clean, unpolluted water, we lose out on seafood as a food source. The 2010 BP Oil Spill brought water somewhat back to the consciousness of the average American. Hundreds of Louisiana fishermen found themselves unable to do business thanks to this unprecedented ecological disaster.

Thus, water problems are as likely to bring about a famine as any other sort of problem we can name, whether it ceases to fall from the sky like we'd wish it to, whether we contaminate it, or whether we exhaust it as a resource.

Water for Crops

We can't control the rain. Droughts come and go without much human intervention and have throughout the course of history. But the bulk of our water-for-crops problems do not arise from a lack of rain, but from a massive strain being put on the groundwater and irrigation systems. FoodAndWaterWatch.org offers a succinct explanation of our groundwater issues.

Farmers in the western United States are drilling ever deeper to water their crops...In communities all around the country citizens are seeing the effects of a decline in one of our most crucial but least understood natural resources: groundwater.

The water that settles between rocks and dirt under the earth's surface after it rains accounts for 40% of our drinking and agricultural water supply. Through the watershed, it links to surface waters, which share sources of water from both above and below the ground. When it disappears, pumping through wells becomes harder and more expensive; rivers, lakes, streams and wetlands dry up, and even the land itself can cave in.

Today, our groundwater resources are disappearing in many parts of the country. In some regions, underground water levels are falling because we are pumping water through wells faster than it is naturally replaced by rainfall. This might permanently damage our aquifer's capacity to hold water, and can have broad consequences for our entire water supply. [153]

Many times the freedom movement gets a little bit uptight about water conservation issues. On several of the constitutionalist independent media sites, you will hear a great deal of sound and fury about low flow toilets (the government's in our bathrooms now!) and other measures taken to conserve water. Yet if there is a problem with generating enough water to produce enough crops to feed human beings, then it's rational to think that we should do something about the problem. Once again, this does not take a totalitarian regime. It doesn't even really take government regulations—each of us who owns our own home, for example, can install a low-flow showerhead. The quality of the shower doesn't change very much; the streams of water are somewhat thinner but it's basically the same shower. Again, these are voluntary measures that we can take because we have chosen to take them in response to a problem that we see. We do not support measures by the government to create or enforce any kind of "eco-police" who might show up to tell you how to manage your personal water consumption. Yet (and forgive the pun) refusing to have anything to do with any such measures because a wide-eyed Malthusian green supporter also suggests them is throwing the baby out with the bathwater.

The Malthusian can do it because he thinks there are too many people. We can do it because God called on us to be good stewards of the resources He gave to us, and because our grandparents and great-grandparents didn't think waste and excess were good ideas, either.

Besides, some of these methods *are* seeing success.

A promising alternative to developing new sources of groundwater is implementing intelligent water conservation and demand management programs that make better use of groundwater that's already available. Water conservation has already produced significant reductions in water use in many domestic, agricultural, and industrial applications. Use of low flow toilets, more efficient washing machines, and less water intensive landscaping can significantly reduce domestic groundwater needs. Many of these water efficient appliances and technologies are now widely used across the United States and around the world. Agricultural irrigation systems are becoming increasingly efficient. Drip irrigation has been shown to cut water use by 30%-70% over the standard conventional irrigation procedures, and has allowed some farmers to achieve irrigation efficiencies as high as 95%.

Water re-use has also helped meet demand without having to tap additional sources. Groundwater is utilized for potable and domestic needs while lower quality surface waters and wastewater are being used to satisfy lower quality demands like irrigation. Israel currently reuses 65% of its domestic wastewater for crop production, freeing up additional freshwater for households and industries. [154]

Making sure water is used in a responsible, sane manner is just as important as stocking up on canned goods or heirloom seeds. It is all part of stewarding our resources in a way that ensures an ability to feed ourselves in the foreseeable future.

Fishing Issues

Fish are in short supply. We've been overfishing our waters for decades, and as a result of doing so, many species are disappearing. Now we are faced with fish that eat exactly the same way cows and hogs do—grain fed fish in factory fish farms. Again you see some of the same problems: developing countries losing food in order to feed richer people the tastes they love. Companies, who continue to profit simply by hiking prices, don't show a lot of concern for disappearing species [155].

However, there has been a greater awareness of the problem in recent decades, enough that several species of fish are sustainable choices that you can eat without being party to destructive trawling and overfishing or putting further strain on the grain markets. You can, for example, buy sustainable fish online at ILoveBlueSea. com. You can also double check your fish choices on the Environmental Defense Fund or Monterey Bay Aquarium's sustainable fish watch pages. If you've taken the vegetarian route, of course, you avoid the fish question altogether.

Topsoil Erosion

Most of the soil's nutrients are found in the topsoil, which is exactly the soil that winds up in trouble. Topsoil erosion is not a new problem - Plato was talking about it back in the 4th century BC. And while we're losing topsoil at a slower rate due to conservation tillage, this is still a problem we need to keep an eye on. It takes 500 years to form just one inch of topsoil [156]!

Farmers have a great deal of impact on this problem simply by the practices they choose. Crop rotation, leaving fields fallow, contour plowing, strip cropping, terracing, and organic composting all offer some protection to the topsoil. There's also conservation tillage, which involves leaving crop residues in the soil to partially cover the topsoil, which helps to hold the essential top layer in place [157].

All of these resource management issues are issues for God-fearing people as well as those who are concerned about the ability of the world to feed itself. In fact, Christians should be wary of allowing purely secular, often Malthusian, interests to co-opt every aspect of this debate. As Ghillean T. Prance mentioned in *The Earth Under Threat: A Christian Perspective*:

> *The dominion in [Genesis 1:29-30] was not God's authority to use up all the earth's resources for human needs alone. A problem in the Western world has been that many Christian people have taken God's command of dominion as a divine authorization to exploit the earth with no thought for the welfare of cultures, other creatures, the landscape, the mineral resources, the oceans or the atmosphere.* [158]

2.3 Fundamental Disruptions in the Infrastructure

℘•℃

If you walk into your local Kroger or Safeway, you'll see row upon row of food. It's hard to imagine that those rows of food only represent about a three day supply for whatever section of the area that grocery store services. Yet it's true—if the trucks stopped running for even 3 days, you would begin to see most of the items you rely on disappear from your grocery store shelves.

Strikes, civil unrest, war, terror attacks, contaminated food, and spikes in fuel prices—all of them have the capability to throw your ability to get food out of whack. And depending upon the scope and identity of the problem, this food shortage could translate into a full scale famine. The disruptions would be there even for those of us who typically eat "locally," or eating with a 100 mile radius of your hometown—quite a significant distance if you suddenly lack the ability to simply hop into a car or truck and drive it.

The entire system is a very fragile spider's web.

To eat is to participate in a global food system. Our 800 million tons of food are shipped around the world annually. Food today travels an average of 1500 miles from harvest to table, a distance that is representative of the industrialization and globalization of the food supply and the dearth of knowledge consumers have about how and who is producing, processing, and transporting the food they eat. From grower to consumer, food often changes hands a dozen times or more, moving along a food supply chain that links producers, packagers, shippers, food manufacturers, wholesale distributors, food retailers, and consumers. With this modern industrialized agricultural system, the farmer is no longer at the center of the production process; farming is one component of a complex agribusiness system composed of agricultural inputs, farm production, processing, distribution, and consumption. [159]

This system is also a fragile spider's web that relies on a very small number of very large farms. 70% of our food supply is produced by a handful of big agribusiness producers. That other 30%, held by small-to-medium sized farmers across America, would look mighty small if any of these large businesses were forced out of business or lost their monoculture crop to any of the myriad of dangers that threaten such a set-up. Yet our government, social, and business policies are still structured in such a way as to make it very difficult for this network of smaller farmers to stay in business; they survive through a series of co-ops, farmer's markets, and even roadside stands where fruit is sold from the back of trucks.

Over the past four decades, concentration in the ownership and management of food production has dramatically restructured the agricultural and food industry in the United States... Through mergers and acquisitions and fortified by farm policy, companies achieve economies of scale to produce or control a larger share of commodities. With economies of scale, companies are able to achieve cost advantages and undercut competitors by forcing the price of commodities below the cost of production. Cost advantages are achieved through larger-scale production, an increase in the number of units produced results in a decrease in the cost of producing each unit.

The trend towards larger farms is tied directly to profit margins and to the U.S. system of farm subsidies, which rewards gross output and encourages a "get big" strategy. On average, smaller farms have negative farm operating profits and frequently combine on-farm income with income from off-farm sources. As farm size increases, profit margins also increase. Larger farms average an operating profit margin of greater than 10%, but this profitability is tied to a large extent to farm commodity programs. By their nature, commodity programs encourage farmers to expand operations in order to obtain more acres and higher guaranteed government payments. In addition to leaving the concentration of production in the hands of fewer and fewer farmers, this subsidy system—applied primarily to five crops (corn, wheat, soybeans, cotton, and rice)—benefits the operation of food manufacturers and other food marketers who have access to a steady supply of cheap farm commodities, which reduces costs and boosts of profits. Artificially cheap corn, for example, underwrites the "supersizing" of fast food processors as well as the production of high fructose corn syrup and ethanol. [160]

It's all about food supply, and whether and how those food supplies can be cut off, contaminated, endangered or disrupted. The set-up of our current food infrastructure is remarkably vulnerable simply because it is both so complicated and large. We can focus the bulk of our attention on three areas: transportation, importation, and contamination. Note that any one of these areas can be disrupted or aggravated by any long term war or civil unrest.

Transportation

There are, of course, two prongs to any discussion of the food transportation infra-structure. The first is the fuel prices and the second is the trucks and railways that get our food to us. There are approximately 21 million trucks involved with getting food across the United States every day; rail transportation also plays a large role [161].

Because of this fact, any spike in fuel prices impacts the price of food. When you go to your local supermarket, you aren't just paying for the food itself. You're paying the cost of the food, the cost of getting the food to the wholesale distributor, the cost of getting the food from the distributor to the retail store, the cost of shelf space and other fees associated with shelf space, and in some cases, the cost of packaging as well. Given your average apple has racked up 1500 travel miles, and given the average price of fuel these days, your apple has spent about $200 in gas just reaching your front door. The cost is spread around a bit of course, as your apple made the journey with thousands of other apples, so that at the end of the day you only pay the few cents share of that apple's cost. The U.S. Energy Information Administration estimates that gas prices could top $4.00 a gallon by September 2011; your food prices will rise accordingly.

Each increase in food prices means another bracket of people who can't afford to buy food. Some families will be able to continue buying food, but less of it.

Others absorb the price increase without much pain, but the numbers eventually become a cage. Truckers are also being laid off; that means fewer trucks are running. That will translate into higher food prices as well.

Rising fuel prices bring trouble, however. They put truckers out of business, or the truckers wind up striking. In almost every case of trucker strikes around the world, high food prices have wound up cited as one of the pressing reasons. Your average urban center is not producing its own food, so when the trucks stop, the grocery store shelves empty out, too. Those trucks also bring the gas that you use, so, if you are one of the millions of people who have a long commute to work, you might find your ability to get to your source of livelihood dries up—and corporations are not known for being understanding and flexible towards the bulk of their employees. If you had a one-month food supply, you would have a better chance than most people of surviving a short-term strike.

A truly organized long-term strike, however, would be absolutely devastating. It would, in fact, be enough to bring the entire country to its knees.

Trucking advocate and activist Allen Smith of TruthAboutTrucking.com offers an extremely vivid picture of what would happen to the nation if all of the truckers ever banded together for a serious strike that was not announced and circumvented. It would start with a mass panic as people began to rush the stores for supplies; store shelves would wind up empty and stay that way. Within several hours the gas stations would be out of fuel. Schools and universities would shut down because school buses could not run. Law and order would deteriorate because law enforcement vehicles would be left on the side of the road. All of the approximately 145,381,402 vehicles in the United States would become useless. Livestock would die out for want of feed. There would be trash everywhere because the garbage trucks wouldn't be able to run. Hospitals would swiftly run out of medicine and food. Banks and ATM machines would be devoid of cash. Power plants would eventually shut down, which in turn would shut down the internet and other communication mediums. In short, all of society would break down, with global repercussions [162].

Of course, it's unlikely the United States government would allow themselves to be dismantled in this way. It's far more likely that FEMA would activate the top secret Continuity of Government plan. We'd see martial law declared, all of the trucks seized, and FEMA labor camps opened with the striking truckers likely ending up as among the first detainees [163]. Neither scenario is pretty.

Importation

As of right now, 27% of the fresh fruit we eat and about 38% of the vegetables we eat come from Mexico, with other imports streaming in from around the world (164). As our own ability to produce food continues to dwindle, our dependence on foreign food will have to rise with it. It's not necessary to import all of our food for us to become, essentially, dependent on imports. When we allow other countries become the suppliers of vital commodities, we essentially hand them a collar to put around our necks.

Imagine what would happen if we broke out into a full scale war with any of the countries from whom we currently import food? At the very least, they'd stop sending their food. We'd have to wait for all military action to be completed before things would return to normal. Given that war could destroy a great deal of the production capacity of any nation, that might not be for a long, long time.

Imports, too, depend on the fragile web of energy and oil: oil for ships, oil for planes. It wouldn't take too many more hikes in energy prices to start driving food import companies out of business, or to turn prices prohibitive. In a sense, our energy dependence already translates into food dependence—we are now making a bad situation worse.

It would not even take a war or a spike in oil prices to cut off our import supply, however. In truth, as more and more countries face famine on their own soils, they will have to face the decision to cease exports. India has already banned exports to account for a growing food problem [165]. Russia has made noises in this direction as well. Those goods will not be available to us no matter how little malice is inherent in the act. Individuals who are in control of at least a part of their food supply will fare better than those who are caught completely unprepared.

Contamination

We already see a fair amount of contamination of our food products simply because they're coming in from foreign nations where standards are more lax and safety procedures less observed. Throughout 2010, many products were recalled from the shelves because they were found to be infested with salmonella and e. coli. Yet those are simply individual products, and most people absorbed their lack with a fair degree of grace, choosing simply to eat the myriad of other choices on the shelves until those food items returned.

A terrorist threat against the food supply, however, where a group comes in to *deliberately* contaminate the food supply with poisons or pathogens, could represent an entirely different story. The Kansas State University Food Safety Network outlines the terrorist threat in a report titled *Safe Food: From Farm to Fork.*

> *Large farms and food processing plants with widespread distribution networks are vulnerable targets for food terrorism. Potential weapons range from sophisticated bio-engineered pathogens to other agents that are part of the natural environment. The US Centers for Disease Control and Prevention has cited the following biological agents as potential weapons that could be used to deliberately poison the food supply: cloistridium, botulinium, salmonella spp., e. coli. 0157itt7, vibrio cholerae. An attack could occur at any point along the food supply chain, from farm to fork. Terrorists could create harm through (1) final product contamination using either chemical or biological agents with the intent to kill or cause illness among consumers, (2) disruption of food distribution systems, (3) damage to the agricultural economy by introducing devastating crop pathogens or exotic animal diseases such as foot-and-mouth disease or (4) hoaxes, using the mass media or Internet, which create anxiety and fear.* [166]

Though there are questions about exactly how much terrorism is actually a threat, at least as it pertains to angry Muslims acting independently, the fact remains that these things could happen. Ultimately, it won't matter to us as consumers whether it's a false flag attack launched by subversive, treasonous elements in the United States government as an excuse to take a little more control, or whether an angry jihadist takes his stab at the food supply. And many people who now fall under the heading of domestic terrorists, from pro-life activists to gun owners to anyone who ever thought voting for Ron Paul was a good idea, would end up squarely in the sites of the government as easy scapegoats.

2.4 Natural Disasters and Weather Patterns

ଈୠ•ୡଔ

Good crops rely on good weather, and the weather system has always been beyond mankind's ability to control, though not for lack of trying. Weather patterns have been confounding us and creating famines since the dawn of time. For all of our technology and for all of our attempts to understand meteorology, we're still at nature's mercy.

What the Heck is Going on With Our Climate?

Concern over some sort of "global climate change" is nothing new, especially when the weather starts acting in ways we don't expect it to act. *Time Magazine* ran a June 24, 1974 headline which read: Another Ice Age? Now in the early 21st century, we're afraid the planet's getting too hot, and we've allowed this idea to lead us down some really dark paths. A sick video released by the 10:10 organization, for example, showed teachers blowing up kids in their classroom who dared to disagree with climate change. Meanwhile, Al Gore, the poster-child for global warming, buys houses (in the plural) that would fail any eco-friendly test you'd care to give them.

The evidence, though, shows that humans seem to flip out over *any* perceived shift in temperature and spin it into a number of crazy apocalyptic scenarios, as in 1974 when the media was sure we were all about to be covered over by the glaciers. Global temperatures did spike in 1999, to an eyebrow-raising degree, but began to fall again after the turn of the century [167]. It was this sort of thinking that led author Holly Lisle to acerbically note on her blog, "Global Climate Crisis— means that we will have rising temperatures around the world, followed by falling temperatures around the world—all going on at the same time—with storm systems, hurricanes, tornadoes and so on happening somewhere all the time. The ice caps and glaciers will expand, and then retreat, and then expand, and then RETREAT!!!! (Oh, God, whatever shall we do?) The other name for the Global Climate Crisis? Weather" [168].

That's not to say there aren't some serious ecological and environmental problems, and as we've observed in the previous sections, many of the solutions for those problems overlap with things the climate change proponents would get behind—and many don't. Many people beating the drums for the global climate crisis are beating the drums for a totalitarian government with Malthusian aims. Others are well-meaning people who truly do care, people who have been duped by a lie that, if nothing else, serves people who want to profit from cap and trade. It's important to go through all of this, because you can't sit down and have a conversation about weather without tripping over whether or not the entire world is in danger from events that would fit right into some cataclysmic summer disaster movie.

If anything, some researchers have given us reason to think the current, small warming trend might even be a good thing. We've tracked the history of famine in this book enough for the same pattern observed by David Zhang of the University of Hong Kong to come to light—colder periods typically result in far more danger. The Little Ice Age, for example, was part of the force that drove Asian rats to carry the plague down into Europe. As for our modern warming, it's interesting to note that both the Roman and Medieval warmings were a bit warmer than what we're getting now. We've had less than 0.7 C degrees of warming in the past 160 years. Historically, warming cycles typically deliver about half their total warmings in the early decades, implying that only another 0.7 degrees of warming will be on its way during the next several centuries, which is not likely to disrupt modern crop production on a global scale [169]. On a regional scale, certainly, we've seen freak weather, much as we've already observed, and that freak weather has wiped out harvests enough to put pressure on the global food system. But there's reason to believe we've got a little bit more to fear from the movements of El Nino than the carbon in the atmosphere.

When Natural Disaster Strikes

About the only natural disaster we've not seen in the United States in recent years is a tsunami. The number of, and the intensity of, natural disasters seems to be on the upswing. Wildfires, mudslides, earthquakes, tornados, hurricanes, blizzards and ice storms—we've seen it all. Because of that fact, it only stands to reason that you should take the time to create a sense of preparedness for whatever natural disaster might occur in the area where you live. [170]

On a regional scale, natural disasters tend to bring hunger hard on the heels of the original event. This hunger can be short term as the infrastructure winds up disrupted, but longer-term hungers can also be the result. Even assuming a benevolent government, we have seen how often food aid goes awry, even in our own country. For example, $5.3 million worth of food aid from Britain sat in an Arkansas warehouse, some of it going bad, during Hurricane Katrina. Rather than distributing it, officials passed the buck and bickered over whether or not the food was safe [171].

During a disaster, food and bottled water wind up at a premium. After the 2010 Haitian earthquake bottled water was almost as good as gold. It can take time for aid to start to flow, or even natural functions of the infrastructure. Those who are prepared to weather such disasters can face them with less stress and have a better chance of coming out on the other side.

Natural disasters can also destroy crops, destroy food stores, and thus create food shortages that can have more implications across distance and time than might initially be expected. And recovery from a natural disaster can take a lot longer than people think. Usually the news is done talking about whatever the problem is before the rebuilding is complete. And even our government advises that you need to be able to take care of yourself for at least a week.

But natural disasters are usually brief, and if they don't disrupt crops over a wide area and in the long-term, they generally do not bring on full-on-famine conditions. Food shortages, though, and your personal ability to get to food when you need it, might be very different.

Unlike the other famine causes we've evaluated, there's nothing you can do about a natural disaster but be prepared. We can't predict the climate with total accuracy; we can't predict droughts or storms, floods or fires; we can't predict earthquakes or hurricanes. These events will happen. The only question is when and where.

2.5 Economic Depression

ଓ • ଓଃ

At this point, we're starting to come full circle. The reasons for famine tend to go hand in hand with their causes. There's a reason the Four Horsemen ride together—because any one of them can bring all the others. To a certain extent, by the time you've begun delving into one cause of famine, you've touched on all the others. For example, we've already noted how spiraling food prices can result in a "slow famine," and how the economic depression conditions are already putting a massive strain on food banks and food stamp programs across the countryside.

Just like those Third World regimes, famine as a result of recession, depression, inflation and collapse is not a result of bad harvests. There's food—you just can't buy it, because the price of food has skyrocketed out of the reach of the common man or woman. We ended up discussing some possible scenarios for this back in the section on infrastructure.

It really is all related. You can't tug on one part of the spider's web without tugging on all the others. You got to see the effects of an Economic Depression famine both during the French Revolution and during the Great Depression.

There are few "solutions" that a common man or woman can use against economic depression. We don't control the markets: the IMF, the World Bank, and the Federal Reserve do that. What we *can* control is our mindset. Slowly but surely, Americans are coming to understand that we cannot depend on our employers, the government, or general prosperity to save us. We have to save ourselves.

This can mean taking control of our own food supply. For some, it will also mean becoming self-employed so as not to rely on Big Corporate for money ever again. It can mean trying to get "off-grid" as much as possible so that skyrocketing prices affect you less and less. You won't much care about energy prices, for example, if you're safe in a snug home with solar power and well water. Food prices won't bother you so much if you've got chickens in the yard, a garden full of tasty food growing just outside, and a store of canned goods to see you through the winter. This is how most Americans would have been living prior to the 1930s, but social, political, and economic shifts have changed matters.

More and more, it's looking like it's time to get back in touch with our self-reliant roots. The value of our currency is plummeting. Pundits talk about economic recovery "just on the horizon," but how good does the picture look really?

In spite of a three trillion dollar "stimulus" package, unemployment is at 9.8% and, according to MSNBC, "the highest since June of 1983" [172]. The dollar is still extremely weak. The rise in fuel and food costs that we have already documented means that, on the whole, we will all be cutting back somewhere.

And there's evidence to support the fact that there are people out there profiting from all of this misery and uncertainty. Profit means a motive to continue making it happen. How can this be so? Well, take JP Morgan, which is one of the largest processors of food stamps in the country; who, incidentally, outsources their public assistance call center work to India.

> *JP Morgan is the only one today still operating public-assistance call centers overseas...JP Morgan provides food stamps in 26 states and the District of Columbia. It also provides child support debit cards in 15 states and unemployment insurance cards in seven states... The 130,000 food stamp families in West Virginia have their calls routed to India...the 488,000 households in Tennessee also have their calls sent to JP Morgan call centers in India...In Michigan, JP Morgan allows unemployment recipients two free withdrawals from its network of ATMs. For each additional withdrawal, the bank takes a $1.50 fee. If somebody loses their card, the first replacement is free. The second costs $7.50. The banks also get a fee for each case they handle. Take Indiana. JP Morgan gets 62 to 64 cents for each food stamp case handled monthly there. With 296,245 cases right now, that means the state is paying JP Morgan $183,672 a month on top of any other fees it collects.* [173]

Thank you, Washington, for spending $3 trillion to bail out these "too big to fail banks," so that they could profit further off of American joblessness and underemployment while continuing to ship jobs overseas because, with all that money, the best they can afford to pay is $3.00 an hour to a person who can't even speak English well enough to get through any basic customer service call! We can expect the entire farce to proceed for some time. Why wouldn't it? The corruption reeking off of these maneuvers benefits the people who are powerful enough to pull them off. Big Corporate and Big Government *does not care* about Main Street and never will. These are the same people who perfected the vacuum cleaner art of sucking wealth out of other countries and putting it in their own pocket. Why not the richest country in the world?

There are plenty of Americans who will survive this period of economic depression without much problem, but you might not be one of them. You have to see this period of economic instability as an actual threat to your own food supply. Think of it this way: let's say you end up losing your job. All of your payments stay the same: housing, utilities, food. But typically, an unemployment check only represents about 2/3 of the original income. Unless you were living in a scenario where one third of your income was disposable, and you're in no debt, you'll be feeling the pinch. That's if you get unemployment at all—and these days, companies are better and better at wriggling out of unemployment payments. States are all too happy to support them in this because the unemployment office is having trouble paying all of the checks they need to write, too.

In any case you may be in a scenario where you have little or no money coming into your home. When you've taken the time to build a personal food supply, however, you will at least have one stress off your mind: keeping the family fed. You can then focus on keeping your home, perhaps through odd jobs or working through savings. Your savings, if you're using them, will last longer, and you'll be less tempted to reach for your credit cards to keep your family afloat.

And even if you don't lose your job, those food stores can still come in handy. Even if we don't see martial law; even if we don't see wide scale famine; even if we don't see wars and civil unrest and more natural disasters sweeping across the landscape. Food is already growing more expensive. Nothing indicates that prices will come down any time soon. Remember our example where a single loaf of bread 'fed' one family? The family who already has a little bit of peanut butter stored to go on that bread is going to be nutritionally and physically better off. They are less likely to be weak and sick and will recover first. If you've already got some groceries, then you can buy staples and use those groceries as a light supplement until the price of food begins to adjust once more. If you've started even a little apartment garden, then you'll have a source of food for free.

And as if all of this weren't enough, total economic collapse could be on the horizon, a point where everything in our country ceases to function simply because there is literally no money to pay for it, in which toilet paper comes to be more valuable than paper money (though it may be the only proper use for it). How likely is it? More likely than you might think.

If China starts dumping all of the United States debt, our debt crisis will skyrocket to massive proportions; low interest debt is about the only thing keeping our government functioning. QE2 raised interest rates instead of lowering them as promised. The entire global economy is now based on debt. In 2000 it was at $57 trillion. In 2009 it was already at $109 trillion. Inflation is already out of control. "Paper gold" and "paper silver" have been sold all over the earth; unfortunately there's more paper precious metals than precious metals. In fact, there has never been as many precious metals on earth, ever, as have been sold in "paper" form. The real estate market is flooded with homes that nobody can buy. In Detroit, you could buy a fairly nice 3 bedroom house for $10,000 if you were willing to live in the wasteland of the city where crime runs rampant—*if* you had $10,000. Investors are bailing out of municipal bonds just as fast as they can, and the derivatives gambling bubble could burst any day now [174].

Most people are holding on by their fingernails. It wouldn't take very much to knock most of us off of a cliff. While the mainstream media shuffles their feet and mumbles about how much better things are getting, the entire world teeters on the edge. The implosion to come might be God's way of righting some of the imbalances and injustices that this complex global system, built on bricks of greed and thoughtlessness, has created. When the dust settles, we may all have a second chance to build a republic once more, to build a world that does not let bankers and businessmen become the informal tyrants of the globe. But we all have to survive to that day. Many won't. Even some of those who prepare won't. There just aren't any guarantees. But those that don't prepare *surely* won't. The time to come will require the courage and intelligence of heroes. Nearly every cause for famine seems to be ramping up at the same time, even in the absence of any natural disaster or weather problems. A perfect storm, indeed.

PART 3

ഔ•ഏ

MORE
THREATS
TO THE
FOOD
SUPPLY

As if having some of the specific and historical conditions for famine breeding in our world and nation weren't enough, there are some strange and unique new problems to worry about. Some are brought on by science, such as the threat of GMO (genetically modified) foods. Others are explorations into ways in which our own country has gone awry, and how it has been seized and manipulated by new Stalins and Maos. It's also necessary to take a more specialized look at Agribusiness, as well as agriculture's dependence on "better living through chemistry." Finally, we have to take a look at the United Nations and its stated plans for food.

These specific threats go beyond generalizations and historical record. Some of them, in fact, are beyond anything we've ever encountered before, requiring us to think our way through them. Genetically modified foods, for example, are nothing that our forefathers ever experienced or even dreamed of, but we now find ourselves faced with the task of trying to cope with them and make decisions with them.

Opposing the public's right to understand what's going on with their food is a massive PR and spin machine that is eagerly spouting lies in the name of profits. The mainstream media is largely silent on all of these issues. Double-speak and double-think are the order of the day, and it takes a very careful reading to see past carefully constructed, glowing "feel good" language to the issues beneath.

3.1 American Farm Control

ಐ • ಐ

American farm control, and the scheme of paying farmers to avoid production, began in 1933. To properly understand the threat of farm control you have to understand its origins; how and why it came to be, who wanted it set up the way it was, and who benefited from it. This will help you see how an "emergency measure" can literally stay on the books and get used to forward other people's political aims years and years after the crisis has passed.

You will see the roots of many of our current problems unrelated to farms or food but intricately related to our ability to access food being born. You will see how decisions made 78 years ago led to American jobs being shipped overseas today. You will see how we lost our ability to make wages at an American cost of living price so that we would instead have to rely on cheap imports from China.

Why did America change so dramatically? Was it the inevitable course of history? Unintended consequences of policies that seemed like good ideas at the time? Or was it all a matter of design? Were there political and business interests that had a specific plan in mind when they forwarded these policies, and if so, what was the plan and what were the ideologies that shaped the plan?

The "sold" or original intent of the Agricultural Adjustment Act was likely what you've read about in textbooks and heard all your life. It was an emergency measure meant for one year's worth of surpluses when the export market dropped off. It was meant to preserve the wages of the farmer, to preserve or create jobs, and to make sure that prices stayed stable enough to avoid depressing the market further. Those surpluses were not of every crop across the board and they certainly weren't expected to continue year after year.

George Peek was the Administer of the AAA for one year. He quit in disgust but had an awful lot to say about the Act and what went on there. Here is his understanding of the intention of the Agricultural Adjustment Act—the intention which he felt was betrayed by the time he resigned.

> *My preliminary drive…was to dispose of depressing surpluses and, if possible, to raise domestic prices by agreement. These were emergency measures and defensible as such.* [175]

Though Peek recognized the problem of falling prices, he was still suspicious of pinning the source of the problem on surplus. His observation on this count was this:

> *The question is not one primarily of surplus. We in the farm movement had talked so much about surplus that surplus is looked on as a curse. I am afraid that our desire to get rid of certain surplus production which temporarily hurts prices has been so great that we have been led into a position where we have seemed to advocate the abhorrent and un-American doctrine of scarcity.*

> *When I was a boy, that farmer was regarded as a rich and provident man who carried over a crib full of corn or a bin full of wheat. We*

gauged a man by the size or condition of his herd. That man had real wealth, he had something for a rainy day—he was insured against a bad crop. 'As good as wheat in the bin,' was our measure of real worth. Those principles must always hold good, and there can never be a solution for the farm problem—or any other social problem, for that matter—if plenty is held to be a curse. [176]

The Senate Committee hearings surrounding the problem included a statement by the Chairman that there wasn't really a problem of overproduction. The problem as he saw it was "purely the inability to buy." Yet an emergency measure meant to jump-start the economy continued unabated for 63 years, long after the close of the Great Depression. It was put into active use and continued to guide policy, it was used far beyond its original stated intent, and it wound up forwarding the agenda of Communists. This can be said with confidence simply by going back to the documented facts—no Conspiracy Theory required. To understand how and why "the farm problem" became a cancer of Communism running through our system, you have to know about the Ware Cell.

In fact, if you were reading this between 1948–1952, a cell of communists in the Agricultural Adjustment Administration would not seem like conspiracy theory to you at all. It would, in fact, be ongoing news. Over the next few years a slew of names would come out, all connected to the AAA in some way: Alger Hiss, Nathan Witt, Lee Pressman, John Abt, Henry H. Collins, Jr., Harry Dexter White and Lauchlin Currie.

According to Moscow directives, cell members never remained stationary; they moved to higher and higher places of policy-making and authority in government. And as each cell member advanced, he pulled others up by recommendations and appointive authority. Original members of the Ware cell soon spread out to other government departments and committees. Today, the nerve fibers of this first Communist cell in the Federal Government influence and shape many parts of our domestic policy. [177]

It is impossible to think that a group of Communists could sit in highly placed government positions and not influence policy. It's also ridiculous to think that it would not happen again. Furthermore, one unnamed Communist remained uncaught, ready to grow the cell again. Peek himself observed the Communists in action for some time. Peek's comment below also helps sum up reasons why viewing the world through a two-party lens is such a fallacy.

> *I eventually found that I was not in a Democratic Administration but in a curious collection of socialists and internationalists who were neither Republicans nor Democrats. They, fanatic-like, believed that their objectives transcended the objectives of ordinary human beings and therefore could not allow themselves to be hampered by the codes of ordinary mental honesty, by platform pledges, by the Constitution or by any other rules of human conduct.* [178]

In point of fact, speaking as to his role and the role of his co-administrator Charles J. Brand, Peek went on to wonder:

> *...whether or not Mr. Brand and I were ever anything more than window dressing to give confidence to Congress and the farmers until the secret plans could be matured. It will be remembered that Congress—and especially the Senate—was against the Act if it were to be administered by Wallace and Tugwell Had the Wallace-Tugwell plans been known in the beginning, most certainly neither the farmers nor Congress would have accepted the Act. It would seem that Mr. Brand and I were kept in front only until public funds could be used to organize a machine and purchase the acquiescence of enough of the farmers to establish the system of regimented production.* [179]

Why the AAA though? Why, out of all of the places where the Communist party could seek to infiltrate the government, was agriculture chosen? What did the behind-the-scenes maneuvering of the AAA seek to accomplish, and did it manage its primary goals?

First, you must remember that the primary struggle against collectivization in Russia came from the countryside. That is, it came from the farmers. Second, farmers guarantee food supply. By placing farmers under the direct control of the government, the Communists built a framework by which food could be used as a weapon in America. Socialism is considered by Communists to be an intermediate step on the way to communism, so any socialist plan or program must be viewed with an eye towards the vision of Communism which may well be emerging under its hand.

The secret aim of the AAA was to place control of farms in the hands of the government and to force the farmer into a dependency relationship with the government by placing him on the government dole. Once government funds became the source of the farmer's livelihood, government control became inevitable. This is the principle of Keynesian Socialism, a brand of Socialism which helps to keep control by maintaining the illusion that there is no control. The appearance is that of democracy and ownership, but the government keeps control—the ability to tell the farmers what to farm, for example, or the ability to set the prices. The government throws money at the farmer and allows him to "own" his farm on paper, then continues to pile more and more regulations and more and more intrusion upon his head.

The primary requirement for the institution of a Socialist society is a society in which all or most of the citizens are dependent upon the government in some way, so that they look to the government for solutions and obey to continue receiving the money or goods upon which they depend. You can certainly see this playing out in our very own 21st century society, a little bit louder and a little bit worse, as they say.

Another secret goal of the AAA was to break up the profit system so that it could eventually be replaced by a Socialist system, then a Communist one. We know this was a stated goal of the Communist infiltrators because they said so. The knowledge begins with Dr. William Wirt, a school superintendent that got invited to a dinner party of Communist sympathizers. Four of the guests were government officials; the fifth guest was a Russian reporter for *Tass*, the Soviet news agency. Wirt was initially brushed off by government officials, but he persevered until he managed to open up a Congressional investigation (180). Snippets of his testimony are telling.

'Brain Trusters' insist that the America of Washington, Jefferson, and Lincoln must first be destroyed so that on the ruins they will be able to construct an America under their own pattern. ... They wish to

put the common man back into the feudal society of the Dark Ages...I was told they believe that by thwarting our then-evident economic recovery they would be able to prolong the country's destitution until they had demonstrated to the American people that the Government must operate business and commerce. By propaganda they would destroy institutions making long-term capital loans, then push Uncle Sam into making these loans. Once Uncle Sam becomes our financier He must also follow his money with control and management. ... [They said] 'We believe we have Roosevelt in the middle of a swift stream and that the current is so strong he cannot turn back or escape from it. We believe we can keep Mr. Roosevelt there until we are ready to Supplant him with a Stalin. [181]

Lest you have trouble believing that anyone in the United States could ever possibly admire Stalin or want a repeat, note another observation from Peek. It is chilling, and directly relevant to the topic of famine and food shortage which we have been following. "Another group," Peek reports, "was against relief on the grounds that hungry men revolt sooner than fed men. They would have starved the people on the same theory that the Russians used to force the farmers into collective farming. One, in a position of prominence, was reported to have expressed deep regret over the food distribution as only delaying the great revolution" [182].

An April 2, 1934 a *Time Magazine* article headlined National Affairs, Underlings on Revolution also revealed testimony from Wirt, including this particular statement: ***"They were sure that they could depend upon the psychology of empty stomachs and they would keep them empty. The masses would soon agree that anything should be done rather than nothing. Any escape from present miseries would be welcome, even though it should turn out to be another misery"*** [183].

If the government's continued control over our farming system does not worry you in light of such statements, then go back and read them again.

A third secret aim of the AAA was to break down international trade barriers to move the world closer to a collectivist, one-world government structure, the end result of which was the dismantling of American business in favor of shipping jobs overseas, among other things. George Peek actually predicted our 2011 plight way back in 1933, when tariffs were being lowered or done away with wherever possible. The idea behind the move was that this would somehow make the world, as he put it, "one big happy family." Instead, all that happened was that the protections which helped keep American wages high and American jobs in place were removed.

Many brush aside the idea of a planned world government that stretches back through so many administrations, but they would do well to pay attention to another observation from George Peek: "Those who most ardently desire our membership in the League also advocate the lowering of tariffs and the cancellation of war debts" [184]. He went on to note that the World Peace Foundation and the Foreign Policy Association, both dependent upon largesse from the Carnegie Peace Foundation, backed a book by Secretary Wallace that stated a relationship between world peace, world trade, and agriculture. All of these organizations were deeply involved in the League of Nations and, though the League of Nations ultimately failed, there is no denying that the United Nations is its spiritual descendent.

How do we know that a totalitarian world government is within the plans of these communist thinkers? They hide in plain sight! It's a matter of paying attention. Here's a snippet of an article from *The Palm Beach Post*, November 12, 1939, headlined, Only Two Active Lobbies Work For a World Peace in Washington.

> *[The groups] back a six point program to keep America out of war, procure a just peace and **work for a permanent world government. ...Wealthiest of all the peace groups is the Carnegie Endowment for International Peace**, organized in 1910... It conducts extensive researches on the problems of war and peace and issues a number of publications on peace and international affairs, which it distributes gratis to libraries and other institutions around the world.* [185]

So to sum up, you have a Communist brain trust touting world peace through the lowering of tariffs and international boundaries to trade in the pursuit of a world government. We can infer these interests did not, at any point, envision returning to a democratic government after receiving the world government they were working so hard for. We can also take a look at our current situation and stop to wonder if the Communists did not achieve their aims of keeping everyone in poverty after all. From the moment we began exporting our jobs the aim of this group was realized in living color. Considering we are seeing the stated aims of the communist infiltrators playing out in our current events, it would be naïve to assume that everything ended with the Alger Hiss case. It would be naïve to assume that it all ended with the Cold War, or that any attempt to point out these facts is "Cold War propaganda." The Agenda is alive and well.

Nobody believed Dr. Wirt, either. In fact, a July 1st, 1935 issue of *Time Magazine* called his attempts to warn the nation a "puff of flatulence" on the Roosevelt administration. By 1948, of course, the famous Alger Hiss case had begun and Wirt was vindicated. Unfortunately, Wirt didn't live to see his victory. He died under suspicious circumstances just two years after that fateful dinner party.

Overproduction was a hoax. The numbers, in fact, were not good even back in 1932. George Peek lamented the lack of book keeping on the movement of commodities internationally, and 33 years later Dan P. VanGorder would note the following: "If we had not exported a single pound of farm commodities during those eight years, domestic consumption would still have totaled 25 million tons above production. In other words, we had underproduction rather than overproduction" [186]! Peek didn't find his way to those numbers; he had a hard time getting anybody to look at any numbers at all. His diary would record his frustration that few people in Roosevelt's administration were particularly interested in facts. If we truly had an overproduction problem, we would hardly need to import nearly 30% of our food from Mexico and China! We would simply produce it, sell it here, and export it to make a profit.

We haven't fundamentally changed the Act, in spite of revisions in 1996 and 2002. Supposedly, the farm reform of 1996, called the Federal Agricultural Improvement and Reform Act (FAIR) was supposed to put a stop to AAA subsidies, which encompasses both pay-outs to working farmers for high-demand commodities like corn or soy and payouts to people who do not farm in order to reward them for failing to produce. Supposedly, the bill was to eliminate target prices, eliminate the Acreage Production Program, and eliminate deficiency payments. This would then place "greater" (notice, not total) decision making in the hands of a farmer. But there were plenty of farm welfare recipients who wanted no such thing (notice how the ability to basically write themselves a check through supporting basic government programs leads big business to contribute to socialist aims as well. One might well suppose that your average CEO doesn't even really care what happens with the currency or profit system if he gets to continue living like a King at the end of it). So what happened? A $47 billion dollar package that did absolutely nothing to create reform. The measures would take place over the course of 7 years in a "phase-out" program that allowed for renewals, delays, more reforms and renames. The rules of subsidies changed slightly, and there was a lot of re-naming going on. Meanwhile, farm welfare payments actually tripled between 1999 and 2001 to the tune of $21 billion per year. 66% of that went to the richest 10% of Big Agribusiness. In 2002, so that Congress could appear to be "doing something," there was a FAIR rework that did little more than go around renaming the same programs and basically made sure that subsidized farming, and thus government controlled farming, was here to stay [187].

Even Obama draws parallels between Roosevelt and Obama. Given the fact that we now know that "reformists" in the Roosevelt administration saw Roosevelt as little more than a placeholder for the Stalin to come, we can view Obama's administration in a new and chilling light. Once again, hunger, deprivation, and unemployment stalk the land. The conditions are ripe for the same sorts of sweeping "reforms" that changed our nation in the 30s. It's too much to hope that there are no more collectivists, communists, one-worldists, socialists, and wild eyed theorists in his administration, even without the evidence that there are quite a bit of each.

You can hardly pull up a newspaper article about Obama these days that does not mention him in the same breath as FDR. Obama models his presidency after FDR and made similar noises to FDR in his speech of January 20, 2009.

The really sad part about all this is that FDR didn't even end the Depression, though he is popularly credited with doing so. He managed to take full political credit for that, though it was actually WWII that successfully ended it. It's interesting to note that during the Hoover Administration, unemployment averaged 6.2 million annually. In the first two Roosevelt Administrations, average annual unemployment was *9.9 million people.* And, of course, Roosevelt spent untold billions on his programs [188]. How's Obama stacking up? In spite of spending *trillions* of the taxpayer's dollars, our "new Roosevelt" has created an interesting parallel. Unemployment in November of 2008 was 6.7%. In 2011 we're up to 9.4%. It's probably safe to say Obama's plan isn't working, but it has gifted us with a bunch of new controlling legislation much as FDR's New Deal did, from Obamacare all the way down to the Food Safety Modernization Act, which grants the FDA broad new powers. One wonders if he will attempt to duplicate FDR's 13 years in office (or more) in spite of the 22nd Amendment, which was in fact passed *because* of Roosevelt. Our current leaders have already shown themselves to be largely contemptuous of the Constitution, and the machinery is in place to allow Obama or anyone who comes after him to be the "second Stalin" for whom the collectivists in the AAA looked for so long ago.

3.2 The Oppressive Regime We've Failed to See

಼⊙•ಌ

1933 was an awfully big year for punching freedom right in the nose. Not only did we get the communist-authored AAA but we also got the *War and Emergency Powers Act of 1933*. This act placed the United States under a "state of emergency" and *actually suspended the Constitution*.

We've apparently been in a "state of emergency" for the past 78 years, because the War and Emergency Powers Act of 1933 was never rescinded. Presidents to this day have retained the powers granted to it by this Act. While Article 1 of the Constitution of the United States grants Congress the right to make federal law, this process has now been circumvented. In point of fact, the War and Emergency Powers Act created a *de facto* dictatorship by allowing presidents to make extensive use of Executive Orders to bypass every check and balance which our founding fathers put into place during the formation of our Constitutional Republic.

How do Executive Orders work? Paul Begala, advisor to President Bill Clinton, said it fairly succinctly when he said, "Stroke of the pen, law of the land. Pretty cool." But it's not cool. It is, in fact, high treason. Even had the Act been rescinded in due time, right around the time the "emergency" was over, it still would have been high treason. Why? Because it set the precedent that it is "okay" to suspend our God-given, inalienable rights whenever our government decides there is a sufficient "emergency."

This was a concern shared by Congressman James Beck in the Congressional Record of 1933. He wrote:

> *I think of all the damnable heresies that have ever been suggested in connection with the Constitution, the doctrine of emergency is the worst. It means that when Congress declares an emergency, there is no Constitution. This means its death. It is the very doctrine the German chancellor is invoking today in the dying house of the parliamentary body of the Germany republic, namely, that because of an emergency, it should grant to the German Chancellor absolute power to pass any law, even though the law contradicts the Constitution of the German Republic. Chancellor Hitler is at least frank about it. We pay the Constitution lip-service, but the result is the same. But the Constitution of the United States, as a restraining influence in keeping the Federal government within the carefully prescribed channels of power, is moribund, if not dead. We are witnessing its death-agonies, for when this bill becomes law, if unhappily it becomes a law, there is no longer any workable Constitution to keep Congress within the limits of its Constitutional powers.* [189]

Though it boggles the mind to think we lost our grip on the Constitutional Republic just 157 years after 1776, we must turn around and face the facts. Now we enjoy the freedoms we enjoy on the whim and the largesse of the American Presidency.

> *The President isn't the only one. The judiciary has also overstepped its bounds. Court decisions have mandated tax increases, reverse discrimination, preferential treatment, and a host of other ills that the citizenry has no recourse against. Instead of our legislators making law as the Constitution provides for, and who are in their position by the will and good graces of the people, unelected judiciary now make law from the bench at the thump of a gavel.* [190]

In addition, there are a slew of administrative agencies such as the IRS, OSHA, Social Security and the infamous FEMA that are appointed, unelected positions with the power to create rules and regulations and enforce them as if they were law [191].

Americans are pretty trusting and naïve. We tend to believe that nobody will use such powers for dark aims. Surely it was all on the up and up. Most people cannot imagine doing anything psychotic or cruel even if some emergency order granted us the power to do so. Yet Roosevelt himself signed Executive Order 9066, which gave us concentration camps on our own shores, much to the horror of the Americans of Japanese descent who found themselves enslaved there.

The Patriot Act violates no less than six Constitutional Amendments. If our Constitution hadn't effectively died 78 years ago this might be more surprising. Still, it's worth noting whenever a broad, sweeping policy brings changes to America, it also brings us that much further from the free nation that we were meant to be. This pernicious Act brings us the following abominations:

- The government can search and seize your papers and effects at any time, with no probable cause whatsoever. They can also conduct "sneak and peek" searches of your home with no warrant, no notification, and no probable cause, all in the name of conducting "investigations of terrorism." They can also tap your phone line and read your e-mail without any warrant, notification, or probable cause. If they want to know what you've been checking out from the library lately, they can go get those records too, again with no notification or warrant.
- The ability to snatch you up off of the streets and drag you away to a gulag to be tortured without trial for an indefinite period of time, with no access to a lawyer, your family, or the outside world. If you do get a lawyer, the government now reserves the right to listen into your consultations with your lawyer. No due process is necessary, and even civilians can be tried by a military court (if they are tried at all).
- The Patriot Act allows the government to monitor religious institutions without any probable cause whatsoever.
- If your friendly neighborhood librarian happens to let slip that the government subpoenaed that book list then she can also be grabbed and thrown into prison without trial. The same goes for any other record keepers who might seek to warn you that you are now the subject of a terrorist investigation.

- The Patriot Act allows the government to set up "free speech zones." You can say whatever you like—in a stadium about 5 miles away from whatever event you might happen to be protesting.
- The Patriot Act defines terrorism very broadly, to the point where civil disobedience, protests, and marches are all potential "acts of terrorism." Let's restate that: ***exercising your First Amendment rights is now considered a potential act of terrorism***.

Senator Russ Feingold of Wisconsin sounded eerily like Senator James Beck as he tried to sound the alarm about the Patriot Act on October 25, 2001.

Of course, there is no doubt that if we lived in a police state, it would be easy to catch terrorists. If we lived in a country that allowed the police to search your home at any time without a reason; if we lived in a country that allowed government to open your mail, eavesdrop on your phone conversations, or intercept your e-mail communications; if we lived in a country that allowed the government to hold people in jail indefinitely based on what they write or think, or based on mere suspicion that they are up to no good, then the government would no doubt discover and arrest more terrorists.

But that probably would not be a country in which we would want to live. And that would not be a country for which we could, in good conscience, ask our young people to fight and die. In short, that would not be America.

Preserving our freedom is one of the main reasons that we are now engaged in this new war on terrorism. We will lose that war without firing a shot if we sacrifice the liberties of the American people. (192)

And Feingold's words fell on deaf ears as surely as Beck's did. He was the only Senator to vote against the Patriot Act.

Uninformed Americans believe it's only "brown people"—Arabs—that are being targeted with this Act. They would be very wrong. Though, as Feingold also noted, quoting jurist Learned Hand during World War II, "The spirit of liberty is the spirit which seeks to understand the minds of other men and women; the spirit of liberty is the spirit which weighs their interests alongside their own without bias." That is to say, even if the Arabs were the *only people the Patriot Act ever targeted*, it would *still be wrong*. The Propaganda Machine which makes "Arab" or "Muslim" a synonym for "Terrorist" is bigoted and ugly, and is a direct slap in the face of all the Muslims who have lived and worked in our great country as good citizens. These people want to live, work, and enjoy their families just as we do, and should not be penalized for the actions of the few any more than the Americans of Japanese descent should have been penalized over Pearl Harbor.

But it's not just brown people. Just ask the Missouri Information Analysis Center (MIAC) how they would identify a "domestic terrorist." There are some groups, such as white supremacist groups, that indeed have engaged in dangerous, terrorist activities in the past. However, most of the assertions that you can find in the MIAC report border on naming specific thought crimes.

- People who are concerned about gun control.
- Constitutionalists, particularly the ones who are concerned that Barrack Obama does not meet the citizenship requirements to hold office as the President of the United States.
- Those who believe in the New World Order, that forces are trying to set up a one world government, or that the elites are controlling and exploiting the world to their own personal gain.
- Those with concerns about the Federal Reserve System.
- Those who protest high taxes.
- Those who are worried about the presence of FEMA camps or concerned about the broad, sweeping powers granted to FEMA.
- Those who believe the government is working to set up a North American Union.
- Those concerned about the use and abuse of RFID micro-chipping devices.
- Christians. This is couched in the language of "Christian Identity" and anti-Semitic sentiment, but could easily go to cover all Christians.
- States' Rights advocates, or those who see themselves as "Sovereign Citizens," or those who recognize the rights of the county Sheriff or seek to appoint strong, constitutionally educated county Sheriffs.
- Anti-abortionists.
- Those opposed to immigration or open borders.

- Members of the Constitutional Party, the Campaign for Liberty, or the Libertarian Party.
- Supporters of Chuck Baldwin, Ron Paul, or Bob Barr.
- Those who display a Gadsen Flag, or other flags such as the 9 Stripes of the Sons of Liberty.

To this, the Southern Poverty Law Center would add members of the Patriot Movement, those who would quote the *Possee Comitatus Act* that states that the military may not engage in police actions (these are also demonized as anti-Semites) and members of the Oath Keepers group or We Are Change.

Now of *course* it goes without saying that there are some *real nut jobs out* there who are not nice people who do believe in some or all of the points above. Yet now everyone who has ever had these sentiments or spoken out against the government is painted with the same brush, and the government now has a law that allows them to drag you off into a gulag if you voted for the wrong person. Furthermore, you can find nut jobs who are willing to hurt others for their beliefs on just about any political or social platform you care to name. There are nut jobs who are willing to kill people over global warming, too. The existence of insane people, or insane cruel groups who happened to vote for Ron Paul, does not logically create a scenario where *everyone* who voted for Ron Paul or who is concerned about the Constitution is a wild eyed revolutionary ready to gun down innocent people. This is, however, exactly how these viewpoints are demonized, ensuring that many sober, objective people who might otherwise be willing to take a look at valid arguments do not, because the media has gotten them so associated with the crazy radicals that they are literally afraid to look at or dismiss everything that is said. And yet there are people out there who believe the power to throw dissenters into prison would *never ever be misused*! One shouldn't be asking why it would be misused; one should ask why it *wouldn't*. Governments like power. They like keeping any power they can get and don't tend to give up power once they have it. They also aren't too fond of dissent. You do the math.

President Barak Obama promised to rid us of the Patriot Act. Instead, he has renewed it, very quietly, and the media has kept silent.

We are exhibiting classic signs of a despotic regime. In conducting a historical survey of fascist societies, including societies that had working, functional democracies when the hammer of tyranny came down upon them, author and political consultant Naomi Wolf identified ten basic things that "every would-be dictator, whether they're on the Left or the Right, does...There's a blueprint to closing down an open a society or crushing a democracy" (193). By observing the steps, we can peel back the layers of the modern-day onion to determine whether or not our fears of a despotic, closed-society ushered in by martial law are valid ones. Here is her list, taken from her speech "The End of America: A Letter of Warning to a Young Patriot," given in the Kane Building on the University of Washington Campus, October 11, 2007.

1. *Invoke a terrifying internal and external threat*. The threat can be a hyped up false threat or it can be a very real threat. In our case, our government has the handy threat of "terrorists throughout the globe." We are told various stories on all of the horrible things they intend to do to us, from photographs of blue eyes staring out from burqas to total world annihilation. There is also a tendency to use fake documents as an excuse; we saw this when the "yellow cake" documents "proved" weapons of mass destruction in Iraq, allowing George W. Bush to invade.

2. *Create a secret prison system, outside the rule of law, where torture takes place*. Establish military tribunals to strip the people of due process. Not only do we now have Guantanamo Bay thanks to George W. Bush (which Obama promised to shut down but did not), but there are CIA "black cells" around the world. It has been conclusively proven and admitted that torture takes place at these facilities. Wolf goes on to note that this always starts with abusing people (such as Arabs) that nobody in the mainstream identifies with, but the list finally expands to include journalists, editors, activists, labor leaders, and clergy. As it stands right now, the President of the United States can look at any citizen for any reason and declare them an "enemy combatant," a status offense for which there is no defense, not of innocence nor of political affiliation.

3. *Create a paramilitary force*. We can take a look at Blackwater and the TSA and look no further to find examples of a paramilitary thug group threatening and intimidating American citizens. As Wolf observes, it doesn't much matter if all of the trappings of democracy are in place if the people are too scared to push back. From the massacre of Iraqi citizens to Blackwater operating in

New Orleans in the wake of Katrina and shooting our own citizens, we indeed have our very own set of thugs.

4. ***Create a surveillance apparatus for ordinary citizens***. FISA and the Patriot Act took care of this one for us. Defense contractors in the military-industrial complex now ensure their source of profit by creating surveillance equipment and naming us as the enemy. They're hard pressed to run out of "us."

5. ***Arbitrarily detain and release citizens***. You can see the beginnings of this apparatus in the TSA "No Fly" increased security list. There have already been cases of those who have criticized our government being disallowed from crossing the border into other countries, another common tactic. Pretty soon, job opportunities and other opportunities end up closing down to people on "the list." You can see anybody who criticized the government publically on that list. You can also see multiple news articles detailing the abuses of the TSA in which citizens are grabbed, held, and shouted at for hours for attempting to fly.

6. ***Target key people***. People in the press, academics, celebrities—all of these have faced unemployment or worse for failing to "toe the government line." These people are targeted so that we may see the consequences of their dissent. We've seen a military lawyer who pressed for fair trials for detainees lose his job, people in academia lose their jobs for criticizing Bush, and a CIA contract worker who, in a closed blog called waterboarding torture, lose hers. There are other examples.

7. ***Harass citizens groups***. You will find government infiltrators and agent provocateurs worming their way into just about any group you care to name, from antiwar groups to environmental groups to the Tea Party. The government not only now has people in place to cause problems that legitimate group members can then be blamed and arrested for, but indeed this tactic removes a citizen's ability to organize with other citizens, simply because citizens cannot trust one another.

8. ***Restrict the press***. Arrests of journalists are at an all-time high, and in the case of Bill Keller, editor of the New York Times, there was an open movement to see him charged with treason and espionage and executed. Brandon Manning sits in solitary confinement and is on a no-sleep torture schedule because he is accused of giving documents to Wikileaks, an independent journalism site that

has provided evidence of government misdeeds. The Federal Government informs anyone working for them that reading Wikileaks is breaking the law. In addition, the Cybersecurity Act gave the government a way to shut down independent media in the future.

9. ***Recast dissent as treason***. You have already seen this running through other events named; from placing people on "the List" to grabbing up journalists and accusing them of treason.

10. ***Subvert the rule of law...A.K.A. martial law***. We're not here yet, thankfully. But the government certainly has the ability to enact martial law at any time. The Continuity of Government program and a slew of executive orders have the entire framework in place [194].

So what country do we live in again? And given this is the blueprint used by Mussolini, by Lenin, by Stalin, by Mao, and by every manner of petty dictator, what is your guarantee that you will be able to feed your family through a prolonged period of martial law, oppressive government, and food-as-a-weapon?

The Continuity of Government Program established FEMA as a "Shadow Government;" it not only gives powers to FEMA in the event of an emergency, such as a hurricane or earthquake, but gives it what it needs to "maintain the existing social and political order." How can it be said any plainer than that? The existing social and political order is nothing less than the current dictatorial regime! But understanding the FEMA connection does require a bit of back-tracking. After all, most people do not associate FEMA with guns, detention camps, or troops, even though FEMA became a part of the U.S. Department of Homeland Security in 2003.

FEMA began in 1979 when President Jimmy Carter signed Executive Order 12127. This order merged many agencies into one:

- The Federal Insurance Administration
- The National Fire Prevention and Control Administration
- The National Weather Service Community Preparedness Program
- The Federal Preparedness Agency of the General Services Administration
- Federal Disaster Administration activities from HUD
- And civil defense responsibilities, transferred from the Defense Department's Civil Preparedness Agency [195].

Documents released by the Freedom of Information Act have painted a disturbing picture. These documents are available for public consumption. The United States has contingency plans for establishing martial law in this country, not only in times of war, but also if there is what the Defense Department calls, "a complete breakdown of the exercise of government functions by local civilian authorities. What's more, there is a little known 1971 memorandum prepared by the Deputy Secretary of Defense which also provides justification for military control similar to martial law...Martial law was defined in an internal Federal Emergency Management Agency memo written in 1982...The memo, written by FEMA official John Brinkerhoff to agency director Louis Giuffrida, notes that Martial law "suspends all prior existing laws, functions, systems, and programs of civil government, replacing them... with a military system. By 'all' systems one means all: courts, mails, garbage collection, fire fighting, agricultural extension services, schools, aviation control, toll bridges-- in a word, all. Martial law is expected to be proclaimed by the president, although "senior military commanders" also enjoy the power to invoke it in the absence of a presidential order. [(196)]

Those who are relying on the Possee Comitatus Act of 1878 (the act which prohibits military personnel from acting in a civilian police capacity) will be disappointed. A 1971 Pentagon document offers so many "exceptions" to Possee Comitatus that it might as well no longer exist. This was a modification of the "Code of Federal Regulations, title 32, Volume 2, Chapter 1, Part 215, Section 6 with the "Employment of Military Resources in the Event of Civil disturbances," a modification made by Deputy Secretary of Defense David Packard [(197)].

"Well of course," you might be thinking, "the government would only do this in the event of a nuclear war or something, or a really, really bad crisis." If you're thinking that, then you are failing to understand that a "really, really bad crisis" is *now whatever the President says that it is*! He has to make it convincing enough, of course, but he's spoiled for choice: terrorist threats, health threats, economic threats...

All that really matters is that he has the power to call martial law whenever he wants to. You can find no greater demonstration of this than in 2008 when the

$13 trillion bailout was under discussion. Addressing the House of Representatives during the debate, Representative Brad Shuman (D-California, 27th District, Shuman Oaks, Northridge, U.S. House) offered the following chilling words, and you can find this C-Span clip right on YouTube:

> *Many of us were told in private conversations that if we voted against this bill on Monday, that the sky would fall, the market would fall two or three thousand points further, another couple thousand the second day, and a few members were even told that there would be **martial law in America if we voted no.** [(198)]*

So let's follow the bouncing ball here. Recognizing that much despotism keeps all of the trappings of democratic society about them, choosing instead to simply corrupt them, we have to ask ourselves a question: if our elected representatives can be brow-beaten into passing a bill, any bill, simply by wielding the threat of martial law, then do we really even have elected representatives? No, we have a puppet-government who dances for the amusement of those in power, who is there for no other reason but to make the majority of the American people feel *comfortable* that they still live in a free society. *All that matters is the power.* The government need never use it! They can get everything they want with the big stick, the threat, and at any minute they could use that power to do anything they want, from starving citizens to enslaving them (or starving them to enslave them).

Of course, it doesn't have to be communism or socialism. What's so confusing about our current mess is that there are communists, socialists, collectivists, internationalists, and corporate tyrants who are *all about(!) the capitalism*, all putting the same pressure on the same pressure, trying to pull it around to benefit them directly. Liberals? Conservatives? Left? Right? It takes two wings to fly an evil Nazi eagle! We have to start thinking about "liberty and justice for all," and ignore all these other labels.

In the case of the bailout bill, the Wall Street and Banker hyper-capitalist, corrupt twisters of the free market who were meant to protect us pulled one heck of a coup. Let's take a serious look at the Cui Bono (Latin meaning 'who benefits') of this bailout bill, which we now must remember was passed under threat. Let's remember that We The People were sold the bailout bill on the premise that it would help save jobs, it would help the government create programs to save homes, and it would otherwise generally stimulate the economy and help everyone out. Did you get a new job after the bailout bill passed or did any of your neighbors? Was your house saved or the house of your neighbor? Well of course not. Unemployment rose from 6.7% to 9.4% right? It nearly peaked to 9.9% during 2010. It was sold to us as a measure to keep all those "too big to fail" banks from failing so we wouldn't wind up with Great Depression bank closures and bank runs. There might not have been any bank runs, but banks have closed, they have failed, and they have been absorbed by the much larger banks who were beneficiaries of this bill. So it's very, very, obvious that the bill did not work as sold.

"This bailout," says former Goldman-Sachs managing director Nomi Prins, author of *It Takes a Pillage*, "was never meant to help consumers...if the government wanted to get the money to consumers, it could have given them bailout assistance directly, or at least directed it to banks that were eager to give out or renegotiate loans...for all the money we threw at the problem, we still got the worst case scenario: barely solvent and under-regulated institutions" [199].

Former Minnesota governor Jessie Ventura pointed out in his book *American Conspiracies, Lies, Lies, and More Dirty Lies that the Government Tells Us* that the price tag of the bailout was *so high* that you could literally have paid off every mortgage and every student loan in America, paid for every American to have an insurance policy from a major insurance company with no particular legislative sidestepping, and still had three trillion dollars to spare [200]. As socialist of a program as that may sound, it surely would have been of more benefit to We the People than what actually happened and certainly would have been more in line with the program as sold.

> *Wasn't the expectation that, once it got rescued, Wall Street would then be good sports and send money into creating jobs and initiating a major recovery? But the big banks didn't start lending again, instead they hoarded the cash and paid out huge bonuses to their execs. The behemoths got even more beastly.* [201]

So when you put all this information together with the fact that martial law literally got threatened if this bailout didn't pass, what do you get? The workings of a Constitutional Republic? A government by the people, for the people, and of the people? A government that is capable of basic concern for its own citizens?

Well no. No you don't. You get a Mafia. A bunch of thugs who are content to threaten you with their army of jackbooted Guido-clones if you don't fall into line and cough up all of your money. You get school bullies who slam the smaller kids into lockers and relieve them of their lunch money every single day. Bullies hold sandwiches over weaker kid's heads every single day. Can you really imagine the government won't withhold food from you if they can benefit from it?

It gets worse.

Thanks to Hitler, the worst nightmare of any society gone to despotism goes way beyond anything King George did to the original 13 colonists—which is frightening enough considering British soldiers and mercenaries were routinely breaking into the homes of colonists, harassing, molesting, and thieving from them. Thanks to Hitler, our worst nightmare involves millions of people being shipped off to prisons at gunpoint, to be worked to death, half-starved, and sometimes killed in massive gas chambers.

We've had concentration camps before, though we did not, at least, gas the Japanese-Americans. Still, the shadow of that history looms large across our nation. If only we could say with any amount of certainty that such a thing could never happen on our soil again. It's too bad we know it's not true.

From *The Miami Herald*, July 5, 1987. Headline: **Reagan Aides and the Secret Government.**

*From 1982 to 1984 [Oliver] North assisted FEMA, the U.S. Government's chief national crisis-management unit, in revising contingency plans for dealing with nuclear war, **insurrection**, or massive military mobilization.*

...A government official familiar with North's collaboration with FEMA said then-director Louis O. Guiffrida...mentioned North in meetings during that time as FEMA's NSC contact.

*...The plan **did not define national crisis**, but it was understood to be nuclear war, **violent and widespread internal dissent**, or **national opposition against a military invasion abroad**.*

The official said the contingency plan was written as part of an executive order or legislative package that Reagan would sign and hold with the NSC until a severe crisis arose. The national law portions of the plan were outlined in a June 30, 1982 memo by Guiffrida's deputy for national preparedness programs, John Brinkerhoff. A copy of the memo was obtained by the Herald.

*The scenario outlined in the Brinkerhoff memo resembled somewhat a paper Guiffrida had written in 1970 at the Army War College in Carlisle, PA, in which he advocated martial law in case of a national uprising by black militants. The paper also advocated the **round-up and transfer to "assembly centers or relocation camps" of at least 21 million "American Negroes."***

When he saw the FEMA plans, Attorney General Smith became alarmed. [202]

That's right. FEMA's contingency plans involve rounding up Americans—"dissidents"—and putting them into concentration camps. We should of course be concerned about this no matter what color the targets are, but the fact is that the definition has expanded to pretty much include "anybody the government doesn't like," and, if you read our emphasis closely enough, *pretty much has from the moment these camps were conceptualized.*

And did they build them? They most certainly did. From *The New York Times*, February 4, 2006. Headline: **Halliburton Subsidiary Gets Contract to Add Temporary Immigration Detention Centers.**

The Army Corps of Engineers has awarded a contract worth up to $385 million for building temporary immigration detention centers to Kellogg Brown and Root, the Halliburton subsidiary that has been criticized for overcharging the Pentagon for its work in Iraq.

*KBR would build the centers for the Homeland Security Department for **an unexpected influx of immigrants, to house people in the event of a natural disaster or for new programs that require additional detention space**.* [203]

Yes, they just kind of "slipped that in there," all of those "new programs that require additional detention space," but we know that Homeland Security and FEMA are exactly the same people; and, in light of everything else we've outlined in this chapter, the assurances you'll find later in the article that it's "only in case we get a whole bunch of immigrants" reads particularly hollow.

You can even read a full army plan for civilian internment called Army Regulation 210-35, the *Civilian Inmate Labor Program*, available on army.mil. It doesn't get much clearer than reading this document. On page 3:

> **Summary:** *This regulation provides guidance for establishing and managing* **civilian inmate labor programs on Army installations.** *It addresses recordkeeping and reporting issues related to the Civilian Inmate Labor Program and/or* **prison camp administration.** [204]

Those who talk about such things are often labeled "conspiracy theorists." Yet that's an awfully silly label to use when you can read all about it in major news media and on the Army's own website. You can see these things being talked about on C-Span. The problem is that most people tune it out. They look up and they hear the words, but the words sort of filter through their mind without ever hitting on major implications. Double-speak and double-think are really the orders of the day. Everyone is convinced that it doesn't mean "them," it means "the bad guys." Then we all go on with our lives. The few who notice, care, and try to do something about it find their warnings falling on deaf ears, and, at times, find an entire propaganda machine arrayed against them, ready to demonize them in the eyes of the people.

Big Brother really is watching you through a complex system of technological tyranny. He is also listening to what you have to say and reading everything you send.

[Action: Satellite Camera slowly zooming in: the world, the United States, Pennsylvania, then a City View, then a neighborhood view, then a street view. Finally, it zooms in on a house; computerized letters scroll across the screen. Subject: Located.]

Your name is Tom.

You live just off of 5th Street.

Nice car, Tom.

Nice house.

What's not so nice is you owe Pennsylvania $4,212 in back taxes.

Listen, Tom.

*We can make this easy. Pay online by June 18, and we'll skip your penalty and take half off your interest. Because, Tom? We **do** know who you are.* [205]

The Pennsylvania Department of Revenue tax commercial of 2010 was not an exaggeration. The government really does have access to all sorts of information about you. In point of fact, so do private businesses. Collection agents can now pull up a Google street view to see what kind of house you live in and what kind of car you drive as part of a routine practice to push people into paying all sorts of bills, from your back taxes to your credit card bill. They can also often pull up your place of employment with a quick bit of digging on the internet.

Some information we foolishly make public ourselves. Identity theft experts warn that Facebook is the identity thief's best friend, as we usually make our home city and our date of birth public. Some people make their address and phone number public too. That is all a thief needs to put in a forwarding order where they can usually get access to most of the rest of your information as well. In some cases, the date of birth might just be the last bit of information they need to crack your life open like a nut.

Private companies compile all sorts of information about each citizen, creating a data file that basically amounts to a dossier. A swift transaction between those companies and the government means the government can now know more about you than you can possibly realize. Do you use a debit card all or most of the time? Then someone has information on 99% of what you buy, where you buy it, and how you buy it. If you have computerized loyalty cards, like your grocery store card, that links to any of your personal information, it is possible for that private company to sell information about your eating habits to a public entity. Given the government is now firmly entrenched in our health insurance, this should be a concern. Some bureaucrat could, if they wished, call you up to tell you to start eating less salt or face an increase in your taxes.

During the 2010 census there was a new addition to the program. Census workers were sent out with hand-held devices which recorded the GPS coordinates of every home in America. They were sent out about a year before taking the actual census in order to collect this data. This is part of a global effort being promoted by the United Nations. GPS data can, of course, be plugged directly into a powerful satellite in order to get real time camera data from the eye in the sky [206].

There are multiple ways that this information can be compiled and used against you. For example, at one point there were rumors about a bank crossing their customer data with a cancer registry and then downgrading the creditworthiness of every customer who had cancer. Not only does this discriminate against people with certain health risks, but it violates the traditional confidentiality bond between doctor and patient [207].

Certain monitoring activities allow employers to see your computer screen as you work, thus noting exactly what you are doing on the computer all day long. They can track and monitor if you read your e-mail during the day…and they can read your e-mail too.

And of course, it's getting more and more difficult to walk down or drive down any street in America, or to walk into most stores in America, without a video camera recording everything you do. This information can be matched to your vehicle registration and license plate information to simply send you that traffic ticket through the mail, without ever requiring a police officer to pull you over.

Right now, products are all marked with a bar code, but there's a move on to add RFID chipping to every single product in America. A radio frequency identifier chip could, in the future, be picked up and read by various devices, which means that the government could literally reach into your home and make a categorical inventory of everything you have in there [208]. Think about the pernicious potential here! In Stalin's era, in Mao's era, they had to go door to door with the soldiers and make searches to find hidden food stores. Can you imagine how much easier and quicker it would be for the government to pull up a database of your buying records or to scan the RFID chips of the food in your home? This is why you should buy food now, in cash. The loophole here is that with the technologically based methods of searching, there is less of a likelihood that soldiers would come door to door, making food bought prior to these methods somewhat easier to hide (though traditional hiding methods aren't exactly ill-advised).

Your cell phone can be used at any time to pinpoint your location, even if you turn it off. Your cell phone works on radio frequencies, and the government can also use it to turn into a roving "bug" that will allow them to hear everything you say around your phone [209]. That means that if you happen to yell, in a fit of anger, "I'd like to punch the President in the nose, he's so dumb!" and you have your cell phone three feet away on the dining room table, it's conceivable that the Secret Service could knock on your door an hour or two later.

Usually when you point these things out to people you get one of two reactions. They either say, "I'm not doing anything wrong and I have nothing to hide." Or you hear, "Hey, if they want to listen in on my phone conversations they're welcome to. My life is boring." And it's true. Most people aren't doing anything wrong and most people's lives are pretty boring. In point of fact, nobody *is* usually *actively* paying attention to you and what you do. The personalized ads you receive on the Internet, for example, courtesy of Google, are all automated. The problem is that all of this information is being stored and slowly centralized. If anyone did want to know more about you, they could. It's all there at their fingertips. If you're under investigation (whether you've done anything wrong or not), the government can now pull up an extensive dossier. They can use it to find you, to drag you in, and to compile circumstantial evidence against you. Given we are already right on the verge of thoughts being declared crime and of pre-crime profiling, you might not really want the government to know, for example, that you bought a copy of *Rising Prices, Empty Shelves*. After all, "people who believe in FEMA concentration camps" are another class of people that have been labeled as "potential domestic terrorists."

Furthermore, the more capability this technology has, the more ways it can be used against us, to the point where the government could literally "turn off" your ability to move through modern society at the flip of a switch [210]. What does that mean for your food security? It means that if you've expressed the wrong political view, someone could literally starve you without resorting to a million-person famine that would cause an outcry. They can simply deprive you of any kind of access to the ability to buy or sell. If you'll recall, in the Bible, this is the exact method that the anti-Christ uses to demand worship from the world. Those who would worship him get a mark that's required to buy or sell, and those who don't are cut off from the economic structure and are easy pickings for hunting down.

While certainly all that's really required for such a scheme is some sort of stamp or tattoo, one must admit that an RFID chip implanted in the hand is probably a lot more efficient, since stamps or tattoos can be faked and RFID's can be switched off at a distance. Computer data can be manipulated with the touch of a button. This technology literally puts the axe over your head at all times.

Great Britain actually has a program in place right now where the government can put a camera into a private home, monitor people inside their homes, and send private security guards around to do home checks. They've also instituted a "tattle-tale" network where families who are deemed "responsible" can rat on families they don't like [211]. And just in case Pennsylvania didn't think that it was working hard enough to win the "Creepy Orwell Award," in February of 2010 a suburban Philadelphia school was caught using school-issued laptops to spy on students and parents *in their homes*. They certainly had access to the ability to watch students and parents getting dressed and undressed, depending on where the laptop was located in the house. They could certainly hear, and act on, anything said in the home [212].

Furthermore, spying on you or going through your personal business without a warrant amounts to a violation of the Constitution—yet again. Just because we *have* the technology does not mean we should necessarily *use* the technology.

We already know that oppressive regimes starve their citizens, and we already know there was a Stalinist-Soviet influence back in 1933 when this ball really got rolling. There is no reason to suspect that an American dictatorship would be any kinder or gentler than a Russian one. The time for food security is now, before someone flips the switch on all of those "contingency plans" and ushers in a new reign of terror for America.

3.3 The Choking Grip of Agribusiness

ℰꙨ•ℭℛ

More and more it seems that big companies lobby the government, and we lobby big companies. That's because we recognize something fundamental about the way that our country—and indeed our world—has gone. Somewhere along the line, we ended up with a powerful cartel of Big Corporations who, without any election at all, have been able to pass laws, get control of people's lives, and treat people like slaves. In the case of Agribusiness, you will see the Top 4 companies with control of 80% of the farming activity in this nation.

They don't own everything. In fact, they get a lot of their inventory through contracts with smaller farmers. But as you'll soon see, those farmers cannot stay in business without towing the line of these big companies. As it stands, the system basically creates a situation where farmers have no say over the way they do their business. Increasingly, there is also a hidden world of illegal immigrant labor. It keeps prices cheap for the end-consumer, but also creates a hidden underclass, a group of people who "believe they have no rights and will not complain" (213). One reason for immigration control is not so much to "keep those dirty illegals out" as many claim, but because it hurts two people—the people who try to maintain good jobs here in our own country and the people who desperately flee over the border in search of a better life, only to end up exploited because, being illegals, they *have no recourse but to do whatever they are told*. One does not resist immigration through a lack of compassion but through a compassionate recognition of realities. It is not racism that calls for closed borders but an awareness of the pressures those open borders put on *all* people—all, of course, except for that 1% of people at the very top of the ladder that profits so nicely from the entire arrangement.

These companies have taken control of the discourse about food entirely. In the 2008 FAO summit, for example, an amazing thing happened. Those who challenged Big Agribusiness were literally thrown out.

Farmer and civil society leaders carrying out a peaceful action today in Rome, Italy at the FAO summit on the Food Crisis were **forcefully removed** *from the premises. At around 1:30 pm farmers and representatives of civil society organizations staged an action at the press room to deliver a message that* **millions of additional people are joining the ranks of the hungry** *as the* **corporations that control the global food system are making record profits.**

*The issues of corporate control and speculation, which are leading causes of recent spikes in food prices, **are not being discussed by government delegations and the international agencies meeting in Rome to debate solutions to the crisis.***

*...the main causes of the world's food crises are not being dealt with, **and the world's food producers**—the farmers, fisherfolk, agricultural workers and indigenous workers—**have been shut out of the discussion.*** [214]

The Agribusiness industry, of course, has no intention of relieving you of your food—they want you to buy it. But they do not care how many people can buy it so long as their own profits remain high. In addition, they do not care that their unsafe, unsanitary practices have destroyed lives, killing adults and young children alike. They are either in denial about the real effects of their work or they have somehow justified all of this in their own minds. And because they control most of the industry, it's hard to make good choices about your food, choices that protect you and your family.

Do we eat from the farm or do we eat from the factory? Though food advertisements carry slick photographs of family farms, the reality is quite a bit different. Our food has been placed on a factory model controlled by multi-national corporations. "These are enormous assembly lines where the animals and the workers alike are being abused." Our food system values uniformity, conformity, and cheapness, and thanks to the advent of the factory-based fast food restaurant, most of the hamburger meat, potatoes, pork, chicken, and apples worldwide are bought up by major fast food chains. This has completely changed the face of the industry, and even if you choose not to eat in a fast-food restaurant, you are still eating meat that's controlled by a very specific system [215].

We have come to a point that we've literally redesigned our food, redesigned God's design on things like our chickens. Our chickens are now raised and slaughtered in half the time, yet they are twice as big and have much larger breasts to produce the coveted white meat that sells best. This is done by pumping the chickens, for example, full of antibiotics and hormones [216]. There is a great deal of speculation that the rise of "precocious puberty," where girls develop breasts at a very early age (around seven or eight), could be linked to those hormones.

The conditions for the cows and chickens are atrocious, and it's really little wonder we've had such trouble with public health. The animals are packed in so tightly they can barely move. They are sick, often because they have been forced to grow so quickly that their bones and their internal organs cannot keep up. The Big Agribusiness companies prefer their contractors to keep the chickens in complete darkness as it makes them lie down and resist less when it comes time to pick them up. Sick chickens are processed right along with well chickens. In the case of cows and pigs, these animals are force fed corn to make them grow faster. They are left to stand literally knee-deep in each other's manure for days on end. They are caked in manure when they get to the slaughterhouse. These slaughterhouses are processing 400 cows an hour. They are simply spray-hosed off and sent on. *Of course* they can't keep manure out of meat! That's how we wind up with virulent (and deadly) strains of e.coli and salmonella in our meat. It also gets into our vegetables thanks to run-off from factory farms. And because we continue to pump these animals full of antibiotics, the humans which eat them become resistant—sometimes even allergic—to the antibiotics which might previously have saved their lives.

In spite of the fact that letting a cow eat grass—not corn—for 5 days will wipe out 80% of the e.coli in her system, the Big Business answer to the equation is to create hamburger meat filler *drenched in ammonia* in order to kill the e.coli and then mix it up with regular hamburger meat [217]. Most of us would not get a bottle of ammonia, take it off the shelf, toss it in a frying pan, and sauté our meat in it. We'd probably die if we did that. We'd certainly get sick. And if we gave it to our children, we'd be convicted of child abuse. But that's exactly what Big Agribusiness is willing to do. Beef drenched in Pine Sol is perfectly okay for the average American as far as they are concerned.

Pernicious debt and the constant threat of a loss of contract keeps the smaller farmers "in line." The average chicken farmer is about $500,000 in debt after obtaining just 2 chicken houses. That farmer will go on to earn about $18,000 per year. They have to pay off the debt, but, in the meantime, the Big Agribusiness Companies will continue to intimidate them into these dirty practices and will continually threaten to yank contracts if the farmers do not make still more costly "upgrades" as required by Big Agribusiness. We do a lot of talk about the small farmer, but the average "small farmer" is as under the thumb of the multinational corporations as the average factory worker [218].

It's not just our farmers who have found themselves crushed by Big Business, Big Business that in many cases winds up pushing legislation or controlling regulatory agencies meant to oversee their activities.

In Alaska, the crab fishing industry used to be a place where an ambitious, hard-working individual could work 20 or 30 years and make a good living. Boats were family owned and crews were cared for like family. The work was dangerous and the season was dangerous, but the benefits were spread out across communities.

In 2004, a piece of legislation passed that created a system called "crab rationalization." This system quickly consolidated the power to work at all into the hands of a very few large companies, benefiting owners, processors, and those who got into co-ops fast enough while swiftly bankrupting individual boats.

*Rationalization awards a guaranteed amount of catch to boat owners and seafood **processors based mostly on their past success rates**. The intent was to allow quota holders to buy, sell, and lease shares among themselves. ...The aim was also to make the season safer by changing the free-for-all, derby-style race to one that earmarked a guaranteed portion of the catch while allowing more time to catch it.* [219]

If you follow that bouncing ball you'll quickly see what happens. Let's say you, an independent fisherman, caught a 0.01% share of crabs this year. That was a low-catch year for you, barely enough to keep your boat running. It also means that next year you will only be allowed to catch up to that low-catch number—that is, only up to the 0.01% upon which you cannot sustain your business.

Meanwhile, Big Crab Company owns 100 boats. They already have 23% of the quota and a special contract with a processing company. They will always be able to field enough boats to meet that 23% number, and, if they under-fish this year, they can just buy up more quota next year from, say, you. You now have to decide whether to sell your share and leave your boat idle, knowing you can't afford to run your boat, or to try again on even less quota than before. Big companies can stack their quota, take longer to catch it, use fewer boats, and beat out the little guy every single time. In addition, there are now fewer than half the jobs there once were. And while owners and processors make record profits from the new system, the wages of the crew members who risk life and limb catching the crab have steadily declined [220].

Throughout our food industry, there is a move by large companies to force the little guy out of business in the name of "efficiency" or "safety." The USDA often tries to shut down smaller farmers, claiming that their chemical-free, free-range, open-air conditions are somehow "unsanitary" and inferior to dousing our food in tons of chlorine or ammonia. Lab tests, of course, quickly denounce this notion. A USDA initiative to shut down Polyface Farms, for example, was defeated when the farm was able to demonstrate that the factory farm meat carried a staggering *270% more pathogens* than their free-range meat [221].

The new Food Safety Modernization Act isn't a very exciting read, should you take the time to read the entire bill (we did). It looks just about like your average set of state daycare center licensing regulations. In the hands of a *reasonable person*, it would be ho-hum. Keep a clean operation. Keep records to show your operation is clean. Be able to demonstrate this at any time so that we know you're not putting a bunch of deadly pathogens into the food supply. Necessary. Good. Basically yawn-worthy. Not, were we living in a Constitutional Republic controlled by and for the people, worth getting up in arms over. And you would think that it just be something that might get Agribusiness under control at last.

Given the practices of Agribusiness, you'd *think* they'd be afraid of this bill. After all, these are the people putting ammonia and manure into our hamburgers. Why was it supported, then, by every major Agribusiness company and the Agribusiness lobby?

Probably in the hopes that they can send more USDA and FDA inspectors out to more reasonable farming operations and use them to harass them, shut them down, or tie them up in legal battles until those farmers have little choice to stop competing with the Big Guys. Because, you see, just as George Peek noted that the AAA wouldn't be particularly exciting in the hands of a reasonable administrator, like any bill it can be deadly in the hands of malicious business interests, petty bureaucrats and a Big Brother government firmly in bed with said business interests. Our government, which we already know from the previous section, is growing increasingly obsessed with controlling its citizenry. What better way than to consolidate the food supply into the hands of their four or five best friends?

Joel Salatin of Polyface farms perhaps said it best in the documentary film *Food, Inc*. He said, "We've become a culture of technicians. We're all into the *how* of it, and nobody's stepping back and saying, 'but *why*?' A culture that just views a pig as a pile of proto-plasmic, inanimate structure to be manipulated by whatever creative design the human race can foist on that critter will probably view individuals within its community, and other cultures in the community of nations with the same disdain, and disrespect, and controlling type mentality" [222]. And isn't that exactly what we're seeing out of our government and out of the elitist business interests?

We really have a scenario where the foxes are watching the henhouse. Ostensibly, the FDA and the USDA exist to protect American consumers from bad food practices. After all, if we're going to allow any invasive government regulation of the free market at all, it is because we would a) understand the potential excesses of the market as we are now seeing, once corporate interests finally blasted past the early restrictions against their sort of business model (back in the days of Standard Oil) and b) because we believe those agencies are going to protect us. We believe, for example, that a USDA regulator who picks up a big hunk of chlorine, ammonia washed, manure filled beef is going to take that big hunk of beef off to a nice, clean laboratory where objective, scientific men with the best interests of the public at heart are going to make sure it's the right color, make sure it smells okay, and do some tests on it to make sure that it's not full of any nasty little parasites that might send our children to the hospital or potentially kill them. It was meant, originally, as a check-and-balance style system. But you can't have a check-and-balance system when the same interests are manipulating both sides of the system. It is ludicrous to think that we ever could.

Like we saw with Goldman-Sachs and the financial industry, in which former Wall Street bankers and CEOs wound up heading "regulatory agencies," you can find an inordinate number of people moving from Agribusiness into government. In the past years, we have had such luminaries as a former executive VP of the National Food Processor's Association, a former lobbyist for the largest pusher of GMO foods and seeds in the nation, and the former chief lobbyist for the beef industry heading the FDA or the USDA. Earl Butz, the 1971 secretary of the USDA under Nixon who pushed the "Get Big or Get Out" strategy now infecting the farm industry *worldwide*, began as a board member for Ralston-Purina.

If you'd like to know why just about everything we eat seems to be made of either corn or soy, and why these days we have a policy of fostering the biggest farms possible, you really only need look at Earl Butz. He got the ball rolling for us.

He envisioned a hyper-efficient, centralized food system, one that could profitably and cheaply "feed the world" by manipulating... mountains of Midwestern corn and soy. Patron Saint of the Fast Food Nation, Butz lived to see his dream realized.

"Plant fence row to fence row!"

Urged on by Butz and buoyed by high grain prices, millions of Midwestern farmers scrambled to plant as much as they could to take advantage. Midwestern farmers spent the 1970s taking on more debt to buy more land, bigger and more complicated machines, new seed varieties, more fertilizers and pesticides, and generally producing as much as they possibly could.

Then, in the 1980s, the bubble burst. By that time, farms were cranking out much more than the market could bear, and prices fell accordingly. Meanwhile, interest rates had spiked, making all those loans farmers had taken out in the 70s into a paralyzing burden. Farm incomes plunged, and tens of thousands of farms went under.

...Yet the food production machine Butz created kept cranking. Surviving farms responded to low prices by planting more, hoping to make up on volume what they were losing on price. Failed farms got folded into larger operations at cut-rate prices. Throughout the Grain Belt, abandoned farmhouses were burned to the ground, cleared, and incorporated into ever-larger corn and soy fields.

While farmers scrambled to "get big or get out," Butz's beloved agri-business giants cheered. Regaled with mountains of cut-rate corn... [agribusiness] used its political muscle to rig up lucrative markets for high-fructose corn syrup and ethanol...[giving rise to]...CAFOs...and cheap but highly profitable burgers, chops, and chicken nuggets. [223]

Even today, the fast-food industry relies on the parameters which Butz set up. Farmers did indeed "get big or get out." In 1970 5 big companies controlled 25% of the industry; now 4 of them control 80% [224].

Now you take a board like the FDA, a board which is charged with making sure what goes into our mouth is safe. And you take an issue like, "Are GMOs safe," and put a former lobbyist for the GMO food giant in charge of the FDA. It doesn't take a geneticist—or indeed, even a single test—to figure out what answer the FDA is going to come up with. "OF COURSE IT'S SAFE, DIG IN, EAT UP!" It's a symptom of our information overload and America's general exhaustion with the corrupt political system that there wasn't more of an outcry over this—and, of course, a symptom of a media controlled by some of the very same interests who quietly said little or nothing at all.

Bigger still isn't better. Canada took a "bigger is better" strategy too. A study by Canada's National Farmer's Union called *The Farm Crisis: Bigger Farms and the Myths of "Competition" and "Efficiency"* challenged the government policy that "increases in farm size" would result in "a decrease in incomes for farmers...lowering prices for consumers...and better paid employment in the cities for farmers who get out." The report was so bold as to call the assumptions upon which these notions were predicated to be "lies." They discovered that larger farms were not, in fact, more efficient. It did not, in fact, relate back to bigger profits for farmers. Farm expansion, they found, had increased the crisis in farmer incomes more than ever. They also noted that more and more, farmers, especially smaller farmers, were getting squeezed by a huge train of multi-national corporations, including fuel, oil, and natural gas companies; fertilizer companies who turn the natural gas into nitrogen fertilizer; chemical and seed companies; machine companies and banks; grain companies, railways, packers and processors; retailers, and restaurants [225]. Under such circumstances it is difficult to see how a small farmer could possibly win.

Agribusiness literally forms what one might call the Exploitation Nation. Freedom lovers, and indeed many Americans, have gotten suspicious of labor unions and the intent of labor. Big abuses like those shown in GM's labor unions have rendered the public fairly contemptuous of labor's efforts. Well, labor can get too much power. Government can get too much power. Business can get too much power. That is why, again and again, we have a series of checks and balances. Labor unions serve a purpose. Labor unions have given us the safe working conditions under a reasonable number of hours that we enjoy today. They have given us, in many cases, fairer wages (just as often as they have created unsustainable wages that skew the system). So when you're starting to view the practices of Agribusiness when it comes to labor, it's important to realize there has to be a balance.

On the one hand, you do not want a too-powerful union driving up wages into unrealistic stratospheres for too-little work, nor do you want them shutting down vital areas of the nation with a strike.

On the *other* hand, you also do not want child labor, and dirty, unsafe working conditions that leave good, hardworking Americans struggling to support their families. You do not want our citizens forced to work at wages that do not allow them to care for their families.

Once again we must call for a fair and balanced viewpoint. We *must* do so, because that's what the Founding Fathers did. We must recognize that it is *human nature* to attempt to exploit a system and take too much power. When the system works, the market keeps labor in check, and labor keeps the market in check, and everybody (with some grumbling) is more or less happy. *When the system works.*

In examining Agribusiness, we will see Americans working in conditions that we wouldn't force our worst enemies into. And because Agribusiness is a global concern, you will see them going into other countries with a jocular, patriarchal smile about fifty seconds before they slam a boot into the face of the less fortunate and then laugh all the way to the bank.

One would almost have to look at these conditions and ask ourselves, "would God cry out for these people? Would Jesus want us to treat people, and allow people, to be treated in this fashion?"

Delving into any issue can be very frustrating because we all tend to make broad generalizations. They're often our *pet* generalizations. But we just can't do that! We've *got* to look at the human costs. We've got to put ourselves in other people's shoes. We've got to apply liberty and justice, and we've got to ask ourselves how we'd want to be treated, and how we'd want our children to be treated.

So let us walk in the shoes of Agribusiness labor for a while, and see what sort of conclusions we come to.

First, we'll take a look at a worker in an American meat packing plant. "They have," one worker at Smithfield in Tar Heel, North Carolina says, "the same mentality towards workers as they do towards the hogs. They don't have to worry about their comfort, because they're temporary" [226]. So you have this plant, where 32,000 hogs are slaughtered every day. Close your eyes and imagine yourself, or your mother, or one of your children, or your best friend standing there, day after day, doing exactly the same task. They are covered in blood, feces, and urine. The conditions are so dangerous and unsanitary that they routinely get horrific infections and are constantly ill. Wages are low, the lower because the area where this plant has chosen to operate is so economically depressed. These very people have to choose between buying food and buying medicine for their conditions. And many of them will never be able to afford to leave. This is not the respectable, clean, highly paid meat packing plant of the 1950s [227]. How are you feeling about conditions now?

We also talk a lot about illegal immigrants. To us, they are dirty people who sweep in and steal our jobs. We don't realize that Agribusiness and our government stole theirs first. When NAFTA came along, Mexican corn farmers were literally driven out of business by all of the cheap American corn flooding into the nation. So what did the meat packers do? They went in and *actively recruited* illegal immigrants. They bused them in. The government turned a blind eye to the whole thing. Now, of course, there's a crackdown on illegal immigrants. The Agribusiness managers, owners, everyone involved in this scheme—they're fine. They're continuing to make their money. It's the workers that are getting deported [228].

Now let's go across the world. Let's go to Africa and take a look at the picture there.

The corporate rush to industrialize African Agriculture is riding the coattails of the global food crisis. With help from big philanthropy and government aid, agribusiness grants are rapidly expanding their market power on the continent. An $8 million dollar project for soy production in Mozambique and Zambia between Cargill and Gates claims it will raise the income of 37,000 farmers by $200/year within 4 years. If the project works, that amounts to about $0.50/day per farmer, or $7.4 million dollars--$600,000 less than the money invested in the project in the first place. The soy will be used for biofuels and livestock feed. Basically, a contract farming scheme was launched *at the Soy Innovations Africa Conference held in Westin Grand in Capetown, South Africa.*

Meanwhile, Mozambique has been rocked by food riots, because people can't afford bread, much less grain-fed meat or processed feed for their livestock. They don't have cars to fill up with biofuels, either.

...While the corporate colonization of African agriculture is carefully presented in the standard anti-hunger packaging of the Green Revolution, historically, industrial agriculture has left more poor and hungry people than it has 'saved.' [229]

The truly amazing part of this entire debacle is that we haven't even touched on all of the issues yet!

We haven't touched on the fact that cheap food drives all of this—but there are so many families who are making such lousy wages that they rely on that cheap food. We haven't touched on how poverty hits on obesity—how fresh fruits and vegetables are out of reach for many low-income families but the copious amounts of fast-food Dollar Menus are not. We haven't touched on the epidemic of diabetes and heart disease striking at not only our adults but our children as well. We've hardly brushed the surface of Big Pharma's interest in the entire affair. There are so many issues with our food and we haven't even come near all of them.

But if you start tracking your way through this book, you'll start to see a disturbing pattern emerging. Let's recap.

We have a corrupt banking industry that intentionally sucks the wealth out of nations and, on an individual level, the middle and lower class back home. They are in bed with the government, and high level managers, board members, and lobbyists from this industry end up as unelected government appointees on a regular basis.

We have a military-industrial complex that makes its money off of fostering wars as well as by selling the government surveillance equipment and detention centers. This has prepared our government to declare martial law and to force people into slave labor in concentration camps at any time.

We have a food industry that intentionally uses nasty practices, exploited labor, and predatory practices to take total control of everything we eat and drink. They, too, are in bed with the government, and they, too, have an inordinate number of managers, board members, and lobbyists which end up as highly placed, unelected governmental appointees with the force of law behind them.

We have an increasing maze and network of taxes, welfare and corporate welfare, controls, unfairly applied regulations, subsidies, practices, and policies which make it very difficult for a scrupulous small-to-medium sized businessperson to work at all; in many cases, they cannot work without being told exactly what to do and how to do it by much larger, more powerful business concerns whose authority is slowly becoming inseparable from governmental authority.

We have a pharmaceutical and medical industry which is doing exactly the same thing and which is now backed by a positively labyrinthine government-managed health insurance system.

We've got a media who, far from acting as the watchdog of government and industry, is in fact owned by government and industry and in fact prostitutes itself to it. We have a government agency in the form of the FCC which has stated an outright hostility towards independent media and has a host of initiatives on the table to shut it all down.

We've got a Gordian Knot system in which even conscientious people who do not like the practices behind the system find themselves trapped in it, and in which it is going to be almost impossible to extricate ourselves from without hurting someone, a great many of them neighbors and friends, ordinary people like you and I.

If you're not worried yet, you haven't been reading closely enough.

But don't worry.

We're not nearly done yet.

3.4 Chemicals, Chemicals Everywhere

৪ා • ୠ

We have already discussed some of the pernicious effects of antibiotics on the meat industry. These unintended consequences are really only a puzzle piece of the 20th-21st century "better living through chemistry" attitude. We throw chemicals everywhere. We use them in fertilizers, we use them in weed killers, and we use them in pesticides. We've called it the Green Revolution and insist that it has saved lives by bringing yields far above what they ever could be alone. And in this regard, we can indeed tip the hat to the chemical industry. The yields are absolutely amazing. But given the consequences of how they have been obtained, we might well ask ourselves how many lives have been lost in other ways, and whether or not we've really done anything other than replace famine with a long-term pestilence.

We can't just evaluate our chemical dependence in terms of a threat to the food supply; we must evaluate it in terms of its threat to public health as well. In addition, we need to evaluate what it's doing to our ability to produce agriculture well into the future.

There are a few potential future courses. Either we will, and soon, abandon the use of poisons and thus suffer a drop in food production back to pre-chemical (but safer) levels - at that point, we will either finally put more of the productive earth back into production by abandoning the banking, business, and colonial practices that force such a scenario or we will suffer a broad, sweeping famine until production and demand again catch up to one another - or we will continue on in our current madness, and there will be, as we've amply demonstrated in this book, famine *anyway*. *And* a whole lot of people and communities will be sick. And there will continue to be fewer animals and fish to hunt in order to supplement our diets.

Or God in His mercy really *will* return soon to smack all of us around and teach us how to do it right (The argument of this book is not an eschatological one; we do not profess to know the "day or the hour." So we do not say "these *are* the End Times!" We do, however, simply point out that Jesus' return is certainly looking like a more and more urgent occurrence).

In any case, *today* there is a problem.

Before the environmental movement was co-opted by the elite to forward their Malthusian schemes, it was concerned with the activities of the elite. To say that there is no real environmental problem just because evil people have led well-meaning people in the movement to points of insanity would be as big of a fallacy as accepting a totalitarian society based on an unproven environmental "problem" dreamed up by the likes of Ted Turner. Arguably, the movement got its start in 1962 when Rachel Carson wrote her ground breaking book *Silent Spring*.

The primary concern of *Silent Spring* is the very issue which we will discuss in this chapter. In short, this is the idea that pesticides, herbicides, and chemical fertilizers represent a very real threat. It's been nearly 50 years since the idea was first introduced, however, and our agricultural system continues to spread chemical death around with a liberal hand. In her introduction to the 2002 edition to Carson's book Linda Lear points out:

> *The domestic production of DDT was banned, but not its export, ensuring that the pollution of the earth's atmosphere, oceans, streams, and wildlife would continue unabated. DDT is found in the livers of birds and fish on every oceanic island on the planet and in the breast milk of every mother.* [230]

The story of our dependence on poisons is the story of modern America. That is, a story of excess by the elite, of criminal carelessness and of a lack of care. It's the story of sacrificing the substance of safety for the comforting appearance of plenty. It's all mixed in with man's tendency to avoid worrying about anything which does not immediately affect him.

A farmer friend of mine who I greatly respect produces cotton and soybeans. While out in the garden one day his wife was spraying with the chemical herbicide *Roundup*. She got some of it into her mouth and expressed a brief concern, but he said, "Don't worry about it, it's just Roundup." My farmer friend is an extremely intelligent man, so it's easy to see why the bulk of the population just isn't too concerned. He's also a man of exceptional morals who would never intentionally cause harm to anybody at all.

However, familiarity breeds contempt and familiarity is helped along by the media and by slick PR ad campaigns. Indeed, his wife did not fall over dead from this exposure. All the same, the primary ingredient of Roundup is Glyphosate.

> *The active toxicity of glyphosate products to humans was first publicized by physicians in Japan who studied suicide attempts; nine cases were fatal. Symptoms included intestinal pain, vomiting, excess fluid in the lungs, pneumonia, clouding of consciousness,*

and destruction of red blood cells...More recent reviews of poisoning incidents have found similar symptoms, as well as lung dysfunction, erosion of the gastro- intestinal tract, abnormal electrocardiograms, low blood pressure, kidney damage, and damage to the larynx. [(231)]

Obviously you wouldn't want to pour a big old glass of the stuff and have it with your breakfast. The results wouldn't be too good. And yet we're all somehow perfectly comfortable with spraying 30 to 48 *million* pounds of the stuff on our crops, lawns, golf courses and city streets every single year, as if, when it's done its job of killing all the plants we don't want, it's just going to peacefully go away somewhere instead of getting into our soil, our water supply, the plants we sprayed it with and then proceeded to eat, the cells of the animals we also eat, and our own cells as well. Somehow, the slow build-up of the stuff in our systems is not considered to be nearly as pernicious or suicidal as simply pouring yourself a nice glass of Glyhosate would be. Industry would have you believe we sort of harmlessly pass it all out of our natural waste processes if it gets into our body at all.

And as you will soon see, as with all the other issues, this issue ties so very tightly into everything else we've been discussing. In Part 2, for example, we noted the increasing difficulty of finding water that we can use for good agriculture. Most of Earth's water can't be used; in this chapter you will learn how we've come to remove even more water from our capability to use it. As Rachel Carson offers:

By strange paradox, most of the earth's abundant water is not usable for agriculture, industry, or human consumption because of its heavy load of sea salts, and so most of the world's population is either experiencing or is threatened with critical shortages. In an age where man has forgotten his origins and is blind to even his most essential needs for survival, water, along with other resources, has become the victim of his indifference.

The problem of water pollution by pesticides can be understood only in context, as part of the whole to which it belongs. The pollution entering our waterways comes from many sources: radioactive wastes from reactors, laboratories, and hospitals; fallout from nuclear explosions; domestic wastes from cities and towns; chemical wastes from factories. To these is added a new kind of fallout—the chemical sprays applied to croplands and gardens, forests and fields. Many of the chemical agents in this alarming mélange imitate and augment the harmful effects of radiation. (232)

Issues of chemical agriculture are issues of inalienable rights. There is now literally no way to keep yourself from exposure to the effects of chemical agriculture. We have no freedom to choose whether or not we want to be exposed to them. Informed consent is withheld from us (233).

Rachel Carson would also come to note this in her book. "If the Bill of Rights contains no guarantee that a citizen shall secure against lethal poisons distributed either by private individuals or public officials," she noted, "it is surely only because our forefathers, despite their considerable wisdom and foresight, could conceive of no such problem" (234).

Yet one might argue the forefathers did have such foresight. "We hold these truths to be self-evident, that all men are created equal, that they were endowed by their Creator with certain unalienable rights, that among these are life, liberty, and the pursuit of happiness." If the uninhibited spraying of lethal poisons is a threat to life, as the preponderance of evidence seems to suggest, and given the bulk of the population exposed to such poison is neither in the chemical industry nor the agricultural industry and thus has had no say or choice in whether or not such things are used, then we would have to state that the continued knowing use of such chemicals represents a violation of the basic right to life.

Now the market might argue that we the consumer make these decisions through our buying habits, and this is true. We do. The reason you can now walk into any Wal-Mart in the nation and pick up some organic foods is because we the consumer have demanded organic foods on our shelves. If we began buying nothing but organic food, eschewing all other options, then in another decade you would see Wal-Mart begin stocking nothing but organic food. However, you have to note the lack of public information. And you have to note the pricing factors that put poisoned broccoli at an affordable price but organically grown broccoli at a price that soars out of the reach of a great many American families.

While each of us bears a bit of the responsibility for the situation as it stands, we have to note that responsibility in terms of two factors. First, if one has no knowledge or little access to knowledge that can help them make a good, informed decision, then it follows they bear less responsibility for that decision than those who have such access and are fully informed. It also follows that responsibility grows with ability to make an impact. You, when you go spend your food dollar, have an average dollar impact of $6133 per year, to a greater or lesser degree depending on how close you are to the $49,000 income average. You can impact the agricultural industry by exactly that much. The chemical-agricultural mogul, however, can make a million dollar decision about whether or not to buy the chemicals, when and whether or not to spray them, what to spray, and how to spray it. "To whom much is given, much is required." Thus we can argue that the man with the ability to make that million dollar decision does bear more responsibility than the man with the ability to make a six thousand dollar decision.

Toxic sludge is now routinely being passed off as a beneficial fertilizer. If you think poisonous fertilizers, weed killers, and pesticides are bad, you ain't seen nothin' yet.

Imagine you're a small farmer in an economically depressed town. Representatives from a big city—New York, say, or Houston—come in and tell you they're going to help you. Not only are they going to relieve you of the crushing financial burden of buying fertilizer by providing it to you for *free*, but they're also going to inject some money into your town if you decide to go with their fertilizer product. Maybe your town needs a new fire station or a new school. The Big City to the rescue!

The fertilizer, they say, is called "biosolid" fertilizer. They make it out to be little more than simple compost. A time honored practice, of course. Organic, even. Safe.

Except it's not safe.

"Biosolids" are another word for sewage sludge. It's the PR word for sludge, sludge that's been taken, blasted with heat, dried, and attractively repackaged as a farm product. It can take several years for the negative effects of spreading this stuff on fields to rear its ugly heads. This hasn't stopped Big Business and Big Government from pushing the stuff.

If the 'Water Environment Federation' has its way, you'll be routinely eating fruits and vegetables fertilized with sewage sludge containing heavy metals, dangerous viruses, PCBs, pesticides and hundreds of other toxic chemicals.

The WEF, whose pleasant sounding name conceals its true identity as the main lobby association for U.S. sewage treatment plants, is working closely with the Environmental Protection Agency to persuade farmers and food processors that sludge is a 'beneficial fertilizer.'

...Spreading sludge on farm fields happens to be the cheapest disposal method available, and the WEF and EPA claim that it is also the most environmentally sound method—that it "recycles" sewage waste by converting it into a valuable resource. [235]

Of course, the National Food Processor Association lobby is against labeling food grown in sludge. We wouldn't want you, the consumer, to feel under-confident about eating a tomato full of poison. "Biosolids" are chock full of lead, which can cause severe retardation or death. There's also viruses, bacteria, protozoa, fungi, and intestinal worms. A vast number of diseases not only get into the ground water but are also taken straight into the crops. Try sitting down to a great big bite of salmonella, shigella, e.coli, encephalitis, meningitis, roundworm, hookworm, and tapeworm just to name a few [236]. Tasty! It's as if Rachel Carson set out to warn us about DDTs, and so the chemical agricultural industry decided to see if it could come up with anything worse. And they did. With flying colors, in fact.

And if you pick up an apple, or a tomato, or a head of lettuce and put it in your mouth, and that apple is full of things that are going to make you sick, *it is not food anymore*. It is a poison, cleverly packaged and designed to look like food. You are no more eating food than Snow White was when she bit into her own fateful apple. You simply are the beneficiary of the proceeds of a *silent famine*—one in which people think they are eating but are in fact slowly killing themselves.

In fact, it could be argued by those who like to compare the past to the future and to try to make predictions that there's no need for the government to pull an open Stalinization Starvation if they can simply slowly poison us all to death while sucking us dry of whatever wealth we manage to produce during our short time on earth.

Greedy companies and our government have used the "delayed reaction" of these effects to repeatedly deny any connection so that they may continue with their practices. At least one company has used genetic engineering to all but ensure that at least one crop will slowly but surely stay out of production without the application of dangerous chemicals. Often these companies have undertaken their practices knowing the dangers. People have died as a direct result of their actions. Don't we generally hold murderers accountable for their actions? Why aren't we now?

And the danger is multiplying. In 1962, 500 new chemicals were being added to our environment every single year. In 2011, we've brought the number up to 1,000. At that rate, we could postulate 2,000 added each year by 2060, except that we already know that at some point we are going to reach a tipping point—a place where we've added so much to our air, water, and soil that we will cause calamity on an unprecedented scale. Though the calamities will no doubt put a stop to this injection, it does seem a poor way to go about it.

Issues of chemical agriculture are also the issues of exploitation of poorer communities. We saw this with the biosolid issue. We've also seen how the agricultural industry of America secretly relies upon a large number of illegal immigrants who are underpaid, exploited, and quietly, actively recruited. It is not the owners of the huge agribusiness farms and the contributors to the farm income numbers (which place average farm income around $76,000 a year) that bear the brunt of the problem. It is the farm workers, who mix the pesticides and herbicides, apply them, and then go out in the fields to work with the plants liberally sprayed with them. There are also a great many farms and food operations in otherwise economically depressed rural areas where communities with few resources to fight are routinely exposed to whatever chemicals the big companies want to apply today. "2/3 of the [toxic] hazards," according to a report by Lynn R. Goldman, MD, MPH of the John Hopkins School of Public Health, "occur in rural areas." This is actually a worldwide problem, but the illnesses go largely unreported. The poorest nations typically use the riskiest pesticides and "within nations the agricultural workforce is often economically disadvantaged" [237].

The Pesticide Action Network UK gives us another vivid picture of the incalculable harm that chemical agriculture causes year after year. "Pesticides," they report, "have become increasingly expensive. The cost of chemicals can be as much as 60% of a farmer's production costs, which leads to severe indebtedness. Pesticides often lose their effectiveness after a few years because pests are able to adapt and become resistant to them. Farmers are then trapped in an endless cycle where they must buy an ever-increasing quantity of pesticides or switch to newer, more expensive chemicals. Each year, thousands of farmers commit suicide because they cannot pay their debts. Ironically, they often do so by ingesting the pesticides which have caused their despair" [238].

It also goes without saying that these poorer communities are less likely to be educated about the risks of the chemicals they are either using or being exposed to, thus making it very difficult for them to make an informed decision— even when they have any choice. When you cannot afford to do anything else, it becomes an act of intolerable cruelty to assume that it is "their choice" to work in those industries or not.

Chemical agriculture threatens our ability to continue to produce any agriculture or to locate any food at all. Ironically, one of the main effects of chemical pesticides is to produce more insects. Not only do the insects grow resistant to the chemicals, but there is often a resurgence of insect numbers after spraying. In the meantime, the health of the birds that eat the insects is threatened. Fish die and wildlife dies which cuts off hunting as an avenue of food production. Livestock is similarly threatened.

We've explored the way chemical fertilizers strip the soil of essential nutrients and render large areas of land useless for agricultural production. We've demonstrated the ways in which herbicides, pesticides, and chemical fertilizers destroy our ability to use water for drinking and agriculture, as well as killing off birds and fish which we might otherwise eat.

And so the very thing which is sold to us as famine prevention may indeed cause a famine in the long run. There will come a point where our chemicals just can't get any more virulent—or rather, they can, but the application of the chemicals at the strength necessary would be so virulent as to render food immediately inedible and to sicken humans to the point where there would be no question of a cause-effect relationships. At that point you have no choice but to live with the insects and manually pull the weeds, or to fertilize in more traditional ways. At that point, however, it might well be too late. This is why anyone concerned with issues of long-term food security would do well to start growing their own organic garden.

3.5 The Threat of GMO Foods

ℰ•℘

As mentioned earlier, for the first time in human history we could be facing a new kind of famine. A famine in which food is freely available, but which is so dangerous to eat that it ferments a new pestilence all its own. A famine in which you can eat, feel full, and even get fat—but in which your future and your children's future is systematically being ripped away from you. Yet another permutation of this threat lies in Genetically Modified foods, also known as GMs or GMOs.

If you shopped at the grocery store this week, went home, and prepared a meal, at least 70% of what you prepared, if not more, contained GMO foods. If you went to restaurants over the course of this week the number could be even higher. That is, unless everything in your shopping cart carried a "certified organic" or "made with organic ingredients" label, because those sorts of foods are required, by law, to avoid GMOs. You may have also avoided GMOs if you found products labeled, "No GMOs" or "Made Without GMOs" because companies are still legally able to simply voluntarily label their food products. You'll never, in the United States, find any food product that tells you it *does* have GMOs, however. That's because the Big GMO companies have managed to make that illegal. Products containing corn, soy, canola, and cottonseed are the big four for GMO content. Almost every processed product in America is made with corn and soy. GM beet sugar is also entering the food supply at an alarming rate [239].

Even when farmers try to avoid GMOs, there's a problem. 80% of our soy farmers, for example, voluntarily use GMO seeds. It's unfortunate that those few farmers trying to look out for our food interests can't do anything about involuntary contamination. When pollen or seeds blow over from neighbor's fields, the farmers who try to avoid GMOs could be producing GMO crops without meaning to or wanting to. This, of course, makes genetically modified food *extremely difficult* if not *impossible* to avoid altogether.

We've already noted how Big GMO has managed to get their major lobbyist in charge of the FDA. The truth of the matter is that many of the representatives of this company have gone on to wind up in highly placed positions in appointed government positions. At least one Supreme Court justice—the one that wrote the majority opinion on whether or not seeds could be patented—had strong ties to Big GMO. You'll see why we're being so vague as to the who, when, and where when you start reading about "Veggie Libel Laws." For now it's enough to say that the information is freely available if you want to go hunt it down for yourself.

Thanks to these foxes in the henhouse, the numerous studies which have questioned the safety of GMO foods have been ignored, glossed over, and buried. Even without these studies, most consumers in the United States say, unequivocally, that they would refuse to buy GMO foods if they knew that's what they were buying [240]. To this one might add, rather cynically, "And if they had a choice."

Studies show extreme health risks from GMOs. From rat testicles that turn blue to gut flora that churn out pesticides, the results of the mostly-ignored studies are alarming. Here are a few from the Seeds of Deception website, which lists a total of 65 studies.

- Rats fed GM potatoes developed potentially pre-cancerous cell growth in the digestive tract. Their brain development was inhibited and so was the development of their testicles. The liver partially atrophied and the pancreases got larger.
- The stomachs of rats fed GM tomatoes began bleeding.
- Workers exposed to GM cotton reported reactions of the skin, eyes, and upper respiratory tract. Some laborers required hospitalization.
- After the cotton harvest in India, a quarter of the sheep that grazed on the GM plants died within a week.
- In 2003, approximately 100 people living next to a GM cornfield in the Philippines developed skin, respiratory, and intestinal reactions, as well as other symptoms during the pollination season. The symptoms reappeared in exactly the same season in 2004; they also appeared in four other villages who planted the same variety of corn.
- GM foods may have a sterilizing effect. Some pigs fed GM corn had low conception rates, false pregnancies, or incidences of giving birth to bags of water.
- When given the choice between GM foods and non-GM foods, animals such as cows, pigs, geese, squirrels, elk, deer, raccoon, mice, and rats will uniformly avoid the GM foods.

- The liver cells of mice fed GM soybeans showed significant changes. Most of the irregularities went away when the GM soy was removed from the diet.
- Female rats fed GM soy starting before conception and continuing through pregnancy and weaning wound up with 55.6% of their offspring dead, compared to 9% from the non-GM soy controls. Some pups from the GM fed mothers were significantly smaller. When offspring from GM fed rats were mated together they were unable to conceive [241].

There's also evidence that toying with the genetic material of our food could lead to epidemics of viruses and antibiotic resistant diseases on a scale which is absolutely unprecedented. So why the rush to get these dangerous genetically modified crops on the market? It's simply this: you can't patent a seed that occurs in nature. You *can* patent a seed that's genetically modified. Once that happens, you have total and complete control over that type of plant. Get enough, or all, of the plants wrapped up in your seed control scheme, and you have just earned yourself control of the global food supply, placing all farmers and consumers directly at your mercy.

Therefore, Big GMO has slowly but surely begun creating an oppressive and dangerous monopoly. Collecting and saving your own seed is a time-honored practice of farmers, but if you use any of Big GMO's patented seed it's against the law. But the law doesn't only apply if you buy the seed and use it on purpose. If any of that genetic material blows into your field from a nearby farm you're still on the hook for it. That means the moment Big GMO can prove that some of their genetic material got mingled in with yours, you're stuck buying your seed over and over again year after year—right after they get done suing you and trying to run you out of business.

These companies devote gigantic budgets to investigating and prosecuting farmers. Big, intimidating men show up and follow farmers around to try to catch them at saving their seed. Farmers can spend hundreds of thousands of dollars defending themselves before they ever enter the courtroom. Further, Agribusiness sometimes patents plant varieties for the purposes of removing them from production. Year after year, farmers find they have fewer and fewer choices on what to plant [242]. Farmers who want to stay out of the grip of Big GMO, at least in the United States, may well find they have the choice to either get out of business entirely or capitulate to the powers that be at last.

The actions of the Big GMOs defy reason. It would be one thing to create seeds and leave a free and open choice on the market as to whether or not farmers are going to buy them, and to ensure that farmers did buy them. But as Big GMOs buy up all of the smaller seed companies, it gets more and more difficult to obtain any seed at all that isn't held in their crushing grip. They've stepped in to make it illegal in some counties to block the planting of GMO seeds. They've made seed-cleaning equipment illegal because they're trying to paint seed-cleaning as a source of "gene-contamination." In some communities, Big GMO has gotten law enforcement to help them intimidate entire communities of farmers, to the point where neighbors do not talk to neighbors. That is because Big GMO encourages neighbors to "turn one another in" for seed saving, as if they were in Nazi Germany whispering criticism of the government to the Gestapo. And yes, there have been instances where one neighbor with a grievance against another will falsely accuse them of seed-saving just to bring the hammer of Big GMO down upon them.

Like the Gestapo, Big GMO maintains lists. These lists have "blacklisted" farmers on them, and those farmers are not allowed to buy from their company in the future. So at some point, should Big GMO be allowed to get control of every single seed in the world, those farmers are automatically out of business [243].

Essentially, these companies are acting like Mafia thugs. They are not acting like any company in any semblance of a constitutional republic ought to be able to act. They're not acting like anybody with a shred of human *decency* ought to be expected to act. They are worshiping at the altar of cold hard cash without ever bothering to think about the long term consequences of their actions, let alone the short term harm they cause.

Because, you see, there's more danger still.

Many of these seeds have what's called a "terminator switch" in them. The "terminator switch" makes the seed-saving argument even more of a simple act of intimidation. Once you've planted the seed and grown the first crop the seeds switch off. You could save 165,000 seeds from terminator switch crops and you'd never get a single plant. Not one. The danger here is this: as these crops continue to contaminate the supply, you could reasonably end up with a scenario in which there are *no seeds left* that do not contain this terminator DNA. That means no seeds, whatsoever, that are not produced like the Frankenstein monster, off in a laboratory somewhere. In the event of any major human disaster where the laboratories lost their ability to function, we could potentially face a scenario where *we can't get anything to grow*. No food, for anybody, anywhere. It sounds like science fiction. It sounds like a bad movie. But the longer we play God, the more likely such a scenario becomes. This wouldn't just be a famine. It would be some sort of epic mega-famine far beyond anything ever seen in human history.

Fortunately, many other countries have outright banned the growth and sale of GMOs. They don't want them. This hasn't stopped Big GMO from attempting to force their mad science upon them, however.

Big GMO wants to strong-arm the countries that have been smart enough to ban them. January 4, 2011. CBSNews.com. Headline: **WikiLeaks: U.S. Wanted Trade War Over GM Crops.**

> *The U.S. ambassador to France urged George W. Bush's administration to wage a trade war against European Union nations over their resistance to genetically modified crops, according to diplomatic cables released by WikiLeaks. Europe's reluctant to accept genetically modified crops, or GM foods, into the market has threatened to cut off a key export market for American farmers.*
>
> *GM foods are still viewed with far greater suspicion in most of Europe than in the United States, where they've been common on dinner tables for years.*
>
> *According to the leaked cable, Ambassador Craig Stapleton, a friend and former business partner of Bush, sent a message to Washington in 2007 suggesting the U.S. Government 'calibrate a target retaliation list that causes some pain across the EU since this is a collective responsibility, but that also focuses in part on the worst culprits.*
>
> *'The list should be measured, rather than vicious, and must be sustainable over the long term...Moving to retaliation will make clear that the current path has real costs to EU interests and could help strengthen European pro-biotech voices.'* [244]

And, of course, if some of the forces among world leaders who are pushing for world government have their way, those sorts of protections for our biodiversity—

the kind of protections that come from having at least a few countries that refuse the advances of Big GMOs—will be virtually eliminated. Given Big GMO's MO of placing their officials in the highest ranks of government to look out for their interests, you could expect total corporate-government control of your food to follow immediately after.

Labeling has turned into libeling. Big GMO—indeed, the entire Agribusiness structure—doesn't really like labeling. As you saw with the "biosolids" debacle, they don't want you to know that your food has been grown in dried sewage. They don't want you to know that your food has been irradiated. They don't want you to know that your food has been genetically modified or cloned. Their excuse is that it would cause "unnecessary alarm to consumers." They don't feel we need to know because, if we knew, we might not want to eat their food. They might lose profits.

It's not enough for them to have near-complete control over our food. No, Big Agribusiness and Big GMOs want to intrude on your First Amendment rights as well. In fact, in some states they've been absolutely successful. In many states you can be sued for saying the wrong thing about food. In Colorado, "food defamation" is actually a felony, which means you could literally *go to prison* for saying the wrong thing about food.

Under the common law, it is only possible to defame a person or corporation, not an object such as an apple.

The veggie libel laws broad sweep and lax standards cast an intimidating shadow over citizen activists and independent- minded reporters and publishers, including book publishers.

In states with food-disparagement laws, comment on the health dangers of bacteria in meats and poultry, the threat of bacterial infection from raw oysters, sulfates in salads, nitrates in bacon and other processed foods, cholesterol in eggs, fat in milk and meat, food dyes, polluted fish, Alar-sprayed apples, pesticide treated foods, non-pasteurized juices and contaminated grapes, among many other examples, could subject the speaker to a lawsuit. '

The realistic objective of the frivolous 'veggie libel' statutes and lawsuits is not money,' says consumer advocate Ralph Nader. 'It is to send a chilling message to millions of people that they'd better keep their opinions to themselves.'

...'Food disparagement laws are the descendents of criminal sedition laws, which made it a crime to criticize public officials,' says American Civil Liberties Executive Director Ida Glasser. 'Today, such laws are used almost exclusively by the powerful to silence their critics.' [245]

Slowly but surely, evil is closing in on every facet of our lives, especially our food. The doors to freedom are closing. The opportunity to get clean food that is good for you, that is not tainted in any way, is diminishing, where it isn't already gone. And when you have corporations with the power to control our very food supply, what stops them from banding together and pulling a complete coup over the government, over the very world, because they alone hold the keys to the basic building blocks of survival? Then again, they're already walking government's halls. Government's already gotten behind them. They don't really need the coup, do they? More and more, it seems they hold all the cards. The time to try to wriggle through those last closing gaps is now.

3.6 The United Nations
℘•℃

Governments and companies have gotten great at Orwellian double-speak. That's how you get a sewage lobby calling itself the "Water Environment Federation," for example. Sometimes, when evaluating their actions, you have to do some translation and reading between the lines, and that isn't always easy. Sometimes, of course, they arrogantly state their intentions outright.

It's worth noting that the same people pursuing destructive, evil policies of government and business here in the United States are tied directly into the United Nations; they also have their hand in supporting and shaping those policies. You cannot suddenly expect people who have shown nothing but greed and malevolent intent to become abruptly benevolent when presented with the capability and power to rule, or at least, at this time, greatly shape the events of the entire planet. It just doesn't happen that way. Therefore, you can start to apply the "actual results" and the clear evil intent of many of these actions to statements which sound otherwise bland and benign. Again, these interests, these people, are absolute masters of taking things already in the hands of good, trustworthy people (things which would put you to sleep to read or think about) and turning them into nightmares for all involved.

You must remember that this is the same group of people that threw the farmers out of the meeting for suggesting that corporate control and record corporate profits could be correlated with the 800 million hungry people around the globe.

You must remember that the bulk of the nations making up the United Nations are *not* free and democratic societies, and many of the ones that are, on the surface, free and democratic societies have become as thoroughly corrupted as our own, the American Empire which so deftly influences the actions of the entire globe.

You must remember that the pernicious IMF and World Bank, who we have conclusively proven to foster the starvation and misery of nations around the globe, are unequivocally United Nations institutions.

These people do not suddenly get benevolent when you sit them down at a meeting and call it a United Nations Meeting, A Summit on Such and Thus, or a resolution, or an agenda.

The reason we suppose or imagine for one minute that the United Nations is somehow "different" is the result of a propaganda campaign begun on us in our K-12 years. At some point, we're all taught that the League of Nations, and then the United Nations, was formed in the wake of the world's most terrible wars so that war would never happen again. It's absolutely devoted, we're told, to peace and the Brotherhood of Man. We attend mock United Nations meetings when we're still idealistic teenagers and discuss how to make the world better, believing in our heart of hearts that UN meetings are like this summer club where all the world leaders put their differences aside, hold hands, sing campfire songs, and talk about how to make life better for everybody. It would be nice if it were true.

It's worth noting, of course, that not everything in every UN plan is going to sound or even be horrible. Part of the perniciousness of the entire affair is that you can find things to agree with. That does not mean, however, that those parts of the program will be where the emphasis lies. It also sometimes means that yes, there are some ethical voices within a program and yes, they got some things passed with real compassion in mind. That's what makes understanding any government or corporate agenda so difficult. It's our natural tendency to put a read on these things that over-emphasizes the parts that sound good while mentally glossing over the parts that are rather frightening.

There is a population reduction agenda brought on by elitists, Malthusians, and Eugenicists that the United Nations is intent on carrying out. We can start teasing through the agenda by working our way through the language of Agenda 21. It's not an easy task. There's so much double-speak, fluff, and legalese in these documents that it's sometimes hard to figure out what they're talking about. You almost need a Rosetta stone to crack the codes! But you can also take a look at the actual realities of policies they've already successfully implemented, either directly or through their subsidiaries, policies which share some of the same language. When you do that, a disturbing picture starts to emerge.

So here are some portions of Agenda 21. We'd need a book to go through every single one, so we've picked some of the most relevant. For example, we've already explored how lowering trade barriers destroys economies and lowers standards of living. So what are we to make of this?

*2.7 The commodity sector dominates the economies of many developing countries in terms of production, employment, and export earnings. An important feature of the world commodity economy in the 1980s was the prevalence of very low declining real prices for most commodities in international markets and a resulting substantial contraction in commodity export earnings for many producing countries. The ability of those countries to mobilize, through international trade, the resources needed to finance investments required for sustainable development may be impaired by this development and by **tariff and non-tariff impediments**, including tariff escalation, **limiting their access to export markets. The removal of distortions in international trade is essential.** In particular, the achievement of this objective requires that there be **substantial and progressive reduction in the support and protection of agriculture**—covering*

*internal regimes, market access and export subsidiaries as well as of
industry and other sectors in **order to avoid inflicting large losses
on the most efficient producers**, especially in developing countries.
Thus, in agriculture, industry, and other sectors, there is scope for
initiatives aimed at trade liberalization and at policies to make
production more responsive to environment and development needs.*

*Trade liberalization should therefore be pursued on a global basis across
economic sectors so as to contribute to sustainable development.* [246]

Now, we have already seen how the IMF and World Bank (which are arms of the
United Nations) use an excess of exports to suck the wealth right out of developing
nations. So Agenda 21 2.7 seems to suggest that "sustainable development" means
continuing to suck all of the wealth of nations and to starve people to death,
because that's the end result of their policies in the first place. Of course, if you
believe that there are "too many people," then maybe the side effect of starving a
bunch of poor dark skinned people doesn't matter too much. That's certainly what
the policies seem to suggest.

Here's another one.

*2.13 For developing countries to benefit from the liberalization of
trading systems, they should implement the following policies, as
appropriate: a) Create a domestic environment supporting an optimal
balance between production for the domestic and export markets and
remove biases against exports and discourage inefficient import-
substitution. b) **Promote the policy framework and the infrastructure
required to improve the efficiency of export and import trade** as
well as the functioning of domestic markets.* [247]

When we read this, we think of "optimal balance" as being a balance that's good for
everyone. That doesn't mean that's what policy makers at the U.N. are thinking.
It just as often means "the balance that's optimal for *us*," the policymakers. They
don't know or care if these policies are helpful to the people who have to live under
them. They want to flood the market with their products while sucking all the
wealth out of a country. That's "sustainable." Sustainable for whom? Sustainable

so that people buying $35,000 toilets can continue to buy $35,000 toilets without having to worry about those dirty poor people rising up?

Here's another snippet.

*5.3 The growth of world population and production combined with unsustainable consumption patterns places increasingly severe stress on the life supporting capabilities of our planet. These interactive processes affect the use of land, water, air, energy and other resources. Rapidly growing cities, unless well managed, face major environmental problems. The increase of both the number and the size of cities calls for greater attention to issues of local government and municipal management. The human dimensions are key elements to consider in this intricate set of relationships and should address the linkages of demographic trends and factors, resource use, appropriate technology, dissemination and development. **Population policy should also recognize the role played by human beings in environmental and developmental concerns.** There is a need to increase awareness of this issue among decision makers at all levels and to provide both better information on which to base national and international policies and a framework against which to interpret this information.* [248]

There is just no way to have a "population policy" in a free society. A policy implies a law, and a law implies something that you are allowed to do or not allowed to do. You can potentially decide to just forward a bunch of money to birth control and call it a "policy," but that's not what we've seen either. For example, earlier we mentioned NSM 2000, Kissinger's population memo. In it he said that U.S. aid should be withheld from countries that didn't have the right "population policy."

The results are disgusting and sad. In Mexico, government hospitals forcibly sterilize women after they have three children without telling them. No consent or foreknowledge. In Peru, they offer up 50 pounds of food to poor women if they'll go ahead and get a tubal ligation. Doctors in government hospitals lose their job if they don't do six certified sterilizations per month—which means, if they're a little short, there's little doubt they'll resort to coercion or, perhaps, to doing a "little extra" the next time they're authorized to perform a wholly different procedure within a woman's body [249]. In some countries, poor men and women are targeted simply because the government offers several months wages if they will agree to get sterilized [250]. Malthusianism, as we've explored, has *always been* about targeting the poor—and you can't begin by saying that some people don't have a right to exist without inserting a heavy element of racism as well. We can see this racism in how these "population policies" are applied:

> *The UK is one of the most densely populated countries, with 90% of the population living on 10% of the land and a fertility rate of less than replacement level. Sub-Saharan Africa has high fertility levels accompanied by patterns of labor migration that result in severe labor shortages in areas of origin. Why, then, one might ask, is sub-Saharan Africa a major recipient of population aid and assistance and the UK not?* [251]

The obvious answer is that those in the UK are considered valuable and those in sub-Saharan Africa are not. The obvious answer is racism.

You will also see as you continue to read that human life is considered to be something that has an "adverse impact," that the death panel policy of getting rid of the elderly and a policy of making household income the determinant of right to life runs rampant through UN Policy.

> *5.4 There is a need to develop strategies to **mitigate both the adverse effect on the environment of human activities** and the adverse impact of environmental change on human population...*

> *5.22 An assessment should be made of the implications of the **age structure** of the population on **resource demand** and **dependency burdens**, ranging from educational expenses for the young to **health care and support for the elderly, and on household income generation.** [252]*

We could go on in this vein, but the point has already been adequately made. Now, place all of this against the blanket statement by Catherine Bertini who spent 10 years as the Executive Director of the United Nations World Food Program. She said, "Food is power. We use it to change behavior. Some may call that bribery.

We do not apologize." *Food control and coercion is already a big part of the United Nations strategy, and there is no reason to think the United Nations will suddenly alter their strategy.*

The UN works hard to grab more power, and they have made it clear that they consider an increase in power for them to be a greater part of their "sustainable agenda." Should they be successful, there is no doubt that they will use food and forced sterilization against anyone that they feel to be "undesireable." It could be the birth of one of the most oppressive and technologically advanced totalitarian regimes on the planet, and there will literally be nowhere to run. Those who do not get prepared now will have two choices—to starve, or to get in line. Those who do prepare will have at least a chance of preserving their liberty.

PART 4

ഌ•ഈ

GETTING
PREPARED

Getting prepared does not mean you will come out the winner in every potential scenario. We have to make that clear now because to tell you otherwise would be irresponsible. Getting prepared means you will get the chance to survive where others do not. It's also important to note that you have to put together a multi-tiered strategy. The survival strategy that will take you safely through your next hurricane or earthquake won't take you through long term unemployment or long term price increases. The strategy that will take you through simple unemployment and long-term price increases will not necessarily take you through a period of martial law or totalitarian government where concentration camps are being employed.

You are also going to have to start where you are. You'll never begin if you push your mindset all the way to the worst case scenario and grow overwhelmed. You really have to start with surviving that local hurricane before you can start trying to work your mindset through ever-more complex and dangerous scenarios.

Further, you have to avoid falling into a particular trap, one in which you have the mindset that you're a movie character. There are those who will foolishly charge into the fray because they've watched too many movies and they believe the "good guys" will always win. Those folks will probably be the first to die or to be rounded up in any serious crisis.

Your job is to protect yourself and your family.

This part of *Rising Prices, Empty Shelves* gives you strategies to do so. It will be up to you to employ those strategies in a systematic fashion.

But first, we're going to give a case study to the few holdouts reading this book who still believe that government and industry are basically benign and that they can rely on them if anything goes wrong. We're going to take you back one chapter in our recent history, back to 2005 and Hurricane Katrina.

4.1 Case Study: An Inept Government, a Flooded City

෨•෬

It was not the hurricane itself which destroyed New Orleans but the flooding that happened shortly *after* the hurricane, when the levee system was destroyed.

This turned what would be a routine event for any citizen on the Gulf Coast into one of the greatest tragedies of our modern history. Tragedy turned to travesty through a series of events that demonstrated a lack of concern, care, or even basic intelligence on the part of local and national government.

The government at both local and national levels acted clueless. This is particularly unfortunate in light of the fact that the government had full awareness of everything that could have happened and plenty of time to create some workable plans that would have spared lives. How do we know this? Because on July 23, 2004, *13 months prior to the hurricane*, FEMA conducted an exercise called the "Hurricane Pam" exercise. Its purpose: to assess the results of a direct hit by a Category 3 hurricane on the levees of New Orleans. The exercise assumed a storm with 120 mph winds and it ascertained that the waters of Lake Pontchartrain would surge over the levee system and flood almost 87% of the city. The exercise *also* ascertained that up to half the city's residents would be unable or unwilling to evacuate and would wind up trapped in attics, rooftops, and makeshift shelters for days [253].

So—what happened? FEMA, who devotes just 6% of their budget to their stated purpose of emergency management in the first place, ascertains that there is going to be a problem and then does not coordinate any type of plan? They don't sit down and say, "The mayor needs to do this, the governor this, the president that?" Would that not in fact entail the "management" portion of emergency management?

Instead it seems like they looked over this data, nodded their heads, and agreed, "Oh wow, that would be really bad." Then they walked away and had a lunchtime martini without giving it any second thought.

Of course, one might wonder what else is to be expected. FEMA director Michael Brown was not a disaster expert. He wasn't any kind of expert. He was an unemployed horse show director who happened to be the college friend of Joe Allbaugh, who happened to be a friend of George W. Bush [254]. Perhaps we are expecting a bit too much, as a hurricane indeed bears no actual relationship to a horse show.

It's little wonder then that 5 hours after Katrina struck, internal memos showed that Brown was mostly concerned with maintaining a positive image of disaster operations during the near catastrophe than in actually saving lives. He also seemed fairly confused about simple facts, such as how many people he had at his disposal. In his memo he said he had 3,000 rescue workers. Later, he would tell news outlets that he only had 2,600 workers nationwide and that FEMA generally relies on state workers and the national guard [255].

Governor Kathleen Blanco was little better. When asked whether there was a "toxic soup" of water in the city she said, "No, it is just water. You know. Water." When a reporter pointed out that something could be *beneath* the water her response was, "Pardon?" [256].

Now—every single resident of the State of Louisiana knows a few things about living in Louisiana. There is, for example, one basement in all of South Louisiana, located in a Spanish Town apartment in downtown Baton Rouge. That's because everyone in Louisiana knows that basements flood. The very same phenomena— flooding—is what has caused the citizens of New Orleans to bury their dead *above ground* in tombs rather than below the earth, pretty much since the day the city was founded. Because in the event of even routine flooding, nobody wants a bunch of cadavers playing *piroux* in the streets. In the event of *non-routine flooding*, such as that brought on by Hurricane Katrina, dead bodies in the street, tainting the water, were pretty much going to be a given. How does one get to be the governor of a state where flooding is that much of an acknowledged, yearly reality and *not* be aware that there was going to be more in the streets of New Orleans, Louisiana than "just water?"

On September 1, 2005, President George W. Bush had some amnesia about the "Hurricane Pam" episodes, exhorting that he did not think anybody could anticipate a breach of the levees [257]. Really? Isn't that exactly what wound up being anticipated just 13 months before? In point of fact, the government had a pretty good idea of the potential problems for several decades prior to the landfall of Hurricane Katrina.

The Army Corps of Engineers began shoring up Lake Pontchartrain decades ago. Administrations and Congress controlled by both parties had ample opportunity to insure the task was completed. They had other priorities. When the federal government took over the responsibility to protect New Orleans, it effectively shut out any private or local efforts that may have emerged to upgrade the levee system. [258]

So let us say, for the sake of argument, that all of the figures in this little drama had nothing but the best intentions for the people of New Orleans. We will say, for the sake of argument, that they really cared about their citizens and what was going on. If that's so, then we've got a significant dearth of intelligence or organization in our government, enough that you would never, ever want to rely on them to protect you in the event of a disaster.

*Vital aid was actively **blocked** from New Orleans, in spite of the fact that there were private charities and companies ready and willing to get in there and do the job.* In addition, the city and state had resources that were not used. The parties who were in fact most successful at creating any kind of aid were individuals, private companies, and private organizations.

> *By Wednesday [after the hurricane] the Hyatt Company had sent food and supplies from its Atlanta and Houston hotels to its hotel in New Orleans. The New Orleans Hyatt is less than half a mile from the convention center, an area of the city local and government officials said was inaccessible. Oil companies sent crews in to begin repairs of rigs and refineries on Monday. Television reporters, news crews, even Harry Connick, Jr. managed to navigate through a city the government said was too perilous for relief efforts.*

> *The New Orleans Times-Picayune noted that by Thursday, Wal-Mart had delivered thirteen trucks of supplies while government bureaucrats were still wringing their hands. By the time the federal government finally marched into New Orleans, the Red Cross had sheltered over 130,000 people and delivered more than 2.5 million meals. By the time military boats began rescuing people from rooftops, ordinary citizens had saved thousands with private boats.*

> *…What's worse, in some cases, government prevented the dissemination of aid. Wal-Mart had three water trucks in New Orleans almost immediately after the hurricane hit. FEMA turned them away. The Red Cross reported on its website that federal and local officials had barred the organization from actually entering New Orleans. Same with the Salvation Army.* [259]

One of the major problems of the evacuation was that the people who had no transportation to leave the city ended up trapped there with only the Superdome or the Convention Center to flee to. Many, many more people could have been ferried out, however. Amtrack offered to take hundreds of evacuees out on one of their trains *for free*. Spokesman Cliff Black later told the press that the city declined his invitation and the train left New Orleans without a single passenger on board. Scores of New Orleans school buses sat idle rather than bringing people out and were not even brought to higher ground for later use [260]. Meanwhile, private companies with van or truck fleets tapped and deputized potential evacuees to bring as many people out of there as possible.

As for the bodies, the initial effort to hire a private mortuary to collect them failed when FEMA and the city began bickering over who would pick up the $119,000 price tag. Bodies sat uncollected and open for about two weeks after they were first released into the streets [261].

Is it so difficult for our government to exhibit basic common sense? Does it make sense to turn away Red Cross workers not once, but twice? Why was food and water actively blocked from reaching those stranded by the storm? The answers range from extremely ugly ones to simple incompetence, but it again demonstrates all of the reasons why you do not want to rely on your city, state, or federal government to take care of you in the event of a major life threatening catastrophe.

When the aid did arrive, it was toxic or incompetent, and was at times discontinued without warning. The tales of FEMA mismanagement are legendary. For example, FEMA decided that they would stop issuing the FEMA relief debit cards but didn't think it was necessary to tell the workers at the shelters that this was the case. Tens of thousands of individuals poured into relief centers only to be turned away. Houston Relief Coordinator Robert Fowler would go on to say at the resulting press conference: "We just wanted to make sure everyone understood that every time they change their minds in Washington, D.C., it affects the people here who are trying to deal with tens of thousands of people" [262].

76,000 FEMA trailers were issued, out of the 100,000 purchased, to homeless individuals, but there was a catch. Each of those mobile homes was tainted with formaldehyde.

The Sierra Club began testing the air in some of the trailers in 2006 and found unusually high levels of formaldehyde. The government delayed almost two years, as reports of illness mounted, before declaring in 2008 that those living in the trailers should move out.

Additional testing by the Centers for Disease Control and Prevention and FEMA found that, on average, formaldehyde levels inside the trailers were five times higher than expected for indoor air. "Long term exposure to levels in this range can be linked to an increased risk of cancer, and as levels rise above this range there can also be a risk of respiratory illness," a CDC statement said. Formaldehyde is particularly dangerous for people with asthma or bronchitis. The government did its testing in December and January, when levels of the toxic chemicals would be at their lowest. [263]

In 2010, someone in the Obama Administration would decide it was a great idea to sell the trailers to the public, demonstrating, yet again, a complete lack of concern for the health and welfare of American Citizens. Perhaps the Administration believed that, in two years, we all would have forgotten about reports of children with nosebleeds, or the actual deaths that occurred as a result of these poor conditions.

There is evidence of racism, and there are even rumors that the government made the situation worse—deliberately. This is a difficult claim to prove, of course, but you can't get away from the fact that most of the 100,000 people remaining in the city after the mandatory evacuation had two strikes against them: they were poor, and they were black. Given the United States-sponsored policies in other countries which indeed target populations of poor, black individuals, it doesn't seem difficult to believe that the government was continent to neglect a few more. Perhaps the government saw an outstanding Malthusian opportunity to rid the world of another 100,000 people.

A CBS Radio News report said that New Orleans City Councilman Oliver Thomas said people are "too afraid of black people to go in and save them." And one New Orleans native, Diana Cole French, said that she and other neighbors witnessed a shocking event: "They bombed," she says, "the walls of the levee" [264]. Unsurprisingly, nobody ever followed up on her claims or investigated them. While it's easy to see why people might have had a hard time believing Ms. French, wouldn't proper moral responsibility demand that someone get out there and investigate whether or not the levees were bombed?

The conditions in the Superdome help show chaos in microcosm and help to show what happens to good people when they are caught unprepared. It is a vivid picture of all the reasons why you should take preparations seriously.

On Tuesday...news sources began reporting serious damage to the city's levee system. Water rushed through the crippled barriers. By the end of the day it was clear that approximately eighty percent of the city was flooded. At 10:00 am, Mayor Nagin announced that the levees had been breached. People were trapped in homes, freeways were blocked, and power was cut off.

In the week following the storm, numerous stories emerged from New Orleans. Some flood victims holed up in the Superdome or the Convention Center. Others were trapped in hospitals. Still others wandered the increasingly dangerous streets.

By Sunday, August 28 at noon, the Superdome opened its doors to the public. By 11 pm, between 8000 and 9000 people had entered the shelter. Many of those who sought protection in the dome had physical disabilities that prevented them from evacuating New Orleans.

Sunday night, the Dome was filled with the noise of thousands of conversations. In the early hours of Monday morning, water began leaking from portions of the Dome's roof.

At 5:00 am the Superdome lost electricity. The dome's emergency generators turned on and powered lights, but the generators were not equipped to run the air conditioning system. The building began to warm. **Many refugees had arrived at the Dome without food or water, despite warnings they should bring both.** *As time passed, they became hungry and dehydrated. Some became irritable as a result. Others died.*

On Tuesday, after the levees broke, a fresh wave of evacuees entered the Dome. It was estimated that the dome eventually held as many as 30,000 people.

The smell was overpowering, a mixture of body odor and human waste. Many of the toilets backed up. Dead bodies were on the floor of the Dome, near the living.

*On Thursday, reports began to surface that women were being raped inside the Superdome. Some of the refugees had guns. **People fought for critical resources, like drinks removed from broken vending machines.** Stab wounds and other injuries resulted.*

...Outside, on the streets of New Orleans, however, the situation was just as bad. Stores were looted, not just for essential items like food and bottled water, but also for electronics and luxury items. Reports circulated of gun fights and murders. Some buildings were on fire. [(265)]

As you can see, it does not take a situation outside the realm of modern imagination to locate reasons why it is important for you to be prepared now. While those who were prepared during Katrina still faced miserable, dangerous situations, they had a better opportunity to protect themselves than those who were completely defenseless and taken by surprise. Those were also the people that had the most opportunity to step up to the plate and help the rest of the community when things got truly bad.

4.2 Back to the Community

ဢ • ೞ

These days, it's not unusual for most people in America to have absolutely no idea who their neighbors are, a situation that would have been unheard of 50 years ago. Yet you cannot survive for very long as a single family entity. For a variety of reasons, it's getting more and more vital for us to raise our heads out of our little bubbles and to get to know the people around us.

This isn't just about knowing people in your city. If you attend church or go to a job, chances are you at least casually know quite a few people from within, say, an 100 mile radius of where you live. But do you know the people on your own street corner? That's less likely unless you happen to attend your local Neighborhood Association meetings. Even then it's rare to find neighbors socializing or speaking to each other more than is strictly necessary.

There are a million ways to analyze what has happened, but we can't dwell on them. We must simply reverse the trend. Most of the analysis, however, would revolve around technology. Fortunately, we can also use this technology to assist us in meeting the community need.

Getting to know members of your community will help you to develop a survival network. In *Understanding and Surviving Martial Law*, author Sam Adams placed "developing a survival network" as the 4th survival tip. "You are going," he said, "to need other people, and they will need you. Together you can acquire the skills and resources to survive. Be very careful of who you admit to these networks. The blowhard down the road who can't stop mouthing off may just get you all in trouble" [266]. But the time to develop such a network is not when soldiers are marching down your street and you don't know who to trust. You can only accurately ascertain who to trust before such a scenario strikes.

A survival network, in addition, can help you survive all sorts of other scenarios. They can provide moral support. More people means a greater chance of having clear heads and good organizers to override the panic instinct should you find yourself having a hard time keeping your own cool. It means material support, defense support, and the support that comes with having a wide variety of skills close to hand.

Author Amanda Ripley wrote in *The Unthinkable: Who Survives When Disaster Strikes*:

> *Systematically prepare for...risks. But do it holistically. Don't just stockpile water like an automaton; learn about the history and the science of the risk and try to conduct a dress rehearsal for your brain. It doesn't need to be elaborate. It can just mean taking the stairs out of your office building once a week. **If possible, involve your whole office or neighborhood in this exercise, not just your family. You will all be in this together, so it's wise to get to know one another in good times, not just in bad. You'd be surprised how receptive people are if you give them a chance.*** [267]

Ripley speaks about a sort of informal network in which everyone has at least practiced or thought about disaster together. But it's also possible—even advisable—to join or begin your own network (or to do both at once. There are national groups that you could join today; local groups may not currently exist but may require more work on your part).

Joining an existing network is the easiest part. You can begin by taking a look at a group called A.N.T.S., or "Americans Networking to Survive." You can reach them at http://sites.google.com/site/americansnetworkingtosurvive/. This is a national network of volunteer "preppers" who have, in the wake of Katrina-level disasters, banded together through the power of the internet to create a citizens action network. A.N.T.S. forms citizen-directed supply networks so that members can get supplies to one another when they need to. "When disaster strikes," their website notes, "relief agencies will bring supplies, but they will be supplying everyone. A.N.T.S. members will be looking for you." This is also a good way to avoid feeling powerless in the wake of all the rather grim information we've been sharing with you throughout this book. You'll know that there are literally thousands of other people out there with some of the same concerns you have that are standing up, taking action, and taking responsibility, rather than waiting around for FEMA to get around to deciding they should probably do something.

The network's website also points out an excellent reason to get linked up to a community of likeminded people at all, noting:

> You can have all the stored preps in the world, but if a disaster wipes out your home and supplies, what are you going to do? If you are an A.N.T.S. member, you are going to make a request for supply pods and have them sent to your location. [268]

A.N.T.S. has developed some fairly extensive "standard operating procedures" for disasters and is a good starting position for any disaster preparedness network. A.N.T.S. meets the basic framework for any good survival network, which is to create a method and a team to pool resources and skills so that the group can be stronger together than it is individually.

However, A.N.T.S. is widespread—it doesn't get you involved with your community per se, and it doesn't help you connect to people right there at home who could band together with you in the event of a bad situation. So how do you go about starting your very own survival network?

Generally, you will start with your family and friends, your neighbors, service providers in your area, and church or civic groups. These four types of individuals form the cornerstones of any complete network. You should also take the time to identify any disabled, elderly, or special-needs individuals in your immediate vicinity who might need your help if disaster strikes [269].

Arthur T. Bradley, author of *Handbook to Practical Disaster Preparedness for the Family*, offers these tips for getting your own personal survival network started:

One way to broach the subject is to begin by discussing the tragedies currently affecting others, and to move on to express your concerns about how the threats might affect your respective families. From there, you can suggest ways to work together to prepare for the most worrisome events.

...Inviting neighbors to become part of a disaster preparedness network is very much like inviting them to be part of a neighborhood watch program. In fact, the two can often be combined. Start with a discussion of the need and the benefits, much like a friendly business proposition.

...Your doctor, accountant, hair dresser, pastor, veterinarian and day care provider are all examples of service providers. A person possessing such skills can be extremely valuable during a time when normal services are unavailable.

...A good way to begin is to discuss relevant concerns and preparations with them—perhaps ask your doctor about providing additional medications, or your pastor about providing shelter in the case of a family that becomes suddenly homeless. [270]

Once you've begun the initial discussions, you can begin inviting everyone to an informal group meeting. One purpose of the meeting should be to simply establish friendships which will be the foundation for trust later. The other should be to get every interested person to introduce themselves and tell a thing or two about their profession, hobbies, and families. That will give you, the group leader, a pretty good idea of who can do what in the event of a crisis, but it's not time to start assigning work yet. Instead, get everyone to read a good disaster preparedness book and create another meeting where everyone can talk about it, and perhaps start taking on some specific contributions after working out some very simple emergency response plans [271].

What works during a hurricane or severe winter storms with power outages could give you all the foundation you need to survive an economic crash, a martial law scenario, or any other type of negative situation you can think of. Working on this now means you find out quickly who the loudmouths and the blowhards are, who you can count on and who you cannot. In the most extreme cases of all, the group may even contain enough competent people with the skills to carry out rescues. Should you so choose and your group so agrees, these groups could even become the foundation for a well-thought-out and capable resistance movement in the event of a truly nightmarish scenario.

If possible, with famine kept particularly in mind, you should work on some of the other community activities that are outlined in this chapter together. After all, if you have a survival network in place already, then it's not such a big step to starting a community garden.

You can help the food supply by joining or sponsoring community gardens, and eating local can also help reduce pressure on food prices. If land use and the ability to find good soil to grow crops on is a concern in terms of the global food supply, then ingenious urban agriculture efforts could provide quite a bit of the answer. Cities are not looking likely to get any smaller or more compact. Efforts to fight urban sprawl have been sluggish, at best. Working with what you've got to create something wonderful, though, is a proud American tradition. Community gardens, urban gardens, and vertical farms provide a new framework for the production and distribution of food.

The success of these ventures will never come from the halls of government or the halls of Agribusiness. They come from people like us, at all levels of society. Anyone can gather together their church, survival network, or neighbors to create an organic community garden that provides tasty, safe, fresh food to everyone involved. Those with more resources might consider investing in vertical farm projects or other urban farm initiatives. Urban farming helps to solve problems that might be caused, for example, by a trucker's strike. By rendering our overall food system that much less fragile, we help ensure that more people will survive any catastrophe. We also take our food production out of the hands of the people who want to play God with the genes of seeds, those who want to drench our food in dangerous chemicals, and those who want to farm in sludge. While not every urban garden will be so well managed or community minded—it's certainly conceivable that agribusiness could get themselves involved as soon as they start smelling money, for example—even an Agribiz run farm in the heart of New York City, say, would render us all a little less vulnerable.

These projects may take some serious perseverance. Though community gardens are catching on, for example, there have been times when groups have had to fight for the right to start them and run them.

Can urban agriculture really work and make a difference? In some places, it already has.

Urban agriculture, including food production, is typically practiced over smaller and more dispersed areas than rural agriculture, uses land and water more sparingly and efficiently, integrates systems more effectively and produces much higher yields and more specialty crops and livestock.

As with other land uses, urban agriculture adapts to city development, with the less space-dependent forms surviving in central areas and the more demanding forms migrating to less-coveted locations.

*Urban agriculture benefits the long-term nutritional health of children in poor farming households and **has made food aid redundant in places where it is practiced extensively**.* [272]

A community garden is an especially good alternative for anyone who:
- Does not have a yard or other space for gardening or personal food production.
- Needs or wants a framework to meet or connect with other members of the community outside of the context of a disaster preparedness group.
- As a survival and solidarity building project for the disaster preparedness group.
- Those who want to help community members gain access to fresh, safe, organic produce.

Community gardens have many other benefits as well. They tend to help foster more vibrant communities, which can make for a safer, less isolated area. They can provide positive outlets for youth groups in the neighborhood, opportunities for education, and promote good health [273].

The American Community Garden Association offers a series of tips for starting a community garden. A fuller explanation of these tips is available on their website at www.communitygarden.org.

1. Form a planning committee and organize a meeting of interested people. Choose a well-organized garden coordinator, but also form committees to accomplish tasks; i.e. Funding & Resource Development, Construction, and Communication.

2. Approach a sponsor for contributions of land, tools, seeds, soil improvements, and/or money.

3. Make a list of what needs to be done. Obtain a garden site. Decide on a mailing address and central telephone number.

4. If your garden has a budget, keep administration of the budget in the hands of several people.

5. After obtaining the site, you must prepare and develop it by cleaning the site and developing your design. Then you should organize volunteer work crews and plan your work days. Include plans for a storage area for tools and other equipment, as well as a compost area. You should also have a rain-proof message board for announcing garden events and messages.

6. You also have to organize your garden rules. For example, what are the conditions for membership? How will plots be assigned and how large shall they be? Does the group charge dues and if so, how is the money used? How will minimum maintenance be managed [274]?

If you have more resources, you might get even more ambitious. Though the tendency among preppers is to believe that we have to sort of grit our teeth and strap in for a dark, wild ride, we also know that God can bring about amazing miracles. There is a concept called vertical farming that might be well worth investing in and pursuing over the course of the next century, a concept which could help to divert many of the potential famine scenarios that we have outlined. They could also prevent still more future famines. Our study of history has shown us that famines, droughts, and totalitarian regimes do eventually end. Making things better is a matter of ingenuity and faith.

With that faith, we can perhaps even eventually defeat the Malthusian schemes by proving that it doesn't have to be that way, by proving that population-to-production problems are a matter of intelligently increasing production, and that pollution problems are a matter of intelligently reducing pollution. We can continue to use our own God-given gifts to try to make things better clear up until the day He shows up for us. We might have to be ready for a fight, as obviously the socialist-Malthusian movement of the United Nations and other interests really have no need or desire to get involved with anything which might ultimately save lives. But assuming we are interested, we can begin exploring other options. Not every part of preparation has to be a pessimist's exercise. We're also not likely to suddenly create a surge of farmers returning to rural areas, walking away from the comfort and convenience the city has to offer.

And what, you might ask, exactly is a vertical farm?

We now have in our hands the tools and the desire to convert squalid urban blight into places where we'd want to raise our children.

Sustainable urban life is technologically achievable, and, more importantly, highly desirable. For example, food waste can easily be converted back into energy employing, clean, state-of-the art incineration technologies, and wastewater can be converted back into drinking water. For the first time in history, an entire city can choose to become the functional urban equivalent of an entire ecosystem.

Our solution lies in vertical farms. These farms would raise food without soil in specially constructed buildings...We should not shy away from the challenges of farming vertically simply because it requires cutting-edge engineering, architecture, and agronomy. All of this is within our grasp.

The idea of growing crops in tall buildings might sound strange. But farming indoors is not a new concept. Commercially viable crops such as strawberries, tomatoes, peppers, cucumbers, herbs, and a wide variety of spices have made their way into commercial greenhouses to the world's supermarkets in ever-increasing amounts over the last fifteen years. Most of these greenhouse operations are small in comparison to the large farms of the American Midwest, but unlike their outdoor counterparts, greenhouse facilities can produce crops year-round.

Vertical farms are immune to weather and other natural elements that can abort food production. Crops can be grown under carefully selected and well-monitored conditions that ensure optimal growth rates for each species of plant all year round...The efficiency of each floor of a vertical farm one acre in footprint, could be equivalent to as many as ten-to-twenty soil-based acres, depending upon the crop.

Some vertical farms could act as stand-alone water regenerating facilities. A cold-brine pipe system could be engineered to aid in the condensation and harvesting of moisture released by the plants. Plants in the vertical farm could convert safe-to-use grey water into drinking water by transpiration. The fact that the entire farm would be a closed-loop system would allow us to recover this unrealized, highly valued resource.

Today's cities fail to meet even the minimum standards of self-reliance. No city lives within its own means...but it doesn't have to be this way. [275]

These farms are already being built in Las Vegas and Dubai. One is already functioning in Singapore, where a company called DJ Engineering has set up a company called Sky Farms that sells vertical farm towers for $10,000 each, proving this solution is neither out of our reach nor even out of the reach of say, a dedicated group of investors who buy the towers, the seeds, and the land to put a tower on. You can get an acre of heirloom, non-GMO, savable seeds from Solutions from Science for about $126, which would cover a one acre floor.

Community currency can help economically strapped communities become stronger while circumventing the corrupt Federal Reserve system that has contributed greatly to the problems around us. It would take another whole book to get into all of the reasons why the Federal Reserve is doing its part to bankrupt America. For now we'll just give you the short version: the Federal Reserve is unelected and owned by private banks and foreign interests. The former chairman, Alan Greenspan, told us all on national television that the Federal Reserve is above the law and there's not anything we can do about it.

Ideally, we'd all be able to get back on currency that is actually backed by something of real value rather than printed on thin air. Money that was on the gold standard, for example, could be taken to any bank and exchanged for gold. There was security in that, as well as a handle on inflation.

If you can't do that, what's the next best thing? Supporting your local community and creating a new economy with local currency is one way to get a little of our own back.

A small but growing number of cash-strapped communities are printing their own money.

Borrowing from a Depression-era idea, they are aiming to help consumers make ends meet and support struggling local business.

The systems generally work like this: businesses and individuals form a network to print currency. Shoppers buy it at a discount—say, 95 cents for one dollar value—and spend the full value at stores that accept the currency.

Workers with dwindling wages are paying for groceries, yoga classes and fuel with Detroit Cheers, Ithaca Hours in New York, Plenty in North Carolina and Berkshares in Massachusetts. [276]

If you are in a community that issues this kind of scrip, you can strengthen community bonds by buying it and using it. If you are a business owner in the community, you might consider becoming one of the local businesses that accepts scrip. Even if it doesn't ultimately defeat the Federal Reserve, it accomplishes stronger bonds, as well as creating a framework for a replacement currency should the American Dollar finally fail, a framework that could keep your local community functioning even when other communities are falling apart.

During the Great Depression, one community came together to defeat the tragedy that brought the rest of the world to its knees. Colquitt County in south

Georgia started out as a one-trick farming pony, farming cotton and facing economic ruin and soil depletion when The Great Depression began. So why was a 1930s newspaper able to report the county as being virtually untouched by the Depression?

It was a matter of total community cooperation, one that would be possible with the cooperation of small, local banks and credit unions (we can hardly expect those too-big-to-fail banks to get involved with anything so sensible or compassionate). Here's how it worked.

First, the bankers agreed to renew the farmer's notes, but the farmers had to agree to (and did agree to) a condition under which they would adopt a program which was agreed upon between bankers, farmers, businessmen, and the county agricultural agent alike, all of which was hashed out at a large community meeting. The county agricultural agent was to plan a diversified group of crops that was practical for all concerned. The farmer agreed to abide by his recommendations; the banker agreed to furnish financial backing to the project; and business and professional men were to develop and provide markets for the county's farm production [277].

Thus it was that each farm put 33% of their land to corn, velvet beans, and runner peanuts. 10% went to oats and peavine hay. 6% of the land went to sweet potatoes, sugar cane, sorghum cane, millet, and home gardens. Another 13% went to tobacco. 26% of each farmer's land went to Spanish peanuts, watermelons, or other approved, specialized crops. 16% stayed in cotton. The rest was devoted to pastureland and livestock: cows, hogs, and chickens, particularly laying hens.

The newspaper report said: "Colquitt farmers have meat in the smokehouse, money in the bank, corn in the cribs, peanuts for the hogs to eat, as well as peanuts to sell, hay and oats and velvet beans in plenty; chickens and eggs to ship, butter and cream to sell, beef cattle for the local packing house; sweet potatoes, cane, sorghum and millet crops are making ready for the markets. Bankers say that no business houses cut salaries and no men have been laid off. The banks are doing an excellent business, a substantial increase over last year. The railroads have actually employed more men. The mills are running full time and there is no unemployment problem in Moutrie" [278].

We need more Colquitt Counties. We could use 3070 of them! If you a farmer, banker, or a businessman, and you're taking the time to get to know others in your community, you might just have what it takes to create a Colquitt story in your own part of the country. While you're at it, you might consider working "shunning GMOs and running Big GMO hatchet men out of town, snubbing Big Agribusinesses and avoiding CAFOs at all costs" on the 21st century version of the plan. This might appeal to the more investment-minded among us who are a bit leery of things like vertical farms. However, the Colquitt Plan has been proven to work, and work well; there is no conceivable reason why such a thing could not work in 2011 just as well as it worked in 1924. Good, intelligent men and women have turned things around in the past just by letting their imaginations get fired up about the possibilities, praying to the Good Lord for aid, and then setting hands, mouths, and hearts to action.

If you're not a businessman, farmer, or banker but you still want to support local efforts, you should consider going on the *100 mile diet* in which you patronize local farmers and farmer's markets for your food rather than going to restaurants or getting food from the supermarket. The food will be safer and you'll keep boosting the local economy. It's also usually much cheaper and tastes better, too.

4.3 Taking Control of Your Food Supply

ℰℭ • ℭℛ

It's great to plan with the community and it's great to get involved in community initiatives. Having a disaster network is also a wonderful idea. But any plan that prepares you for famine or trouble of any kind will necessarily involve a multi-pronged strategy to ensure that you and your family have the food and water that you need to make it through a crisis.

It's easy to get overwhelmed by this task, but you have to think of it in tiers.

Tier 1 involves preparation for that really short-term emergency.

Tier 2 involves preparation for the longer-term emergency, a long bought of unemployment or a long spike in prices.

Tier 3 involves preparation for a wide-scale, long-term famine.

Tier 4 involves preparation for a scenario of martial law and totalitarian government that might seek to starve its people into compliance, a scenario of total currency collapse that sends the nation into a situation of anarchy, or a scenario of invasion by foreign powers out to collect on their debts. Many Tier 4 strategies can't simply be covered by taking control of your food supply, but in fact cover things you'll learn about in section 4.5 and 4.6.

We can't know the future. We can't know which of the 4 Disaster Tiers will end up being a big part of your life. We can predict based on history, current news headlines, and current plots and schemes that are floating out of the centers of world leadership. You may wind up preparing for Tier 4 scenarios and never see them. Hey, that's a good thing. Nobody really wants to live through a Tier 4 event, but if you're that prepared then you'll certainly be prepared for anything less.

There's also different considerations for preparedness strategy that have to take into account your living situation, your community network, your physical and mental capabilities, and your income level. It's not realistic to tell you to "bug out" to your fully paid for off-grid rural retreat if you currently make $9 an hour (But in the event of a short-term evacuation, you still need that bug-out kit and emergency-stocked vehicle). It's more realistic to tell you how you might try surviving "in place" under such circumstances. That said there's also nothing wrong with mentioning the off-grid rural retreat strategy for those who find such a possibility somewhat within their reach. Everybody is different and God will place us where He wants us in such scenarios. Your survival network might open up more opportunities for you than you could manage on your own as well. That's why it's important for you to consider each of the possibilities so that you can craft your best survival strategies when the time comes, and so that you can prepare right now.

It starts with food storage. We need to de-mystify food storage a little bit. It's possible to get military grade MREs, a year's supply of freeze-dried space food, five gallon buckets full of wheat ready to be ground, and canned food at the grocery store. There are morons who will tell you that a bottle of ketchup, some oatmeal and a bit of dried milk will get you through anything. What are you supposed to do?

The secret to creating an emergency survival stockpile is to begin with a few items and gradually add items which allow you to increase from week to week and month-to-month. The key is slowly and steadily stock up. The idea isn't to go into debt purchasing items in huge bulk amounts, thinking this will sustain you in the time of calamity. You need to set up a plan and then stick to it.

Many families are doing good just to keep groceries on the table without purchasing anything extra. But you can begin small, by purchasing two of certain items such as condiments, canned items, packages of pasta, cans of tuna and so on. Use one and put the other one in your new stockpile. If you did this every week for a year, you would soon have that extra store that could pull you through a short term emergency. [279]

The easiest way to do this is to think "meals." There are some that would encourage you to think "pounds," and you can do it that way too. That is, the average person in the United States consumes 1950 pounds of food per year. That means we're all consuming roughly 5 pounds of food per day. That means if you want to use pounds, then a one week emergency food supply for a family of four would be 140 pounds of food. But it's just as easy to note the same meals that you'd eat over a one week period—21 meals in all—and stockpile 21 meals for that one Tier 1 emergency week, along with 2 quarts of water per person per day. That's 5 water bottles per person per day if you're talking a regular sized bottle of water and not one of the cute sport-sized bottles meant to slip into a child's lunch. That means 140 water bottles will take your family through a one week emergency. Before you get too overwhelmed, that's 5 cases (roughly $19.95 worth) of bottled water from your local supermarket. You can adjust for your actual family size.

For Tier 1 and Tier 2 emergencies, you don't want to go crazy stocking a lot of specialty foods. You want to stock the following sorts of food:
- Food that you normally eat and that your family is used to eating.
- Food that you don't have to cook in case one of a few things are true: the power is out and you have no other means to cook OR you're worried about looters, thugs, thieves or military people who might be drawn to your location by the smell of cooking food and try to take your food from you. Granola bars and crackers do not draw attention. The smell of a sizzling steak does. The smell of a cooking pot of macaroni and cheese might, if the smell is strong enough.

These guidelines also work for Tier 3 emergencies, and even Tier 4, though by the latter two Tiers you might indeed want to consider getting more elaborate in your planning. For this, you might consider Howard Ruff's plan, which, simplified and for a family of 4, looks a lot like this:

- Dehydrated apple slices, 20 lbs
- Dehydrated apricot slices, 20 lbs
- Dehydrated fruit blend, 40 lbs
- Prunes, 40 lbs
- Dry green peas, 40 lbs
- Assorted beans, dried, 400 lbs
- Dried carrots, 20 lbs
- Tomato crystals, 40 lbs
- Dried potatoes, 80 lbs
- Peanut butter, 40 lbs
- Dried cheese, 80 lbs
- TVP (textured vegetable protein), 24 lbs
- Honey, 5 lbs (local is better, because it provides a natural defense against allergies)
- Wheat, 200 lbs, with a hand wheat grinder to make flour
- Dried milk, 200 lbs
- Protein concentrate, 80 lbs
- Vitamin Supplements, 80 lbs (280)

There are a few other considerations to the food you might want to buy. For example, the American Public Health Association's Get Ready campaign mentions that chips, peanuts, and crackers do store well and do make good comfort foods, but their high sodium content also means a greater need for water consumption. You might wish to go ahead and buy low-sodium versions of those foods for your stockpile. It's also a good idea to keep bulk olive oil around, as a couple of teaspoons of olive oil a day can be lifesaving.

As a primary strategy, freezer food doesn't generally make great stockpile food—but as a secondary strategy, it's not a bad idea to start freezing all your leftovers rather than sticking them in the fridge and hoping they get eaten. Label each food and the date when it goes into your freezer. As not all emergencies or temporary food crises will involve a loss of power, this can serve you very well. Your frozen food stockpile, for example, can feed you quite nicely during a period of unemployment. However, in any scenario where your power is going to go out soon, consume those frozen foods first, until it no longer becomes viable to do so, before moving on to your primary, dried-and-canned food stockpile.

Don't forget to rotate! Food *and* water can go bad. You can rotate your food and water stores one of two ways. One way is the "front of cupboard, back of cupboard" method. That is, anything new goes to the back of the cupboard and anything old gets pushed up front so that it's immediately used. Everything used is used with the understanding that it will be—must be—replaced.

Another method is the sticker method. In general you're pretty safe if you rotate your food supplies every six months. Putting a big, brightly colored sticker on each of your supplies with a Replacement Date on it at the 5 month mark will alert you to use those foods in your cooking and to replace them with new foods and bottled waters.

Be sure you keep your food stockpile hidden if at all possible. Neighbors, cleaning help, maintenance men, babysitters, your kid's friends—a whole host of people come in and out of your house all the time and you probably don't think too much of it. But if you flaunt your disaster-preparedness stockpile, these same people might knock on your door (politely or with the intent to harm and steal) hoping that you'll feed them later down the line. Don't tell people about your stockpile or put information about it where people can look at it. Keep it out of sight, out of mind. In most scenarios, especially ones where you can reasonably stay where you are, the best strategy is to lay low. You can't do that if everyone knows your business.

Growing your own food is good long-term preparation. Almost anyone can do at least some growing, though for some reason most survival and disaster-preparedness guides seem to assume that everyone has a nice back yard or even acres of rural land to plant a small orchard on. That said, almost anyone can grow some food. If you're in an apartment, for example, you can do urban gardening on your balcony with the use of containers and boxes. You can also get indoor fruit trees and hydroponic gardens like the AeroGarden to produce some small stores. There are indoor light boxes and greenhouses available. Some of them are even designed to fit in corners, like bookshelves, and can form an attractive addition to your home as well as a source for extra food in the event of famine or food shortage. You can order indoor citrus trees that you would take care of just like regular house plants.

Those with more space can of course make use of it, but even if you have a yard or acres of land, you might want to consider some indoor options. Simply put, it's easier to lay low if you're not outside. It's easier to defend a food source that is inside, since you have walls, exits that you can bar off, and alarms that you can set. Outside, a thief can just walk up and pluck up your plants; though this isn't necessarily *going* to happen it's wise to be prepared for any eventuality.

No matter what you do, gardening is essential. Simply put, it gives you a renewable source of food. Any food stockpiling carries a flaw with it—it's going to run out at some point. A garden or some indoor fruit trees can help keep you from going through that stockpile quite so quickly and can make sure you have food to eat even if a crisis ends up lasting for years and years.

And, as discussed, this is a good way to enhance your own food safety and to stretch your own food dollar while putting just a little bit less pressure on the global food system. You know exactly how your plants have been grown. You will know what fertilizer you chose to use—chemical fertilizer or good old fashioned organic compost. You will know if you chose to use pesticides or if you chose to let birds and diversity do their work. You will know that your food is safe—or at least be comfortable with the amount of risks taken with it. In addition, you will be able to taste what the food is really supposed to taste like, since it won't have lost all its nutrients and taste value on a 1,500 mile trip.

The importance of Heirloom Seeds cannot be underestimated. If you order seeds from most commercial seed catalogues, chances are you're getting those Big GMO, AgriBiz terminator seeds. Even if you're not getting terminator seeds, you could be getting hybrid seeds which carry their own dangers: second generation hybrids tend to either revert back to their original type or they sort of collapse into unappetizing, tasteless, or even inedible varieties of the fruit or vegetable they used to be.

This won't help you in the event of a long term crisis where there are no seeds available for order and in which society has broken down to the point where you can't get any mail. Heirloom seeds are seeds that have not been tampered with in any way. That means after you eat your heirloom tomato you can carefully scrape the seeds out, dry them, and store them for planting next year. Heirloom plants produce again and again; the plants you buy from your local nursery do not.

There's also the matter of variety and genetic diversity. There are hundreds of varieties of heirloom plants that you may have never seen or heard about before: Black Russian tomatoes, Boothby's Blonde Cucumbers, Bull's Blood Beets. You will literally re-discover vegetables if you allow yourself to taste the wonderful varieties that heirlooms have to offer.

Heirloom seeds carry another advantage, as well. Because there are more varieties of each sort of fruit or vegetable than you may be used to, heirlooms allow you to tailor your growing plan to your particular climate area.

Most heirloom companies only sell the seeds, which can be daunting for people who are not used to starting their own seeds indoors or are used to planting from plants. If this describes you, take heart—there are heirloom companies out there which will sell and ship to you your very own starter plants.

Be leery about cross-pollination. If you plant more than two varieties of any heirloom plant, you run the risk that they'll turn into hybrid seeds, which you absolutely do not want. Try to be careful about planting near your neighbor's plots as well. You don't want any of that GMO seed!

Stealth gardening may become more important as time goes on. Stealth gardening could mean that you're planting things on your own land that you don't want anyone to see, steal, or confiscate (or that you don't want the government coming in to "inspect"). It's also possible to stealth garden on land you don't strictly own. If there is any seldom-visited public land around you, or land where you could hide certain plants because they look similar to the other plants around them (so long as you know the difference), you might be able to pull off growing a few things without being found out. Indoor gardening has already been discussed--if nobody is coming into your home, that's the easiest form of stealth gardening.

You can also make use of camouflage netting, available from army surplus or paintball game stores, by placing this over your garden. Here you must be careful that you are only covering plants that are tolerant to a partial-shade environment.

Since a lot of people aren't even very good at identifying common food producing plants unless recognizable food is sprouting right off of them, you can even stealth garden by planting the plants all around your yard, shrub-like, instead of planting them in neatly arranged and recognizable garden rows that scream 'garden here!'

Just as your food stockpile will not last forever, neither will your water stockpile. Thus, it is very important to give some thought to the gathering and proper treatment of drinking water. If you are facing your disaster in the middle of winter when there's 4 inches of snow on the ground then obtaining water is no problem, but for the rest of the time and in other climates you've got to give this some thought.

First, the goal is always to stay put as your first option over any other survival strategy. Any time you put yourself out on the road you risk running into troublemakers. You're not on your home ground anymore. You can expose yourself to ambushes, soldiers, environmental hazards, and any number of other problems, especially if you have to go wherever you've got to go on foot. Therefore, it's not a bad idea to add a rain bucket or barrel to your survival stock. You can make one simply by stretching a fine mesh over the top of a bucket or barrel to catch leaves and other debris and setting it outside, but there are also many commercially available ones in many different sizes. As long as you're not in the middle of a drought, you should be able to keep a decent supply of water.

Rain barrel companies generally advertise their barrels as being great water supplies for plants, and that's fine. However, you can drink it if you properly purify it.

You will need some kind of purifier or filter. You may have clean, safe water initially, but in the meantime you may need an alternative. You may find yourself collecting surface water. Most people are unaware that a tincture of iodine 2%, common iodine solution found in most first aid kits, and chlorine bleach can all be used to disinfect surface water. [281]

You will need to add the solution and then boil the water, which means, in the event of a power loss, having some sort of camping cooker. Solutions from Science sells a crisis cooker that runs on propane, charcoal, or wood that will fit this bill nicely.

As for water purifiers, you need ones that don't require power to use. The Berkey Lite water filters use reverse osmosis through filters that last for 50 years.

Not only do they carry a larger water filter that you can place on your counter (and you should look into the power-free versions), but they also have smaller "sport bottles" that can be filled and used immediately, on the go.

If you can't collect rainwater and you don't have snow on the ground, you may be facing a situation where you have to travel to your water. You'll need to note your nearest sources of water. This could be from a drainage ditch, a nearby creek, or a lake within walking distance. You'll need to get a map and plot routes for foot and vehicle. Note this needs to be realistic to what you can reasonably walk today. Most of us do not routinely walk 20 miles a day, and even people in reasonably good shape might well find themselves flagging after seven or eight miles without carrying anything at all. You have to account for carrying the water, because you're going to want to gather enough to make that trip worthwhile. Also, the longer it takes you to travel to and from the water site, the more exposed and vulnerable you are to other threats. This is always a last resort situation. If you find yourself having to take to the wilderness to survive, you'll want to set your camp as close to a water source as possible.

Never drink untreated water. There are lots of little bacteria in the water that can make you very sick.

If your nearest water source is a saltwater source, you can actually purchase portable or home de-salinators. For example, 247water.org, which is the site for a company called Manta Ventures, sells a portable de-salinator that will produce 25 liters of water and has a 30 to 90 day filter life.

As with your food supply, your water supply should be a multi-tiered strategy. Ideally, you'd be better served than most people in the water department if you had access to a well on property that you owned, but that doesn't mean you shouldn't at least stock up on some portable filtration systems. Wells can go dry and people can be displaced from their properties in all manner of emergencies. You'll have to spend your time thinking about where you live and what sort of water resources are available to you, even in worst case scenarios. Remember, too, that there can be "water, water everywhere but not a drop to drink." Sure, you can purify rainwater with bleach, but you probably wouldn't have wanted to take your chances with the post-Katrina New Orleans toxic soup, complete with raw sewage and floating cadavers.

There are other supplies and strategies you'll want to consider for any emergency of any tier. Emergency situations can mean evacuations or a situation where you can't, for whatever reason, stay in your home. Therefore, there are a few other things you should think about adding to your supply in the near-future.

- A document box that has all of your family's vital documents: birth certificates, insurance documents, medical records, marriage license or divorce decree, social security cards, deeds, and vehicle titles. This should be waterproof and airtight.
- Blankets
- First aid kits
- Waterproof tarp, rope, and tent pegs, or an extremely portable lightweight tent
- Windproof, waterproof matches
- 100 hour survival candles
- Signal flares and/or glow sticks
- Emergency cash
- Toilet paper
- Signal whistle
- Weather appropriate items for your climate

A good "quickie" survival guide that will give you fuller explanations and an easy checklists to use is the Solutions from Science booklet *Gone Before You Get There: 77 Items that Instantly Vanish from Store Shelves in a Panic and Why Preparing for a Crisis Cannot Wait*. There are lists you can go through with a highlighter as you acquire each item so that you will know exactly what you have on hand—and what you don't.

The "supply pod" method provides another framework for taking control of your life during any emergency which might impact your ability to obtain food (or any other supplies). This is a method that comes from the A.N.T.S. network. Each of these "pods" is made from a 5 gallon bucket with a lid, available from any hardware store (5 gallon buckets actually have a lot of outstanding survival uses and are some of the most useful things you could ever pick up). Each 5 gallon bucket is packed with a specific sort of survival material. The buckets also help you know exactly how much you could carry in your car.

- Water pod: Contains water bottles or pouches
- Food pod: Contains food

- Shelter pod: Contains a tent or tools for making temporary shelter. May have to cut a hole in the lid for tent poles.
- Bedding pod: Sleeping bag, sheets, covers
- Hygiene pod: Washcloths, towels, hygiene products
- Clothing pod: Necessary clothing items
- Cooking pod: Cooking and fire kits
- Medical pod: Medical supplies
- Baby pod: Formula, baby food, diapers, blankets
- Sanitation pod: Toilet, trash, and cleaning supplies [282]

If you could put together one of each type of "pod" and store it in your closet, then you're going to be ahead of most families in America in terms of having each kind of supply on hand. Even if you don't have a baby, you should think about putting together a baby pod as this will give you some items for barter, another consideration you should be pondering for any sort of long-term survival scenario. Of course, if you opt to join the A.N.T.S. network, you may well have some of these on hand for donations to the supply chain as well, since this is part of the network's standard operating procedures.

4.4 Preserving and Storing Your Own Food

℘ • ℭ

If you're going to have a survival garden, raise or hunt your own meat, or generally have control over your own food supply, then you will need to preserve and store that food as your next step. Otherwise you're going to end up with plenty of food in the summer and fall and not much of anything in the winter, which is the most dangerous time as cheap, easily available food diminishes.

My eighty-four-year-old neighbor is an incredibly cheerful person by all other standards, but she will remark of a relative or friend, 'Well, she's still with us after the winter.'

It's not just about icy sidewalks and inconvenience: she lost two sisters and a lifelong friend during recent winters. She carries in living memory a time when bitter cold and limited diets compromised everyone's immune systems.

I watched the rank-and-file jars in our pantry decline from army to platoon, and finally to lonely sentries staggered along the shelves. We weren't rationing yet, but I couldn't help counting the weeks until our first spring harvests and the happy reopening day of the farmer's market. I had a vision of our neighbors saying of us, 'Well, they're still with us after the winter.' [283]

So learning how to can and dehydrate food are vital sets of survival skills. Fortunately, this is neither as hard as it sounds, nor as dangerous. At home, you can preserve anything you might find canned on your supermarket shelves: vegetables, meats, fruits, chicken stock (but nothing with wheat in it). You'll just need some gear, a sense of adventure, and perhaps a little patience to get through the blips. It also doesn't hurt to get a copy of the Solutions from Science *Food Storage Secrets* guide, which will give you a fuller explanation of the process than anything we can provide here in *Rising Prices, Empty Shelves*.

Still, we can give you a head start. First, you'll need the following equipment:
- Mason jars, various sizes, with lids
- Pressure canner with pressure gauge
- Boil bath canner (also known as a really big stock pot)
- Funnel
- Rubber spatula (never metal)
- Lid magnet (check to make sure it's actually strong enough to get the lids, if not, replace with a stronger, more convenient magnet)
- A jar grip
- A trivet, which sits on the bottom of your pot and keeps the jars from sitting directly on top of it.

You can buy all of this stuff separately or you can get a good home canning kit which will contain all or most of what you'll need.

You can preserve fruit in your boil bath canner, including tomatoes. However, you have to be careful about tomatoes. The hybrid variety of tomatoes you usually find in your supermarket don't always have enough acidity to be safe under this method. Thus you'll need to add two tablespoons of lemon juice to give you the acidity you need. Everything else has to be canned in the pressure cooker.

The process is fairly simple. For example, with tomatoes you'd follow these steps:

1. Run jars through your dishwasher without soap, or wash in scalding hot water. Place your lids in a bath of hot water, where they will sit through the entire process.
2. Dip tomatoes in a bowl of scalding water for thirty seconds.
3. Dunk tomatoes in ice water.
4. Pull off the skin.
5. Pack tomatoes into the jar. They make their own juice so there's no need to add anything. This isn't true for all vegetables or meats you might want to preserve; when something doesn't make its own juice you're going to have to add water to it.
6. Mash it all down and then wipe the exterior of the jar. Leave about an inch off the top. Add your lemon juice if necessary. If you're adding any spices or salt you can add them here, but it's not necessary to add any spices if you don't want to (or if unavailable).
7. Use the spatula to work around the jar once or twice, just to get the air bubbles out.
8. Get the lid and lid the jar. Hand tighten it, but don't go crazy because you want to make sure the air escapes. Otherwise your jar will simply break.
9. Place on trivet in the pot and then add water to about 1-2" above the jar. Put the lid of the stock pot on the pot.
10. Bring the water to a boil. From the boil and no earlier, time 45 minutes. Occasionally check your water to make sure that it is still sitting 1-2" above the surface—you'll need to have another pot of boiling water going so you can add more boiling water if need be.
11. Turn the heat off and then leave in for a while as you don't want to shatter the jar by leaving it on the countertop.
12. Set the jar on a couple of towels on the counter for 12 hours. After, check the seal by pushing down on it. If it doesn't move then the vacuum is okay. If it does, then you either have to refrigerate the jar and us it immediately, or you can just go ahead and reprocess it with a different lid.

13. Remove the ring on the jar and leave the seal on. The rings can rust, and you can re-use the rings.

The process is also pretty simple for the pressure canner that you'll use for veggies and meat (though you don't always have to remove the skins unless they get really hard, and you want to use lean meat). You also don't have to can only one type of food at a time. You can't overcook anything, so just use the time for the substance that requires the highest amount of time. Carrots, for example, need 30 minutes; meat needs 90. You can find information on how much time everything needs on the internet.

You're going to let your pressure cooker vent for ten minutes without the little pressure cooker "hat" on (the actual name of the gadget is the 'pressure regulator'). Once you're ready for that step, just drop it on and turn down the heat; you want the pressure to build gradually. You're going to bring this up to 10 pounds of pressure (higher altitudes might need 12-15, so look this up and look up your area on an altitude map before beginning).

You shouldn't let yourself get distracted at this point; you want to keep adjusting the heat to keep the pressure around 10 pounds. Sometimes this can get away from you, but if the pressure gets too high you'll explode your jars!

After you've pressurized your jars for long enough, you need to let it have a cooling off period. Wait until the pressure regulator drops. That will tell you the pressure cooker has become de-pressurized [284].

It's a good idea to check recipes for all the ins and outs (do you add water? How long does it need to cook? Pressure cooker or boil bath) just to make sure you're doing the right process for the right foods. You can also find recipes for slightly more complicated procedures, like making pickles or pickling eggs, or creating jams and jellies. You could look them up online or you could buy a guidebook that will take you through the different procedures.

Dehydrating is even easier. You can buy a basic dehydrator at Wal-Mart, and the instructions for dehydrating almost anything are in the book. The basic procedure is that you put whatever you want to dehydrate in the trays and let them sit there for 20 hours, occasionally rotating the trays according to your dehydrator's directions, which allows the water to leech out by very low heat. That being said, some things will need a bit of advance preparation, like jerky. Some vegetables, too, can benefit from blanching before you begin, and some fruits need a dip into lemon juice to avoid browning [285].

Again, you want a multi-tiered strategy. Things you can at home will last you about a year. That's pretty good for maintaining the contents of your garden throughout the winter after your final harvest. It also lets you do something with all the zucchini that any zucchini-bearing garden inevitably produces! Dried food can last almost indefinitely and can be put away for longer-term emergencies, forming the cornerstone of a continuing stockpile. Therefore, divide up the contents of your garden between what you're going to eat right away, what you're going to eat this year, and what you might want to save for the longer term. Note that dried, dehydrated food is also a lot more portable, making it very useful in the event that you cannot stay put.

Not that we advocate getting drunk, but making wine might be another good way to preserve fruits that you have grown. In the Middle Ages, people drank a lot more alcohol than water simply because good, clean water was so difficult to find. The alcohol was safer. Alcohol also has its uses for disinfecting, medicinal, cooking, and anesthetic purposes. Therefore, a little bit of home brewing isn't out of order either. One wouldn't do this at the expense of having enough food, mind you, but it's a good strategy if you happen to have some surplus.

Don't buy one of the fancy wine-making kits that require specialized equipment or packages that you'd have to purchase from the kit company over and over again. A basic kit that can get you started with just fruit and water runs a little under $200. There's not space to go into the ins and outs of wine making here but, if it interests you, it might be worth pursuing.

If you took our advice and used heirloom seeds in your gardening then you also need to know how to store and preserve your seeds. Otherwise you will lose the primary benefit of having heirlooms at all, which is the ability to produce your own food, year after year, without any kind of outside influence.

Not every plant will produce seed in every year. Some plants, like carrots, only produce seed every two years; you have to leave them in the ground through the winter and wait for them to flower. If the plant isn't hardy enough to survive in your winter soil then you won't be able to save those seeds, so it's a great idea to go ahead and experiment now, when heirloom seeds are still reasonably available [286].

But other than that, you can and should save the seed each year. Pick fleshy vegetables (tomatoes, squash, and melons). When they're fully ripe, then scoop out their seeds and spread them to dry in a well-ventilated place. Beans and peas only need to be left on the vine till the pods are dry and crackly. Corn, likewise, should be left on the stalk till the kernels dent. Other types of seeds may be gathered only when they're fully formed and filled with 'meat'. Remember to collect seeds only from the most vigorous plants in your garden. [287]

After you gather your seeds and dry them, you will want to label and store them. Little glass baby jars, cleaned out, will allow you to look right inside at your seeds, but you can also use regular mailing envelopes. It's more important to keep them in a cool, dry place because you don't want your seed to mold or sprout. You can add a little dried milk to each of your seed stores to prevent this from happening [288].

You can also deliberately sprout your seeds if you're running low on preserved foods (just like bean sprouts at the store), but if you do this you're either going to have to replace your seeds somehow (perhaps through barter) or make do with fewer plants next year. If you end up with *more* seed than you can plant, you can either use it as a barter item (which is going to be way more precious than gold, silver, or paper money during any sort of collapse) or you can save it for another year—most seed will last for about two years before it starts to suffer from a lower germination rate.

At the very least, gather books on how to become self-sufficient in other arenas as well. In the event of a total currency collapse there are so many things that might not be available. In the event of economic disaster, there are things that might be available but too expensive to be within the reach of the average family. Sometimes, in the event of an oppressive government, other basics besides food are either held out of reach or go out of supply. The more you can figure out how to make and do on your own, the better off you'll be.

For example, it's not that hard to make your own soap—from scratch, mind, not with a glycerin kit from the store. You need a big barrel with a spigot, something to mount it on (like concrete blocks), a hose, a way to make ash, and a way to get water into the barrel. That'll get you basic lye. Combining that with animal fat, olive oil, or vegetable oil will get you basic soap. Granted, there are a few more ins-and-outs than this, but that's where gathering up those manuals comes in. Knowledge is power. What you might not need today might not hurt to have for tomorrow, whether to provide for your own family or to barter. Remember to find the most primitive guides you can; you don't want anything that assumes you have things like access to electricity, fancy essential oils that you didn't make yourself, cute molds, or pre-made glycerin. If you have an interest, you can build what you need and start right now. Anything you learn to do now is going to serve you better than things you have to learn how to do under stress.

You want to learn how the pioneers did all sorts of things. The Hillbilly Housewife blog has a method for making reusable, pioneer women's sanitary items that will see the women of your household through should disposable women's gear no longer be available (and the way she's made it doesn't make using it too onerous). As to toilet paper: a little warm water in a ten gallon bucket and some rags will see you through just as well as disposable toilet paper will, though you of course want to keep a good stockpile of disposable toilet paper to see you through Tier 1, Tier 2, and even Tier 3 emergencies.

What about cloth? Now might be the time to learn how to sheer sheep, weave fabric from plants, or tan animal hides. But all of this is advanced stuff, not stuff you need to get too carried away with to start off. Learning how to tan an animal hide might make you pretty useful to a long term group in one respect, but if you do it before you set aside a few canned goods for a natural disaster then you're basically putting the cart before the horse. The idea here is simply to collect as much knowledge and perhaps to get as much practice as possible. You might also consider joining groups devoted to learning how to do things "the old fashioned way." Those who have seen groups like the Society for Creative Anachronisms as nerdy, silly hobbyists might have a different opinion when you realize that there are members who know how to set up a full scale Dark Ages blacksmithy from scratch, and that they can make basic tools like knives that you would begin to miss if all of yours wound up breaking during any long-term emergency.

Survival is really a three-part mindset. The first part of the mindset is the decision to survive, no matter what. The second part of the mindset is practice—taking on skills and habits right now that can help you later so that they are second nature when the going gets tough. That second part includes all the preparation you are doing now. The third portion is imagination and curiosity—the ability to think to yourself, "Now how was that done before Wal-Mart," and then to go gather up the information. Read everything and think about everything, from natural medicine and herbal remedies to asking yourself how your ancestors went about making candles. While you can't possibly learn everything, you can potentially learn enough—especially if you're part of a survival network that has gotten people assigned to learning 2 or 3 overlapping specialty skills.

4.5 Living off the Land
ജ•രു

In some scenarios, you may find yourself unable to stay in your home, and must instead make do off of the wilderness in some sort of make-shift or temporary shelter. This is not ideal.

> *In spite of all of the survival TV shows you've watched it's not easy to 'live off the land,' especially when you are in a high stress and panic mode. You will need to have food with you. Foraging off the land is not simple. It requires years of accumulated knowledge and experience. And even then it's an iffy situation. If you've never gone camping with your family, and say, attempted to start a fire or cook over an open fire, you might want to try that as a family exercise and see how well you do.* [289]

There are some who might have a sort of hybrid strategy in mind here. That is, they can't afford to go buy a fully equipped farmhouse on a remote piece of land, but they can, perhaps, afford to buy a cheap strip of land where they might place some sort of shelter, such as an RV, a yurt, a teepee, a lavuu or even just a military or science grade all-weather tent. This might be done with the intent of storing supplies on that land, caching them nearby in case of being economically unable to sustain a sturdier home, or in the case of feeling the need to hide from an increasingly oppressive government. This has its disadvantages too, however.

These types of shelter, no matter how cozy, are never going to be as secure as a house is. You're going to have additional challenges to keeping them warm (though some of these structures make it easier. A teepee, for example, has smoke flaps) and though you might adapt quite comfortably to the lifestyle (there are those who do this by choice even now), your family will probably feel more comfortable in familiar surroundings if at all possible. These types of shelter could also provide refuge in the event that you find yourself as part of a refugee camp, tent city, or other scenario where your home has been temporarily destroyed.

Even if you stay put, however, knowing a few very easily identified "wild foods" and a few tips about them could supplement all of your other preparation methods. The same is true if you know how to shoot and skin a deer or do some basic fishing to keep yourself alive. All of this could be part of a 'survive in place' strategy. Bunnies run through the suburbs too, and if you know how to trap or shoot one you've just put a little bit less pressure on your food stores.

Remember, in any survival situation, first and foremost you need food, water, shelter, and heat. Any strategy which neglects any part of these items is a flawed strategy.

If you are trying to supply *all* of your nutritional needs off the land, things get a little more complicated than if you're trying to use the land to supplement your other efforts as part of a multi-pronged strategy.

If you don't have shelter with you, you'll have to build it. A few considerations for this include the distance from available water, the tools and materials you have available, how easy it is to hide your shelter (as, in lieu of being able to make it more defensible hiding will be your best defense), and how comfortable and dry it stays. You also want to avoid areas of high wind or insect infestation, areas with the potential for you to get crushed by falling rocks or large, dead branches. The most rudimentary of all shelters is known as a squirrel's nest—you can build one of these by piling as much dry debris as possible into a pile and then crawling inside to stay dry and warm. If you have a tarp you can render this instantly weatherproof by spreading the tarp over the squirrel's nest and securing it through the grommets with sticks, poles, posts, or rope. Tarps are easy to carry and store; they should be part of your long term survival supplies as a result [290].

If you're on your own land or on a piece of land you have permission to be on, you might consider using the short-term shelter to weather you over until you can build something more long term. This is another area where reading as much as you can comes in handy; if you have a basic idea of how to construct a cob home or a dugout, for example, then you have the ability to make a comfortable (though primitive) shelter that is sturdier, more defensible, and stronger against the elements over the long run. This would be a long term project, however, something done over the course of a year, if not longer. If you're not a particularly "handy" person then this will need to be a relatively simple, small structure to avoid creating something dangerous. However, if you're more confident or you have someone with some construction experience in your party, you might be able to build more elaborate, comfortable structures.

People have gotten creative with all sorts of material. Anyone can stack old used tires into a semblance of a home and daub it up with a mud and straw mixture to keep the elements out. You can even stack those tires in a cone to create the roof. In a survival situation, your imagination and working with what you've got is key. You can also keep a lookout for caves and other natural features which might do the job for you.

Finding wild foods isn't always as hard as you think. There are just a few things to worry about. Taking dandelions from a lawn sprayed heavily with pesticides is a bad idea, but if you find a wild cache of dandelions or are using your own, pesticide free lawn, you're probably in the clear. We're only going to cover the very basic, very easily identifiable wild foods in this guide. You'll need a much more extensive study guide or even an apprenticeship under an expert to take it much further than this. In this guide, for your safety, we will try to avoid "things that can be mistaken for other things."

Another thing about wild foods that's worth mentioning is that, in some cases, you can grow them right out in the open because they don't look like food to your average thug. This can help protect you from thieves, including the thieves that claim they're from the federal government, taking everybody's food for the good of the nation. This is another form of stealth gardening.

- Roses: With 6 to 24 times more Vitamin C than orange juice, rose hips are an excellent choice for a wild food or stealth food. Rose hips are simply the seed pods of roses, and they sometimes remain on the vine even well into the winter. There are also about 35 varieties of wild roses growing along streams, roadsides, fences, open woods and in meadows across the United States. They're fairly difficult to mistake [291].

- Since there are no poisonous varieties of blueberries or huckleberries, this is another wild food you can forage for if you live in the appropriate regions [292].
- You've probably picked raspberries and blackberries as a child, and again, these are easy to recognize without danger that you're going to poison yourself.
- Wild strawberries are similar to domestic varieties, only they are usually smaller. Again, they do not typically resemble other more poisonous plants and can generally be taken safely [293].
- Almost every part of a dandelion can be eaten. The leaves make a good lettuce substitute. The roots can be used a bit like potatoes or ground up to stretch coffee. The heads, while still yellow, have a sweet, buttery flavor but a bit of an odd texture (you can't eat the heads once they've gone to seed). The milky stems are not too tasty, but consuming them won't hurt you any.
- Pine needles can be made into pine needle tea, which can keep you warm and keep some essential nutrients in your body. If you can catch the cone before they drop their seeds, close up, and become useless, then you can feast on a variety of different types of pine nuts.
- Clover's easy to identify as well: the seeds, blossoms, leaves, and flowers can all be eaten [294].
- Wild onions look just about like onions from the store do, and can be used and eaten in just about the same way.

You also have to be wary that you know which part of the plant is edible and which stage of its development under which it is edible (295). Some plants require special preparation, though for the most parts the ones above are easy enough. This topic is worth pursuing more in-depth if only because in the event of a famine everyone is going to have the same idea you do, and they will gravitate straight towards the plants they already know (the raspberries and blackberries in particular).

You can also test plants to see if they're safe to eat, but this is a very slow, step-by-step process and you need to be very careful with it. If you're not sure about the pesticide content of any wild food you should try this even for foods you recognize, too. Each step is basically a progressively more dangerous step which stops to check for a bad reaction between steps.

Start by smelling the plant, as that's one of the first ways nature tells us whether or not a plant may be edible. If you don't like the smell, chances are you should keep looking. Next, simply touch the plant and wait about an hour. If you develop any kind of a skin rash or other reaction, this is probably not a good plant to eat. Then decide what part of the plant you're going to try. If, say, it's a leaf, put a tiny bit of that leaf on your lip. Wait another hour. If you didn't burn, blister, or get a rash, you can proceed to testing a tiny bit on your tongue. Hold that in your mouth for a short time and spit it out. Wait another hour to see if you start to feel sick. Finally, try ingesting a tiny bit and see if that makes you sick. This time you're going to wait a full 24 hours. If it doesn't then you can probably prepare that part of the plant. You'll need to try this with each portion of the plant to see which parts are edible and which parts are inedible. Sometimes the whole plant will be edible; sometimes only a part of it will [296]. Obviously this is a method of last resort. Things could still go horribly wrong, so take the time to gain as much of this knowledge as possible before your out in the middle of nowhere sniffing every scraggly bit of green that doesn't frighten you off by sheer looks alone.

Hunting, trapping, and fishing help you get wild foods that are easier to identify. In the self-defense chapter we'll be talking about guns, but we're going to divert from guns for just a second. If you're going to hunt for your food, it's a good idea to use a bow or a crossbow. There are a couple of good reasons for this. First of all, a bow is silent. If you're out in the forest hunting deer with a gun, that gunshot could bring unfriendlies down upon your head very fast. Those unfriendlies could be soldiers intent on disarming you, gang members who want your guns, or people who know that a gunshot could mean food who would like to relieve you of your freshly caught or killed deer. Second, if you fail to hide your guns adequately, they're going to get taken (witness Hurricane Katrina) more often than not. But bows are not considered a threat anymore by most people, and there's a chance you might be allowed to keep your bow, especially if you have a good old fashioned recurve a' la Robin Hood vs. a big bad compound bow that looks like a military weapon in its own right.

If you've never hunted before, this is not going to be the easiest time of your life. First, you'll have to kill your food, perhaps for your very first time. If you don't kill it right away, you're going to have to track the blood through the forest, avoiding all the dangers within, in order to put the poor animal out of its misery and go on to eat it. Then you have to skin and butcher the thing, which means cutting off its head and feet, then cutting off the skin around the genitals, then cutting out its genitals to avoid tainting your meat with all that musk. Then you're going to have to lop off the portions of meat. If you've never done this before, there's a good chance you will do it wrong or ineffectively. Again, seeking out the knowledge before you decide to rely on it for your survival is a good idea.

Trapping can remove a couple of these difficulties, but you want to be careful as traps can hurt humans too. Usually, traps should be set by a source of food or water. There are hundreds of designs, but most traps will either try to strangle the prey, crush the prey, dangle it, or maim it in some way [297]. Three notched sticks in a figure 4, a heavy weight such as a large branch or rock, and some bait can trap you small game, though you'll also need to take the time to remove evidence of your human scent from your trap. The website wilderness-survival.net/food-2.php has some good ideas and pictures for your reference.

Fishing is probably the easiest as most of us have gone fishing at one time or another; if you already have poles and some form of bait you probably already know what to do. You also probably have some idea of how to clean a fish, but cleaning a fish is relatively easy if you don't. Hack off the head. Hack off the tail. Split the thing in half, away from the bone. Carefully separate the skin from the resulting filet of meat. Fish aren't rocket science, and worms and bugs are easy enough to find for bait. That said, "do not eat the organs of any fish, which can be high in both heavy metals and pesticides, and consume only the skinless, boneless dorsal filets" [298].

These days a lot of people are being proactive by trying homesteading. This is a combination of farming and living off the land that begins by getting a little piece of off-grid property. That said, in spite of what many disaster guides will tell you, it is simply not for everyone.

Obviously, it's much easier to be self-sustaining if you live in a rural area where you are away from the metropolitan masses...this is not a decision to be taken lightly. It's a good idea to perhaps rent acreage for a time before making a purchase. Make sure you locate land that can actually sustain a garden. Living in this manner is not for the faint of heart. [299]

There's also a flipside to this story that a lot of people don't consider, because getting "back to the land," "living off the land," and "homesteading" have taken on a sort of emotional, romantic appeal. There's sometimes an idea that "real" preppers or survivors shun the city. To this I would add that the countryside and the farms were Stalin's targets for starvation, and while I wouldn't call anyone living under Stalin exactly happy, there were those in Moscow who weren't even aware a famine was going on. David Morris of the surviveinplace.com website, which offers step-by-step lessons, also noted in one of his lessons that in the event of many disasters, it is the *cities* that are going to wound up getting supplies first, not the rural areas. This may also be the only option for those of us who just don't have the resources to escape to a rural hideaway. He also notes it's reversible if you "jump the bug out gun," which is not necessarily the case if you scramble to your rural retreat before there's really a need.

If you've been in the cities all your life, you may already be equipped with many of the vital skills that would be necessary to life in the city, such as keeping your mouth shut, not looking anybody in the eye, not trusting or talking too much to anybody you don't know, and staying invisible to robbers and thieves wherever you happen to be. Not everyone ends up expelled from their homes or apartments in the event of a crisis—and cities come with ready-made shelters in the form of abandoned buildings, too. In the event of a total-breakdown, there will be gangs, thieves, and bandits roaming through rural areas as well, diminishing the chance of getting help from anyone outside of your family or immediate group.

You can survive anywhere—survival is a mindset—and God needs people everywhere during a disaster, not just out on the dirt roads and secret pathways of the wilderness. There are also often "pockets" of natural areas near urban areas that can sometimes be exploited the same way full wilderness areas could be. If you're going to try the urban route, the Morris course is worth signing up for.

4.6 Self-Defense

ঈ • ৎ

Self-defense is not just for the grimmest of Tier 4 scenarios. As we saw during Hurricane Katrina, depending upon where you are, you might indeed need self-defense for a Tier 1 scenario. But in a famine, let's remember that people are often out to *eat other people*. That means even the kids in your family should have some idea of how to hit someone where it hurts and run really fast, be aware of using a buddy system, and, in severe survival situations, be equipped with the right kind of non-lethal weapons.

Before we begin, we should mention that you need to know your capabilities. You could be a martial arts black belt with a Taser, a #10 pepper spray gun, a hand gun, and a knife and still not be the sort of person who could, psychologically, ever go Rambo on the enemy. If you're a mother with small children, you might want to avoid confrontation as long as you possibly can without endangering your life and their lives; once you get involved in a fight, you've just inserted a huge element of randomness into events. Bullets could fly where you don't want them to because, when you shoot at people, they do have a tendency to shoot back. Once violence escalates, anyone in your home could wind up dead.

A resistance movement might indeed rise up but, if you're that same mother, you might be better off focusing your bravery towards keeping a hiding spot for a moving resistance member to sleep in and guarding him for the night, rather than trying to get out there and play soldier. If you're an elderly gentleman with a knee condition, you might be brave and trained; you might also just be better off sitting at home with your HAM radio or hand crank radio, assisting communications, and slipping things into drop points. It's a personal choice and one only you can make, but don't ever let anybody push or shame you into doing something you're not physically and emotionally suited for. In good people, killing can take a real emotional toll that can add to the emotional and physical stress you're already under. We've all watched too many movies and I'd daresay most of us have daydreamed about "really showing" that bad guy who shows up at our doorstep. If that bad guy is a soldier from FEMA who has shown up to take the guns you didn't think to cache or had registered with the government because you didn't buy them in cash at a gun show, adopting a "you can have it when you pry it from my cold dead fingers" is probably going to lead to one result. You'll probably wind up dead. Even if you defeat that group of soldiers, they're going to send more to your doorstep, this time with the intent to arrest you. That means you're going to have to leave your home and wind up on the run, which is not an ideal scenario for say, someone who has small children to protect.

And, in a martial law scenario, if you do find yourself preparing for armed resistance, know this—people who start shooting at the enemy during the initial days of martial law are not going to constitute any real, organized resistance.

There will be those who want to fight, but unless they can get some cohesiveness to their organization, they're just shooting cap guns at people with tanks. You would do well to mind your own business, be as peaceable as possible, and stay alive. There will eventually be resistance down the road, but at the inception of martial law, that is NOT the time to fight. Those instituting martial law will be looking for people to make examples of in order to quell any type of uprising or protest from the rest of the sheep. Harsh reprisals at the inception of martial law will keep the masses cowed and controlled. [300]

The spearhead of any resistance is most likely to come from people with real military or police training and the ability to give it to others.

You need self-defense because less prepared people might want to come after your supplies and don't mind stabbing you, beating you, hurting you or killing you to get them. In some scenarios, the loss of your supplies could mean death, even if you hand them over peaceably. Remember that during Hurricane Katrina, one of the first things that happened was looting. People start with stores, because stores are easy targets. When they run out of stores, they start looking over at private homes and apartments. An expensive safe simply calls attention to where your valuables are. A good home security system guards the whole house.

Now, during normal times of peace, a monitored security system is best. The reason is simple: if you're incapacitated, your non-monitored, DIY security system is not going to call law enforcement over to help you. This is even true during a famine when the government has not actively turned against its people. You need to look for the following in a home security company:

- Uniformity of equipment. The absolute largest security provider has over 30 different types of keypads and control boxes. That's because they get their size by acquiring lots of different companies. This means that if something breaks, you're likely to get charged an awful lot of money to fix it. If you go to a dealer of such services, you'll get treated to a fine game of pass-the-buck when it comes time to fix or replace that equipment.

- A company that does not buy out other companies! Sometimes a security company buys out another security company and acquires 5000 new home monitoring contracts. Sometimes 500 of them fall through the cracks, and those 500 people don't find out they weren't monitored anymore until the contract is up.
- Really good background checks on employees. Employees need to be squeaky clean because the salesperson helps you set your phone password and the technician helps you set your keypad code. Some systems allow multiple codes. This means that an unscrupulous employee could program a "back door" for themselves. In addition, all employees are very thoroughly trained in the system, enough to know exactly how to defeat them in general. The person who sold and installed your system also knows exactly how to defeat yours in particular.
- A company which picks up signs when they're not monitoring anymore. The sign is what a loss-prevention strategist might call a "deterrent." Thieves are less likely to break into houses with security signage *unless* they know it's the policy of the company to use that sign more like free advertising for their company, little caring if there's monitoring behind it or not.
- Avoid companies that try to sell you on wireless devices. It's so easy to defeat or jam a wireless system. A wired security system that goes into a dedicated, non-cellular, non-radio phone line is the best security system.

If you go with a DIY system you'll want it to have two components—a noise component, certainly, to scare intruders and wake up your whole household, but also a CCTV component. You can set up video camera monitoring with a computer and a webcam these days. Not only are criminals less-than-eager to engage surveillance systems, but you can also catch whoever has stolen from you on camera. If the authorities still care this could really help you. Hey, people are using surveillance against you all the time, so you might as well use it against the bad guys.

In general, you need to cover all the doors with contacts because the most common method of breaking and entering is to kick in the door. It's neither necessary nor cost-effective, generally, to cover every window with contacts *unless* you are building your house right now and can obtain pre-wiring services, at which case it grows very cost-effective and very easy to do. Windows are generally covered with glass-break detectors in areas of the house where your family will continue moving around at night, such as the bedrooms, and motion detectors where they are not often going to move around, such as the living areas and the front foyer. Make sure your security system includes a "motion off" button so you can turn off the motion detectors during the day and while you are actively at home, moving through the house. It's best to have a keypad with a panic button inside your bedroom, as well as by your front door.

Windows can also be protected with window screw locks which make them a lot harder to open. If you're trying to prepare a retreat for a long term survival scenario, you might even want to get metal security shutters for doors and windows that can be rolled down and locked. Run a bead of caulk around the edges of storm windows so that it's hard to remove them quietly [301].

In the meantime, you should also be paying attention to basic ideas of home safety. Don't advertise that you're not home, for example.

If you're foolish enough to leave on vacation without stopping newspaper delivery, leaving the phone off the hook or having the post office hold your mail then expect to come back to a house that burglars have taken their time going through with a fine tooth comb. [302]

You should also get out of the habit, if you are currently in it, of posting your location status to Facebook, Twitter, or FourSquare. Nothing says: "Come rob me," like, "Taking my whole family down to Detroit for the concert tonight!" People do know how to access this information even if you think you've got it friends locked, and all of us have the habit of adding "friends" who really might not be.

You also need to remove dark areas from your house and yard by keeping your hedges trimmed and installing motion-detector lights. Remove and lock-up things that might help a thief, like your ladder. If you don't already have good deadbolt locks and a peephole, then get them installed.

In urban environments especially, *do not open the door at night if you're not expecting to be called upon.* A lot of criminals really don't care if you're home or not. They will knock on the door and, when you answer, they will force their way inside, subdue you, and take whatever they want at their leisure, including your body and your life if they are so inclined. Avoid answering the door if you don't know who is on the other side. If you're worried you'll miss a family member or friend, the solution is easy: inform them of your policy and ask them to give you a call or a text message before they simply drop by. Most burglaries occur during the day, when burglars think you're at work, but most very dangerous *home invasions* occur at night.

If you've got a home of your own and a little more money at your disposal, you can also invest in a panic room.

The most important thing about this room is that it be in a location that you and your family can reach in a hurry. ...Your refuge room should either be close to the bedroom or be the bedroom itself. This room should have a door that can be locked from the inside...Ideally you should have a separate phone line in this one room that isn't tied to the rest of the house. The outside line should be protected by a metal conduit to make it harder for anyone to cut it.

The purpose of a refuge room is to keep the person who has broken into your home away from you and your family as long as possible. To that end, you're going to need to install a solid core door with heavy locks and the hinges on the inside. You're going to want this door to lock from the outside as well, since this is the room you'll be storing your valuables in.

Your refuge room is going to need more than a strong door. Any burglar whose brain isn't fried on dope will know that he can kick through a standard Sheetrock wall and enter a room. Plywood paneling will add sturdiness and greater impenetrability to your refuge room walls. You don't even have to remove the drywall. Just nail the plywood in place over it. Mark your studs so that you're nailing into framing members and not just the drywall itself. [303]

Recognize that none of this functions as a guarantee that you'll be left alone. During a crisis situation it's important that at least one member of your family, if at all possible, should stay awake, alert, and on watch at all hours of the day. In a true crisis situation, you might want to make your place look more abandoned than occupied (but NOT left abandoned and full of tasty food and other valuables), which means running dark, running quiet, and running strong-smell free as much as possible.

Finally, this is where we've got to give the word about feeding the neighbors. You're a good person so when your hungry neighbors show up at your doorstep begging for food, you're going to want to feed them.

Don't.

Feed your trusted survival network, certainly. That's what you created it for. If you've had long enough with them, you know you can trust all those people to not rat you out to bandits, squeal to the occupying forces of martial law, or come back with 18 of their buddies to clean you out of the rest of your food. You don't know that about the neighbor at your front door. Pray for them, but tell them you have nothing and send them away empty handed. You and your family should also be doing your best not to look like you're eating too well either, just to avoid drawing attention to yourself[304].

*Guns, hand-to-hand combat, older-style weapons, and improvised weapons should all be a part of your self-defense strategy. In addition, Tasers and pepper spray guns might be a better choice than regular guns, especially for family members whose main strategy is going to be getting the bad guy down so they can **run**.* Fighting may be necessary. It's also a mindset. Any kind of combat training is going to equip you better for defending yourself rather than going without combat training and picking up a gun or a knife for the first time in a panic situation. In general, getting this type of training means that you get an idea of how to either calm your mind down to the point where you're not making stupid decisions or to focus your emotions into a kind of unstoppable berserker rage that helps you manage pain and scares the crap out of your enemies while giving you a kind of laser focus on your goal of disabling them by any means necessary. If a survival situation starts up tomorrow and you haven't gotten any training at all, you might still have to defend yourself, but this certainly helps.

Guns, especially, require some specialized knowledge. If you don't know how to load a gun, deal with the kickback, and target a gun, you might end up hurting yourself and others. Furthermore, if you're not really committed to the kill when you pick up a gun, it's just as likely your opponent will take it away from you and use it against you.

Tasers and pepper spray guns (that is, 10% pepper spray guns, which are strong enough to take down grizzly bears, and not those little purse keyfab things that you sometimes see) are weapons that are far more effective in the hands of less experienced users. They're meant to put an attacker down so that you can either get away from them or so that you can get the more experienced fighter in your group or family to come over and deal with the guy. They both still have to be handled with a modicum of care and common sense so that you don't end up shocking yourself or shooting yourself in the face with pepper spray. A good pepper spray gun sprays up to 25 feet away, which means you could stand at one end of your apartment living room and blast anyone coming in the door without risking getting too up close and personal.

As always, a multi-tiered strategy that teaches you a number of different ways and methods to defend yourself gives you far more tools to use to help yourself in the event of a disaster or problem. In addition, you need to be aware that anything heavy, long, or pointy can be used as a weapon in a pinch. Flimsy items like shower curtain rods aren't good for swinging, but you can still jab it into a solar plexus like a spear. Swinging a pot of hot coffee at a bad guy will give you a few moments too. Chairs make good weapons. Knitting needles make good weapons too (305). Ask a martial artist to show you how a rolled up issue of Cosmo or a rolled up Sears catalogue can be used to break a board (with the small, blunt ends, not the wide, long body). That can wreak some havoc on a rib bone, the throat, or the solar plexus.

Even knowing the most vulnerable parts of the body can help. Punching the face isn't particularly helpful in reality, but punching the throat is. The solar plexus, groin, back of the knees, and kidneys are all very vulnerable areas. Men do tend to protect their groins, so if you're in a hand-to-hand situation, one good way to deal with this is to feint for the groin with a kick (which, ladies, they are expecting) and then slam your fist or your improvised weapon into their throat just as hard as you can the moment they block their family jewels.

Let's take a moment to talk about martial arts classes, too, because not all are created equal. Some martial arts and self-defense classes are far more focused on martial arts as a sport than martial arts as a defense method. And while a kick is a kick is a kick, the mindset is different. A martial arts school that is training you to score three points in a series of very fair methods is not going to prepare you the same way a more traditional martial arts school that is training you how to strike a throat and deal with a scenario where he has a knife and you have your hands will. You also really have to be on the look-out for self-proclaimed "masters" and "grand masters" who often lump a dozen and one titles on themselves. You can usually steer clear of them just by seeing how much self-aggrandizement they engage in on their ads and websites.

Women who attend a "women's self-defense course" should also be careful. Find one that is taught by a woman who has taken the time to test every one of the moves with a man twice her size who is actually acting like he is trying to attack her. A lot of the times, men who teach those classes really, really mean well, but ladies, they don't always realize that those "simple moves" work great if you're 200 pounds of muscle with a male center of gravity, but don't work so well if you're an 135 pound lady with a female center of gravity. If you can't find a course taught by such a woman, go ahead and take the course with a man and then ask a man you trust, such as your husband, to go ahead and be the bad guy (in safe conditions) so you can find out which techniques are actually good for your size and weight and which techniques are a total loss for your body type. You don't want to try to find out when you're being attacked.

Learning how to use more medieval weaponry like swords and knives (well, knives are used in every day combat *now*, and are a messy, scary, dangerous way to fight) isn't that bad of an idea either. This goes back to the bows, too. Nobody sees a sword these days and thinks, "threat." They think, "replica," and it's often true, but you can go to an ice skate shop and get those things sharpened for real. It's not a good idea to even swing a blunt sword at someone's neck, and a rattan or bamboo practice sword to the neck or solar plexus will drop someone pretty nicely too. You also don't have to buy ammo for these types of weapons, and you can make ammo for bows. It's not the first choice, certainly—you never bring a sword to a gun fight after all—but a multi-tiered strategy tries to prepare for different eventualities and this is no different. Knives and some swords, such as those located in canes, are also somewhat concealable and can give you an element of surprise if you need it. Again, that medieval reenactment group of guys running around with PVC-and-foam swords or rattan swords may look kind of silly now, but combat skills are combat skills, and this can be a cheap way to learn if you can't afford other types of classes. Any of the hand to hand or melee classes will teach you skills that are good in a gun fight, too, such as understanding range and reach, keeping a clear head, knowing your distance, finding cover or protection, dodging, and keeping a clear head. Paintball exercises are fun, but they also give you some of those skills as well.

Don't shun any skill, knowledge, or exercise that might help give your brain a framework for functioning when trouble shows up on your doorstep. If you have *no choice* but to fight, the last thing you want to do is get stuck in a "combat paralysis" mindset. This happens to some people and it's not a function of cowardice. The brain shuts down because the person suffering from this problem hasn't given their brain any framework for personal violence. At best this can mean you don't get to keep your supplies. At worst, this can mean you wind up dead.

Getting into decent physical shape now is good self-defense. It's more about how far you can walk or run, however, than the little number on the scale. Guess what. If there's no gas, there are no cars. You're going to have to walk, run, or bike to anything you need or anywhere you want to go if that turns out to be the case. This is *not fun* if you've never done it before. If you're a couch potato, now is the time to stop.

This isn't about losing weight, though you'll probably lose at least a little bit. In some regards, losing too much weight right now isn't the best strategy if you're carrying around a few extra pounds that aren't threatening your health at all, simply because each pound represents 3,000 calories that can carry you through a famine issue. You don't want to be *obese*, but humans have always carried around a little bit extra during times of plenty to take them through times of scarcity.

This is more about being mobile if you need to be mobile. Can you, say, bike a quarter of a mile without winding up in an achy, breathless state? Can you hike two miles without feeling like your heart is going to burst out of your chest?

Being physically fit will also help you stay emotionally sharper and will give you more resources, right in and on your own body, to deal with periods of stress or privation.

Keeping your head down and your mouth shut IS self-defense. Know your capabilities, especially in a martial law scenario. The best fight, the one you're most certain to win, is the one you never get into. For most of us, that's going to be the first defense of choice. Survival isn't about looking for trouble; it's about avoiding it wherever possible. In *Understanding and Surviving Martial Law*, Rule #1 is this:

> *Keep your mouth shut…it's as simple as that. Don't invite people into your business and don't make yourself a target. Don't say anything that can make you a target, especially with the government. This is the first and most important habit you need to incorporate.* [306]

Remember the old saying: loose lips sink ships. So you're going to avoid writing down or talking about a variety of information, including information on the location, strengths, material or equipment of any caches you create (see below), any hiding places you maintain, or any drop points you may establish with your group. Second, you're going to avoid talking about any plans you're making to protect yourself. Don't stand around the water cooler telling everybody what you intend to do if there's a famine or if the government shows up at your house. Any discussion you do about your preparations outside of your well-chosen, trusted group is likely to find its way directly into the hands of the people you don't want to have it: thieves, looters, scumbags, gang members, and members of the military in particular.

*You will almost certainly want to hide your guns, even if only against conventional robbers. That said, for the most part, you're not hiding them from robbers. You're hiding them from **enemies**. Caching guns, food, and other items may be absolutely vital in a martial law scenario, but this is not a game.* If you are caching weapons in particular, you're not going to dig them up for target practice or go to and from your cache every time you go hunting. You are storing them against a future day where you're either going to have to protect yourself and your family against thugs and anarchists, or you're burying your weapons for future resistance fighters to use in order to throw off the shackles of a totalitarian regime [307].

If you're serious about caching and hiding weapons then you need to get the *Hide Your Guns* survival manual from Solutions from Science, which will teach you every in and out of doing so, from finding places in your home to all of the different considerations you need to take into account while creating a buried weapons cache. We can give you a few pieces of information here. For example, if you have a staple gun then you can fit hidden pockets into your sofas and chairs, and then reattach the padding, using foam padding to make sure the furniture feels correct when someone searches. You can sometimes create a cavity in the hides of tables. You can do all of this without ripping into your drywall or tearing into your house, hiding spaces which are going to be pretty obvious if you don't really know what you're doing [308].

As for caching, you can use 5 gallon buckets or capped PVC pipes to weatherproof your cache. You want to make sure that your cache has positions for lookouts, landmarks for identification, is accessible to you and is likely to be accessible in the future, is out of the way so that nobody notices you burying the objects, and has plenty of escape routes so you can get out if you find you've been followed. You will never be caching in your own back yard. You can even cache in urban areas by finding nasty, abandoned buildings and then remove some blocks or tile to create a little vault. You need to have multiple caches in order to make sure you can get to at least one of them. Don't forget that you may also want to cache forged IDs, unattainable or hard to come by items like ammo, hand tools, medicine, foods, candles, or radios, items that can be stolen and reused easily like your gold or silver, and even an "E&E" cache that can help you get away from trouble, stocked with a little food, a medicine kit, items to change your appearance, a change of clothes, water purification tablets (you're hardly going to wander around with bleach and a boiling pot if you're on the run), cash, silver, and perhaps an additional small weapon. You might even want to put it all inside of a backpack inside of a 5 gallon bucket so you can dig it up, grab it up, and go [309].

Even if you don't intend to cache weapons, as you get further into your survival strategy, you might at least want to cache food in the event that there is a food round-up or that your in-home survival food is stolen or taken from you. If you have that little rural patch of land that you might flee to, you might want to cache things on the way to the land, on it, or near it so that you don't have to carry everything you'll need with you when you go.

Be careful about joining militia groups, movements, organizations, or protests of any kind right now. This is a tough one, because there is an awful lot of stuff going on that Americans who still have their spirit of freedom will want to get out there and protest. It seems counter-intuitive, perhaps, that the last thing you want to do right now is go and join a militia group, even one that seems fairly benign, like your state militia group. But if you've read this far you already know that there's a great big noose tightening around everyone's neck. The time to shout has nearly ended; the time to be affiliated with any organization is passing slowly away. More and more the shouting doesn't matter, and the organizations get you right smack dab in the middle of a little FBI operation called COINTELPRO, or the FBI counter intelligence program.

According to a Senate Select Committee Study in 1975, FBI agents have been instructed to get into most groups with strong beliefs, and their orders are to expose, disrupt, misdirect, discredit, or otherwise disrupt the activities of these groups and their leaders, usually by pretending to be a member of the group [310]. We talked about this earlier, and how this strategy is also used to make sure that citizens cannot trust one another, making it harder to organize. Even your DP network, unless very carefully constructed and presented, could wind up a target of COINTELPRO.

COINTELPRO is the practice of sending what's called an "agent provocateur" smack dab into the group, and this agent might do several things. Some agents go into protests and deliberately start violence to discredit the group and to give the larger body of law enforcement an excuse to move in and start rounding everybody up. Others pretend to be lock-step members of the group. These guys are very good at seeming like your best friend, in getting you to open up and tell them everything so that they can later use your secrets against you or use you to get to other members [311].

If you want to stay below the radar of government, don't even think about adding your name to a membership roster in any group the government could term a fringe military group, a survivalist group, an un-authorized militia or a radical terrorist-type organization.

Most groups, like civilian militias, might have hundreds of level-headed members, but it takes just one hot-head to bring the group and all its members down with him. Most people are followers, not leaders, and one belligerent know-it-all can hold sway over the majority.

If there is a cause you believe in, then donate funds anonymously. The FBI and ATF routinely infiltrate groups they consider fringe or radical. [(312)]

You'd also be very surprised who the FBI considers fringe or radical. For example, if you sit and read their documents long enough, a tour of the Southern Poverty Law Center website will make you think your own best friend is a dangerous, racist, terrorist waiting to happen. They've targeted some organizations that are otherwise mild as milk-water and made them out to be dangerous. You can bet the FBI is probably watching some of those organizations, too. That's why, when you set up your neighborhood disaster preparedness network, you're not going to talk about it on Facebook or form a Twitter ID for it. Keep it quiet, keep it grassroots and, as much as is possible, don't present it, perhaps not even to its larger body of members, as anything concerned about martial law. A group dedicated to making sure everyone has supplies in a hurricane, who *only* looks concerned about that hurricane, is far less likely to receive attention than a group that talks about some of the issues we've covered in this book.

એ • ஒ

EPILOGUE

The purpose of *Rising Prices, Empty Shelves* was not to scare you. It was to help you get a mindset of survival, the very same mindset that our ancestors carried. An attitude of complacency and a bedrock belief that nothing will ever happen to us is a construction of the modern era; a situation caused, for the most part, by a people who have spent a long, long time in comfort and without distress. It is in our nature to believe that life will always go on as life always has. That is, in fact, our greatest wish—for ourselves, and for our children.

Rough times come, rough times go. Empires rise, empires fall. Some see their way to the end of hard times, some fall in the middle. But it's our belief that those who are aware and prepared, and who are not afraid to be aware and prepared, can face the future without fear and with a certain sense of the pride that comes with being strong and self-reliant. Even the very act of preparing changes something in your mentality. It changes you from the sort of person who is willing to wait around for people to help you to the sort of person that is ready to help yourself. At a still higher permutation, you begin thinking about how to help others out.

That's not to say you'll never accept help. Accepting help is going to be necessary. As we've mentioned, you're stronger together than alone. You might need help, for example, to learn some of the skills and capabilities that you don't currently have. Not everyone learns through reading or even seeing. Some of us have to learn by doing.

It just means you expect to pull your own weight, and that you are committed to being resourceful and seeing yourself through if there's nowhere else to turn. Succeed or fail, you'll do it on your feet, in the spirit of the American citizen.

Solutions from Science offers a variety of resources that we'd like to talk to you about in closing, to help you, instruct you, and encourage you on your journey of self-reliance. You can also find a lot of good resources in our resource section, some for survival and some to help you expand your point of view on all of the issues we've raised in this book. It's been a lot—a thorough education on history, economics, agriculture, human nature, and survival skills— yet there's so much more to learn.

Getting the Guns Out of Sight

In the event of an emergency, if and when all hell breaks loose, protecting your guns will be a key element to defending yourself and your loved ones. When hunger strikes and panic arises, so too will the amount of crime. It won't only be criminals, but "desperate" people as well, breaking into your home hoping to find and take your food, water, and especially guns. Learning how to hide your guns should be one of your top priorities. You can find out more about very clever ways to hide your guns at: **www.hideyourguns.com**.

Heirloom Seeds

If you're going to plant a survival garden then you definitely want a good source of non-hybrid, non-germinated seeds. As you now know, big seed companies have engineered seeds with a "terminator gene." These seeds will not reproduce as they have been genetically altered. We've located a company that sells a "Survival Seed Bank" containing enough heirloom seeds to plant a full acre crisis garden. All you have to do is save some of the seeds each fall and this little kit will produce a lifetime supply of food for you and your family and neighbors. You can learn more about it by going to their website. It can be located at **www.survivalseedbank.com**.

Food Storage

Once you plant and harvest your garden, make sure you know how to properly store these foods by drying or canning. One of the best resources for food storing strategies can be found at: **www.foodshortageussa.com**.

Which Items Instantly Vanish From Store Shelves In a Crisis or Meltdown?

Recently one of our researchers completed the definitive report on the top 77 items that literally vanish from store shelves "faster than a rabbit" when hurricanes, earthquakes, and killer snowstorms threaten. Yep. It's the stuff that gets hoarded when people freak out about an unknown future. It's also the stuff that will disappear quickest in the midst of a food shortage or other economic crisis. Every American needs to read this report as soon as humanly possible. You can learn more about this report by going to: **www.preparedforcrisis.com**.

Double or Triple Survival Garden Production

We've found a product that combines all natural fish emulsion with liquefied kelp, allowing the survival gardener to harvest in fewer days with less (or no) herbicides and pesticides. It yields 200-300% more nutrient dense food as well as dramatically increases shelf life of the produce grown with it. Grow giant vegetables quicker than you thought possible. We highly recommend this all natural product. Get the details at www.growlikecrazy.com.

Free Book Reveals How Squanto's Secret Garden Made the First Thanksgiving Possible

Squanto's gardening advice made the First Thanksgiving possible, and now that same advice can help you, too. When it comes to gardening, it's not how hard you work (the pilgrims were hard workers), it's how much you know that determines success and sometimes even saves lives. Now to help you enjoy a unique American heritage, and grow more life-saving nutritious food…we want you to take a look at the gardening secrets used by Squanto, one of America's greatest unsung heroes. We want you to have some of the very best gardening tips from early colonial history, history that has never been told before. To get your free book, visit: **www. firstthanksgivinggarden.com**.

Crisis Cooking

One of the most important areas of surviving a crisis is the ability to cook meals and sanitize water. Without sterilized water you will have big problems with bugs which can make you or those living with you very, very sick. We found an excellent little survival cooker that can use wood, charcoal, or propane as fuel, which makes it a pretty versatile tool. You can read more about it at: **www.crisiscooker.com**.

New Solar Powered Generator Produces "Off the Grid" Back-Up Power

If you have ever wanted to have an emergency "back-up" system that supplies continuous electrical power, this will be the most important website you will ever visit. Here is why: there is now a completely portable (and ultra-high efficient) solar power generator which produces up to 1800 watts of household electricity on demand when you need it most. News of this "solar backup generator" (it's the first off-the-grid breakthrough in 50 years) is spreading like wildfire all across the country! Additional information about this unit can be found at **www. mysolarbackup.com.**

Power Sleep for a Strong Immune System

Getting sleep when the world is falling apart around you is sometimes difficult to do. If you're having trouble getting to sleep, most folks opt for a sleeping pill. One possible way around the sleeping pill dilemma is by a special audio CD that puts you out without any drugs whatsoever. Most folks simply listen with headphones and then fall asleep. In a stressful situation, this CD may mean getting the healthy sleep that is critical to a strong immune response. Check it out at **www. highspeedsleep.com.**

The "One Survival Supplement" You Shouldn't Be Without

One supplement I would recommend having in your survival arsenal is a substance called shilajit. Shilajit comes from the rocky cliffs of the Himalayas. Somewhat of a mystery, it's believed to form as a result of the "mineral drip" from the cracks of the rocks during the hot summer months. This mineral drip runs through plant matter that has been trapped in the crevices of the cliff areas, and along with geothermal pressure, a dark red, somewhat gummy substance is formed. The reason you want this substance in your survival cabinet is because the active constituent of shilajit is a chemical called fulvic acid. This is why shilajit is one of the most sought after healing compounds in Ayurvedic medicine. Probably the best quality and perhaps the lowest priced shilajit can be found at the website: **www.blacklistedherb.com.** The company will ship the product out to you and only require you to pay the shipping up front and invoice you for the balance due 30 days later. Frankly, I don't know of another supply company that operates on the "golden rule" premise of doing business. Make sure you have some of this substance. Oh, one more thing about shilajit. Many researchers also believe that this substance also makes nutrients from other foods more bioavailable. If this is true, it means all of your stored foods will supply your body with more precious vitamins, minerals and vital trace elements when you need them the most.

How to Make
Your Own Herbal Antibiotics

Learn how to make your own emergency remedies for use in any survival situation if and when medical help may be unavailable. The remedies discovered in this report represent the findings and gleanings of thousands of hours worth of research. To learn more about this report, go to: **www.emergencyherbs.com**.

Making Your Own
Herbal Medicines

To monopolize the market, the pharmaceutical companies are pushing for new strict FDA regulations, and whenever possible, a new outright ban on many herbs. A total ban on raw herbs will be difficult, considering that herbs grow wild in practically every field and backyard in the country. What they can ban, however, is the production and the sale of herbal products. And, believe it or not, that is already happening.

Debra Nuzzi St. Claire is a Master Herbalist who has been studying and teaching herbal medicine for the last 20 years. She has taught and lectured internationally on the preparation and use of herbs. She has formulated over 270 products for the natural health care industry. And, she has developed the most phenomenal herbal program I have ever seen. It is called, "Herbal Preparations and Natural Therapies—Creating and Using a Home Herbal Medicine Chest." When you finish watching these DVDs, you'll know more about the preparation of herbs than 99.9% of the doctors in this country. And believe me, it could turn out to be some of the most precious information you'll ever learn. Find out more information at: **www.makeherbalmedicines.com**.

Hard News and Current Events
From Around the World

If you're sick of the biased media coverage then you'll need to consider this remarkable service. With it, you can watch television from all over the world right from your computer. Why spend hours searching for alternative news sources when you can spend hours watching news as it happens around the globe? The unique service also comes with free technical support and the ability to request new channels. You can find out more information about it by going to **www. orderfreetv.com**.

New Manual Reveals in 90 Minutes
How You Can Get Out of Debt
Without Loans or Bankruptcy!

The Debtors Secret Weapon tells you exactly how to help reduce and perhaps even eliminate certain types of debt and change your life without falling into the traps of loans, foreclosure or bankruptcy. In fact, it has been known to work so fast and so completely that it makes some people feel like they are cheating!

But they are NOT cheating! The secrets taught in the manual are 100% legal and 100% ethical. It's just that bankers, debt collectors, and credit card companies don't want you to know about the loopholes revealed in the manual. To learn how to get out of debt quickly, visit **www.outin90.com**.

How to Cut Your College Costs in Half!

If you have ever wanted to earn an accredited degree from the college of your choice at a fraction of the cost paid by other students, visit: **www.collegeloopholes.com**.

Need a Job Fast?
New Book Reveals How to Get Employers
to Line Up and About Beg You to Work for Them

If you are like millions of Americans who've recently lost their jobs, you're in a real pinch and you need to take fast action. We've found a book that allows you to legally steal any job you want. By "steal" the author simply means that getting work this easy will make you feel like you've broken some rule—but don't worry, nothing illegal or immoral here. It simply details the fastest way to cut through the B.S. and get almost any job you want. Visit www.stealanyjob.com for the complete story.

How to Make Money with Your Truck

You can now use inside information to make a good living with a piece of equipment you may already own. Get some quick cash even during times of unprecedented turmoil that will leave others wondering where all your money came from. This book reveals the little known secrets of how to turn your pickup truck or van into a cash machine and never again worry about job security or the economy. Learn more about this very interesting book by going to: www.moneywithyourtruck.com.

T-Shirts, Mugs Expose the Treachery
of the Global Elite

Wage your own campaign against the dark side. These are definitely shirts the police state would like to lock you up for wearing, but they can't (at least not yet!) Stick your neck out and expose the globalists with t-shirts and mugs available at: www.blacklistedgear.com.

The "Stay Alive" Blueprint
Our Elitist Rulers Don't Want You to See...

This new book teaches you how a crippled 92 year-old survived the Katrina Disaster, without government help, and how her secrets can keep your family alive in a crisis. Not only do you receive excellent information on how to prepare for the potential food crisis, but you also get the reprint rights to this book so you can share it with your friends and family. You can learn more about preparing you and your family for the worst by going to: www.survivalstockpiling.com.

෨•ඥ

᧥ • ᧥

REFERENCES
AND
INDEX

References

℘•℃

1. Kingsolver, Barbara. *Animal, Vegetable, Miracle*. New York: Harper Collins, 2007.

2. Ruff, Howard J. *Famine and Survival in America*. Alamo, CA: Target Publishing, 1974.

3. Fox News. FoxNews.com. [Online] April 1, 2008. [Cited: December 28, 2010.] http://www.foxnews.com/story/0,2933,344170,00.html.

4. The Discovery Channel. [Cited: December 28, 2010.] http://dsc.discovery.com/survival/how-to-survive/food-supply.html.

5. Fuchs, Dale. *The New York Times*. June 10, 2008. [Cited: December 28, 2010.] http://www.nytimes.com/2008/06/10/world/europe/10iht-spain.4.13616120.html?_r=1.

6. Garnsy, Peter. *Famine and Food Supply in the Graeco-Roman World*. Cambridge University Press, 1989.

7. Blue Letter Bible. *The Blue Letter Bible*. [Cited: 12 29, 2010.] http:// www.blueletterbible.org/search/translationResults.cfm?Criteria=famine+OR+famines&t=KJV.

8. Jasky, Stephanie. "How Much Does the Average American Make?" [Cited: 12 29, 2010.] http://fedupusa.org/2010/01/07/how-much-does-the-average-american-make-breaking-down-the-u-s-household-income-numbers/.

9. Rosenthal, Andrew. "Bush Encounters the Supermarket, Amazed." The New York Times February 5, 1992. [Cited: 29 2010, 12.] http://query.nytimes.com/gst/fullpage.html?res=9E0CE1D71031F936A35751C0A964958260.

10. Gomstyn, Alice. "Walmart CEO Pay: More in an Hour than Workers Get All Year?" ABC News/Money. June 2, 2010. [Cited: 12 26, 2010.] http://abcnews.go.com/Business/walmart-ceo-pay-hour-workers-year/story?id=11067470.

11. Greenwald, Robert. *WalMart: The High Cost of Low Price*. Brave New Films, 2005.

12. Maloney, C.J. LewRockwell.com. [Cited: 12 29, 2010.] http://www.lewrockwell.com/maloney/maloney26.1.html.

13. Postel, Sandra. "Egypt's Nile Valley Basin Irrigation." Waterhistory.org [Cited: 12 31, 2010.] http://www.waterhistory.org/histories/nile/t1.html.

14. Maloney, C.J. LewRockwell.com 2010. [Cited: 12 29, 2010.] http://www.lewrockwell.com/maloney/maloney26.1.html.

15. *The Dynamics of a Riverine Civilization: A Geoarchaeological Perspective on the Nile Valley, Egypt.* Hassan, Fekri A. 1, London: World Archaeology, 1997, Vol. 29.

16. Maloney, C.J. LewRockwell.com 2010. [Cited: 12 29, 2010.] http://www.lewrockwell.com/maloney/maloney26.1.html.

17. Kirchoff, Sue. "Surplus U.S. Food Supplies Dry Up." *USA Today.* May 2, 2008. [Cited: 31 12, 2010.] http://www.usatoday.com/money/industries/food/2008-05-01-usda-food-supply_N.htm.

18. Gorder, Dan P. Van. *Ill Fares the Land: The Famine Planned for America.* Belmont: Western Islands, 1966.

19. USDA. Extension. United States Government, 3 22, 2010. [Cited: 12 26, 2010.] http://www.csrees.usda.gov/qlinks/extension.html.

20. Calhoun, George M. *The Business Life of Ancient Athens.* Cooper Square Press, 1926.

21. Garnsy, Peter. *Famine and Food Supply in the Graeco-Roman World.* Cambridge University Press, 1989.

22. Riesner, Rainer. *Paul's Early Period: Chronology, Mission Strategy, Theology.* Wm. B. Eerdman's Publishing, 1997.

23. Garnsy, Peter. *Famine and Food Supply in the Graeco-Roman World.* Cambridge University Press, 1989.

24. Stathakopoulos, Dionysios. *Famine and Pestilence in the Late Roman and Early Byzantine Empire: A Systematic Survey of Subsistence Crises and Epidemics.* Burlington : Ashgate Publishing, 2004.

25. O'Grada, Cormac. *Famine: A Short History.* Princeton University Press, 2010.

26. Stathakopoulos, Dionysios. *Famine and Pestilence in the Late Roman and Early Byzantine Empire: A Systematic Survey of Subsistence Crises and Epidemics.* Burlington : Ashgate Publishing, 2004.

27. Ibid.

28. List of Famines. [Cited: 1 3, 2011.] http://en.wikipedia.org/wiki/List_of_famines

29. Ancient History Sourcebook. [Cited: 1 3, 2011.] http://www.fordham.edu/halsall/ancient/410alaric.html.

30. "Frequently Asked Questions about the Roman Empire." [Cited: 1 3, 2011.] http://www.roman-empire.net/diverse/faq.html#romefall.

31. Knoller, Mark "Political Hotsheet." CBS News August 29, 2010. [Cited: 1 3, 2011.] http://www.cbsnews.com/8301-503544_162-20014998-503544.html.

32. Keck, Kristi. CNN, July 16, 2010. [Cited: 1 3, 2011.] http://articles.cnn.com/2010-07-16/politics/obama.vacation_1_obama-vacation-camp-david-oil-disaster?_s=PM:POLITICS.

33. "United States Presidential Election, 2004." [Cited: 1 3, 2011.] http://en.wikipedia.org/wiki/United_States_presidential_election,_2004.

34. Morgan, Dan; Gaul, Gilbert M.; and Cohen, Sarah. *The Washington Post.* July 2, 2006. [Cited: 1 3, 2011.] http://www.washingtonpost.com/wp-dyn/content/article/2006/07/01/AR2006070100962.html.

35. Nelson, Lynn Harry, "Lectures in Medieval History: The Great Famine and the Black Death." [Cited: 1 3, 2011.] http://www.vlib.us/medieval/lectures/black_death.html.

36. Giamietro, Mario and Pimentel, David. "Food, Land, Population, and the U.S. Economy." [Cited: 1 3, 2011.] www.dieoff.org/page40.htm.

37. PBS Newshour. "Hungry in America: New Food Insecurity Numbers are a Wakeup Call." PBS, November 24, 2009. [Cited: 1 3, 2011.] http://www.pbs.org/newshour/extra/features/us/july-dec09/hunger_11-24.html.

38. Van Gorder, Dan P. Ill Fares the Land: The Famine Planned for America. Belmont: Western Islands, 1966.

39. "The Great Famine and Agraian Crisis in England 1315-1322." The Oxford Journal. [Cited 1 3, 2011.] http://past.oxfordjournals.org/content/59/1/3.full.pdf.

40. Smith, Erika D. and Hunsinger, Dana. "Higher Food Prices Here, and Don't Expect A Break Soon." USA Today. November 20, 2010. [Cited 1 3, 2011.] http://www.usatoday.com/money/economy/2010-11-30-food-prices_N.htm

41. Food and Agriculture Organization of the United Nations. "World Food Situation." November 2010. [Cited 1 3, 2011.] http://www.fao.org/worldfoodsituation/wfs-home/en/

42. OnlineHistory.org, "The Waning of the Middle Ages: Crisis and Recovery." [Cited 1 4, 2011.] http://online-history.org/wc1-docs/The-Waning-of-the-Middle-Ages.doc.

43. Ibid.

44. Tanner, Harold Miles. China: A History. Hackett Publishing Co., 2009.

45. Ibid.

46. Ibid.

47. Modern World History GCSE. [Cited 1 4, 2011.] http://www.johndclare.net/Basics_Russia.htm.

48. Farris, William Wayne. *Japan's Medeival Population: Famine, Fertility, and Warfare in a Transformative Age.* University of Hawaii Press, 2009.

49. Ibid.

50. Ibid.

51. Ibid.

52. Ibid.

53. Gill, Richard Benedict. *The Great Maya Droughts: Water, Life, and Death.* University of New Mexico Press, 2000.

54. List of Famines. [Cited: 1 6, 2011.] http://en.wikipedia.org/wiki/List_of_famines

55. U.S. Department of the Interior: Bureau of Land Mangament, Colorado. "Who Were the Anasazi?" August 18, 2008. [Cited 1 6, 2011.] http://www.blm.gov/co/st/en/fo/ahc/who_were_the_anasazi.html.

56. Skopec, Eric. *The Anasazi Guide.* Lulu.com, 2007.

57. Ibid.

58. Fagan, Brian M. *Time Detectives: How Scientists Use Modern Technology to Recapture the Past.* Simon & Schuster, 1996.

59. Skopec, Eric. *The Anasazi Guide.* Lulu.com, 2007.

60. Carrasto, David. *Quetzalcoatl and the Irony of Empire: Myths and Prophecies in the Aztec Tradition.* University Press of Colorado, 2001

61. Ibid.

62. Soustelle, Jacques. *Daily Life of the Aztecs on the Eve of Spanish Conquests.* Stanford University Press, 1961.

63. Usitalo, Steven A. and Wisenhunt, William Benton. *Russian and Soviet History: From the Time of Troubles to the Collapse of the Soviet Union.* Rowman and Littlefield Publishers, 2008.

64. Margaret, Jacques. *The Russian Empire and Grand Duchy of Moscovy: A 17th Century Account.* University of Pittsburg Press, 1983.

65. Orchard, George Edward and Bussow, Conrad. *The Disturbed State of the Russian Realm.* McGill-Queen's University Press, 1994.

66. Ibid.

67. Usitalo, Steven A. and Wisenhunt, William Benton. *Russian and Soviet History: From the Time of Troubles to the Collapse of the Soviet Union.* Rowman and Littlefield Publishers, 2008.

68. List of Famines. [Cited: 1 6, 2011.] http://en.wikipedia.org/wiki/List_of_famines

69. Neely, Sylvia. *A Concise History of the French Revolution.* Rowman and Littlefield Publishers, 2007.

70. Fraser, Evan D.G. and Rimas, Andrew. *Empires of Food: Feast, Famine, and the Rise and Fall of Civilization.* Free Press, 2010.

71. Ibid.

72. Jacob, H.E. and Reinhart, Peter. *Six Thousand Years of Bread: Its Holy and Unholy History.* Skyhorse Publishing, 2007.

73. Fraser, Evan D.G. and Rimas, Andrew. *Empires of Food: Feast, Famine, and the Rise and Fall of Civilization.* Free Press, 2010.

74. Malthus, Thomas Robert. *An Essay on the Principle of Population as it Affects the Future Improvement of Society.* London, 1798.

75. Yahya, Harun. "The History of Ruthlessness, From Malthus to Darwin." [Cited 1 10, 2011.] http://www.harunyahya.com/books/darwinism/social_weapon/social_weapon03.php#dipnot

76. Belasco, Warren James. *Meals to Come: A History of the Future of Food.* University of California Press, 2006.

77. Yahya, Harun. "The History of Ruthlessness, From Malthus to Darwin." [Cited 1 10, 2011.] http://www.harunyahya.com/books/darwinism/social_weapon/social_weapon03.php#dipnot

78. Ibid.

79. Vandermeer, John H. *The Ecology of Agroecosystems.* Jones and Bartlett Publishers, 2009.

80. Yang, Anand A. *Bazaar India: Markets, Society, and the Colonial State in Gangetic Bihar.* University of California Press, 1999.

81. Cronin, Thomas M. *Principles of Paleoclimatology.* Columbia University Press, 1999.

82. Vandermeer, John H. *The Ecology of Agroecosystems.* Jones and Bartlett Publishers, 2009.

83. Heller, Michael. *The Gridlock Economy: How Too Much Ownership Wrecks Markets, Stops Innovation, and Costs Lives.* Basic Books, 2008.

84. USDA. Extension. United States Government, 3 22, 2010. [Cited: 12 26, 2010.] http://www.csrees.usda.gov/qlinks/extension.html.

85. O'Neill, Joseph R. *The Irish Potato Famine.* Abdo Publishing, 2009.

86. Bihar Famine of 1873. [Cited 1 12, 2011.] http://en.wikipedia.org/wiki/Bihar_famine_of_1873%E2%80%9374

87. Temple, Sir Richard. *Men and Events of My Time in India.* London, Murray, 1882.

88. The Great Depression Online. [Cited 1 12, 2011.] http://www.greatdepressiononline.com/.

89. Smith, Aaron. "1 in 7 American Rely on Food Stamps." CNNMoney December 10, 2010. [Cited 1 13, 2011.] http://money.cnn.com/2010/12/21/news/economy/food_stamps/.

90. Genzer, Nancy Marshall. "Food Banks Overwhelmed With Demand." American Public Media November 25, 2010. [Cited 1 13, 2011.] http://marketplace.publicradio.org/display/web/2010/11/25/pm-food-banks-overwhelmed-with-demand/.

91. Edsforth, Ronald. *The New Deal: America's Response to the Great Depression.* Wiley-Blackwell Publishing, 2000.

92. Gorder, Dan P. Van. *Ill Fares the Land: The Famine Planned for America.* Belmont: Western Islands, 1966.

93. Astyk, Sharon and Newton, Aaron. *A Nation of Farmers: Defeating the Food Crisis on American Soil.* New Society Publishers, 2009.

94. Edsforth, Ronald. *The New Deal: America's Response to the Great Depression.* Wiley-Blackwell Publishing, 2000.

95. Conquest, Robert. *Harvest of Sorrow: Soviet Collectivisation and the Terror Famine.* Oxford University Press, 1987.

96. Ibid.

97. Ibid.

98. The History Place. "Stalin's Forced Famine 1932-1933: 7,000,000 Deaths." *The History Place.* [Cited 1 14, 2011.] http://www.historyplace.com/worldhistory/genocide/stalin.htm.

99. Ibid.

100. Ibid.

101. Ellman, Michael. "The Role of Leadership Perceptions and the Intent in the Soviet Famine of 1931-1934." Europe-Asia Studies, 2005, Vol. 57.

102. Ibid.

103. Dikotter, Frank. *Mao's Great Famine: The History of China's Most Devastating Catastrophe.* Walker & Company, 2010.

104. Ibid.

105. The History Learning Site. "The Great Leap Forward." [Cited 1 14, 2011.] http://www.historylearningsite.co.uk/great_leap_forward.htm.

106. Dikotter, Frank. *Mao's Great Famine: The History of China's Most Devastating Catastrophe.* Walker & Company, 2010.

107. Emmott, Bill. "GM Crops Can Save Us From Food Shortage." *The London Telegraph.* April 17, 2008. [Cited 1 15, 2011.] http://www.telegraph.co.uk/comment/3557344/GM-crops-can-save-us-from-food-shortages.html

108. Dikotter, Frank. *Mao's Great Famine: The History of China's Most Devastating Catastrophe.* Walker & Company, 2010.

109. Gorder, Dan P. Van. *Ill Fares the Land: The Famine Planned for America.* Belmont: Western Islands, 1966.

110. Dikotter, Frank. *Mao's Great Famine: The History of China's Most Devastating Catastrophe.* Walker & Company, 2010.

111. Hewitt, Mike. "Who Do We Owe and How Much?" *The Market Oracle.* July 19, 2007. [Cited 1 15, 2011.] http://www.marketoracle.co.uk/Article1571.html

112. Adams, Sam. *Understanding and Surviving Martial Law.* Solutions From Science, 2009.

113. Ibid.

114. Dikotter, Frank. *Mao's Great Famine: The History of China's Most Devastating Catastrophe.* Walker & Company, 2010.

115. CBS News. "'Nowhere to Hide' From Rising Food Prices." *CBS News: The Early Show.* January 15, 2011. [Cited 1 15, 2011.] http://www.cbsnews.com/stories/2011/01/15/earlyshow/saturday/main7249451.shtml

116. AccuWeather. Extreme Weather Events. January 15, 2011. [Cited 1 15, 2011.] http://www.accuweather.com/blogs/news/story/44427/extreme-weather-events-spark-f.asp

117. Bourne Jr., Joel K. "The Global Food Crisis: The End of Plenty." *National Geographic*. June 2009. [Cited 1 15, 2011.] http://ngm.nationalgeographic.com/2009/06/cheap-food/bourne-text

118. Brown, Lester. "The Great Food Crisis of 2011." *Foreign Policy Magazine*. January 10, 2011. [Cited 1 15, 2011.] http://www.foreignpolicy.com/articles/2011/01/10/the_great_food_crisis_of_2011

119. Adams, Sam. *Understanding and Surviving Martial Law*. Solutions From Science, 2009.

120. Lappe, Francis Moore. *Diet for a Small Planet*. Ballentine Books, 1985.

121. Clemens, Walter C. *Dynamics of International Relations: Conflict and Mutual Gain*. Rowman and Littlefield, 2004.

122. Unger, Rick. "What Did the Founding Fathers Really Think About Corporations and Their Rights?" *True/Slant*. January 22, 2010. [Cited 1 18, 2011.] http://trueslant.com/rickungar/2010/01/22/what-did-the-founding-fathers-really-think-about-corporations-and-their-rights/

123. Tabarrok, Alexander. "Famine, Corruption, the Media, and Democracy." 2005. mason.gmu.edu/.../Famine,%20Corruption,%20the%20Media%20and%20Democracy.ppt

124. Dhabjiv, Al. "Who Owns the Media?" *Journal of Law and Economics*. Vol. XL: VI, 2003.

125. Clemens, Walter C. *Dynamics of International Relations: Conflict and Mutual Gain*. Rowman and Littlefield, 2004.

126. Go, Julian. *American Empire and the Politics of Meaning: Elite Political Cultures in the Philippines and Puerto Rico during U.S. Colonialism*. Duke University Press, 2008.

127. Truth in History Ministries. "Characteristics of an Empire." 2005. [Cited 1 18, 2011.] http://www.truthinhistory.org/characteristics-of-an-empire-2.html

128. Layne, Christopher and Thayer, Bradley A. *American Empire: A Debate*. Routledge. 2006

129. Kissinger, Henry. "NSSM:200 Implications of Worldwide Population Growth for U.S. Security and Overseas Interests." 1974.

130. Lappe, Francis Moore. *Diet for a Small Planet.* Ballentine Books, 1985.

131. Boucher, Douglas H. *The Paradox of Plenty: Hunger in a Bountiful World.* Food First Books, 1999.

132. Ibid.

133. Ibid.

134. The World Bank. "What is the World Bank?" [Cited 1 19, 2011.] http://web. worldbank.org/WBSITE/EXTERNAL/EXTABOUTUS/0,,contentMDK:2004055 8~menuPK:34559~pagePK:34542~piPK:36600,00.html

135. Hartmann, Betsy and Boyce, James. *Needless Hunger: Voices form a Bangladesh Village.* Institute for Food and Development Policy, 1979, 1982.

136. Boucher, Douglas H. *The Paradox of Plenty: Hunger in a Bountiful World.* Food First Books, 1999.

137. Essential Information. "How The IMF Bails Out Big Banks." [Cited 1 18, 2011.] http://www.essentialaction.org/imf/big_bank_bails.htm

138. Evans-Pritchard, Ambrose. "The G20 Moves the World a Step Closer to a Global Currency." *The London Telegraph.* April 3, 2009. [Cited 1 19, 2011.] http:// www.telegraph.co.uk/finance/comment/ambroseevans_pritchard/5096524/ The-G20-moves-the-world-a-step-closer-to-a-global-currency.html

139. Carr, Patrick J. and Kefalas, Maria J. "The Rural Brain Drain." *The Chronicle of Higher Education.* September 21, 2009. [Cited 1 19, 2011.] http://chronicle. com/article/The-Rural-Brain-Drain/48425/

140. Clean Water Action Council. "Land Use and Urban Sprawl." [Cited 1 19, 2011.] http://www.cwac.net/landuse/index.html

141. Gorder, Dan P. Van. *Ill Fares the Land: The Famine Planned for America.* Belmont: Western Islands, 1966.

142. American Farmland Trust. "Sustaining Farms on the Urban Edge." 2009. [Cited 1 20, 2011.] http://www.farmland.org/resources/sustaining-agriculture-in-urbanizing-counties/default.asp

143. Ibid.

144. Weber, Karl. *Food, Inc.: How Industrial Food is Making Us Sicker, Fatter, and Poorer.* Public Affairs, 2009.

145. Kleinman, David S. *Human Adaptation and Population Control: A Non-Malthusian Perspective.* Rowman and Littlefield, 1980.

146. Shuman, Michael. *Going Local: Creating Self-Reliant Communities in a Global Age.* Routledge, 2000.

147. Mason, John. Sustainable Agriculture. CSIRO, 2003.

148. Nikiforuk, Andrew. *Pandemonium: How Globalization and trade are Putting the World at Risk.* University of Queensland, 2007.

149. Green Planet Ethics. "Crop Rotation Versus Monocultures: The Dangers of Monocultures." [Cited 1 19, 2011.] http://greenplanetethics.com/wordpress/crop-rotation-versus-monocultures-the-dangers-of-monocultures/

150. Walters, Kerry S. and Portness, Lisa. *Ethical Vegetarianism: From Pythagoras to Peter Singer.* State University of New York Press, 1999.

151. Ibid.

152. United States Department of Agriculture. "United States Department of Agriculture: Agriculture Fact Book." USDA, 2001-2002.

153. Food & Water Watch. "Unmeasured Danger: America's Hidden Groundwater Crisis." [Cited 1 20, 2011.] http://www.foodandwaterwatch.org/reports/unmeasured-danger-americas-hidden-groundwater-crisis/

154. Lawford, Richard G., Fort, Denise E., Hartmann, Holly C., and Eden, Susanna. *Water: Science, Policy, and Management – Challenges and Opportunities.* American Geophysical Union, 2003.

155. Clover, Charles. *The End of the Line: How Overfishing is Changing the World and What We Eat.* University of California Press, 2006.

156. Prance, Ghillean T. *The Earth Under Threat: A Christian Perspective.* Wild Goose Publications, 2004.

157. Ibid.

158. Ibid.

159. Pernett, Allison S. *The Infrastructure of Food: Procurement and Distribution Implications for Farmers in Western North Carolina.* Appalacian Sustainable Agricultural Project, 2007.

160. Ibid.

161. Department of Homeland Security, Department of Agriculture, and Food and Drug Administration. *Agriculture and Food: Critical Infrastructure and Key Resources, Sector-Specific Plan as to the National Infrastructure Protection Plan.* 2007.

162. Smith, Allen. "Long Term Trucking Strike Would Devastate U.S." February 10, 2010. [Cited 1 21, 2011.] http://www.askthetrucker.com/long-term-trucking-strike-would-devastate-u-s/

163. *Camp FEMA: American Lockdown.* William Lewis Films & Gary Franchi Productions. 2009.

164. The Utah Department of Agriculture and Food. "Self-Sufficient America." [Cited 1 21, 2011.] www.agriadvocates.org/self-sufficiency

165. International Centre for Trade and Sustainable Development. "FAO and USDA Warn of New Surge in Global Food Prices." *Bridges Weekly Trade News Digest.* Volume 15:1, January 19, 2011. [Cited 1 21, 2011.] http://ictsd.org/i/news/bridgesweekly/99373/

166. University of Guelph. "Is the Food Supply Safe From Terrorist Attacks?" March 26, 2003. [Cited 1 21, 2011.] www.foodsafety.ksu.edu/articles/533/food_terrorism_factsheet.pdf

167. Brahic, Catherine. "Climate Myths: The Cooling After 1940 shows CO2 Does Not Cause Warming." *New Scientist.* May 16, 2007. [Cited 1 21, 2011.] http://www.newscientist.com/article/dn11639-climate-myths-the-cooling-after-1940-shows-cosub2sub-does-not-cause-warming.html

168. Lisle, Holly. "'Their' Reality, and the REAL Reality." November 16, 2008. [Cited 1 21, 2011.] http://hollylisle.com/writingdiary2/?s=global+warming

169. Avery, Dennis T. "War, Pestilence, Famine: That's Climate Change…When It's Cold." *PJ Media.* May 10, 2010. [Cited 1 21, 2011.] http://pajamasmedia.com/blog/war-pestilence-famine-thats-climate-change-when-its-cold/2/

170. *Gone Before You Get There: 77 Items That Instantly Vanish From Store Shelves in a Panic.* Solutions From Science, 2010.

171. Connolly, Ceci. "Katrina Food Aid Blocked by U.S. Rules." *The Washington Post.* October 14, 2005. [Cited 1 21, 2011.] http://www.washingtonpost.com/wp-dyn/content/article/2005/10/13/AR2005101302084.html

172. Montanaro, Domenico. "Looking to 2011: Unemployment and the Presidency." *MSNBC.* December 31, 2010. [Cited 1 21, 2011.] http://firstread.msnbc.msn.com/_news/2010/12/31/5742528-looking-to-2011-unemployment-and-the-presidency

173. Mayerowitz, Scott. "Food Stamps Create Jobs…in India." *ABC News.* April 29, 2009. [Cited 1 21, 2011.] http://abcnews.go.com/Business/Economy/story?id=7452561&page=4

174. Snyder, Michael. "12 Economic Collapse Scenarios That We Could Potentially See in 2011." *Benzinga*. January 19, 2011. [Cited 1 22, 2011.] http://www.benzinga.com/11/01/792254/12-economic-collapse-scenarios-that-we-could-potentially-see-in-2011#

175. Peek, George Nelson and Crowther, Samuel. *Why Quit Our Own?* Cornell University, 1936.

176. Ibid.

177. Gorder, Dan P. Van. *Ill Fares the Land: The Famine Planned for America*. Belmont: Western Islands, 1966.

178. Peek, George Nelson and Crowther, Samuel. *Why Quit Our Own?* Cornell University, 1936.

179. Ibid.

180. Stormer, John A. *None Dare Call It Treason*. Liberty Bell, 1990.

181. 73rd Congress, 2nd Session. "Hearings, House Select Committee to Investigate Certain Statements of Dr. William Wirt." April 10 and 17, 1934.

182. Peek, George Nelson and Crowther, Samuel. *Why Quit Our Own?* Cornell University, 1936.

183. "National Affairs: Underlings in a Revolution." *Time Magazine*. April 2, 1934. [Cited 1 25, 2011.] http://www.time.com/time/magazine/article/0,9171,747281-2,00.html

184. Peek, George Nelson and Crowther, Samuel. *Why Quit Our Own?* Cornell University, 1936.

185. "Only Two Active Lobbies Work for a World Peace in Washington." *The Palm Beach Post*. November 12, 1939.

186. Gorder, Dan P. Van. *Ill Fares the Land: The Famine Planned for America*. Belmont: Western Islands, 1966.

187. Sperling, John A. and Helburn, Suzanne Wiggins. *The Great Divide: Retro vs. Metro America*. Polipoint Press, 2004.

188. Gorder, Dan P. Van. *Ill Fares the Land: The Famine Planned for America*. Belmont: Western Islands, 1966.

189. Beck, James. *Congressional Record*. 1933.

190. Adams, Sam. *Understanding and Surviving Martial Law*. Solutions From Science, 2009.

191. Ibid.

192. Feingold, Russ. *Statement of U.S. Senator Russ Feingold on the Anti-Terrorism Bill.* From the Senate floor, 2001.

193. Wolf, Naomi. "The End of America: A Letter of Warning to a Young Patriot." Speech given at Kane Hall on the University of Washington Campus, October 11, 2007. http://www.youtube.com/watch?v=RjALf12PAWc

194. Ibid.

195. U.S. Department of Homeland Security. "FEMA History." [Cited 1 26, 2011.] www.fema.gov/about/history.shtm

196. Lindorff, David. "Could It Happen Here?" *Mother Jones Magazine.* April 1988.

197. Lang, Robert. "1878 Posse Comitatus Act Destroyed." 2010. [Cited 1 26, 2011.] http://sites.google.com/site/robertlangforsenate2010/1878-posse-comitatus-destroyed

198. Sherman, Brad. Remarks on floor of the House of Representatives. C-Span, 2008. [Cited 1 26, 2011.] http://www.youtube.com/watch?v=HaG9d_4zij8

199. Prins, Nomi. *It Takes a Pillage: An Epic Tale of Power, Deceit, and Untold Trillions.* Wiley, 2010.

200. Ventura, Jesse and Russell, Dick. *American Conspiracies: Lies, Lies, and More Dirty Lies the Government Tells Us.* Skyhorse Publishing, 2010.

201. Ibid.

202. Chardy, Alfonso. "Reagan Aides and the Secret Government." *The Miami Herald.* July 5, 1987.

203. Swarms, Rachel L. "Haliburton Subsidiary Gets Contract to Add Temporary Immigration Detention Centers." *The New York Times.* February 4, 2006.

204. Schoomaker, Peter J., "Army Regulation 210-35: Civilian Inmate Labor Program." United States Army, Washington D.C., 2005.

205. Pennsylvania Department of Revenue. Pennsylvania State Tax Commission Commercial "Find Us Before We Find You." 2010.

206. Jeffrey, Grant R. *Shadow Government.* Cloud Ten Pictures, 2010.

207. Ibid.

208. Ibid.

209. Ibid.

210. Ibid.

211. Little, Alison. "Sin Bins for Worst Families." *The Daily Express.* July 23, 2009. [Cited 1 27, 2011.] http://www.express.co.uk/posts/view/115736

212. Stanglin, Douglas. "School District Accused of Spying on Kids via Laptop Computers." *USA Today.* February 18, 2010. [Cited 1 26, 2011.] http://content. usatoday.com/communities/ondeadline/post/2010/02/school-district-accused-of-issuing-webcam-laptops-to-spy-on-students/1

213. Kenner, Robert. *Food, Inc.* Hungry for Change, 2008.

214. Food First. "Farmers Bringing Message of 'Stop Corporate Control Over Food' to the Food Crisis Summit in Rome Were Expelled." June 4, 2008. [Cited 1 27, 2011.] http://www.foodfirst.org/en/node/2143

215. Kenner, Robert. *Food, Inc.* Hungry for Change, 2008.

216. Ibid.

217. Ibid.

218. Ibid.

219. Lewis, Mike. "Crab Fishing Reforms Divide Industry into Haves and Have-Nots." *Seattle Post-Intelligencer.* October 1, 2005. [Cited 1 28, 2011.] www.seattlepi. com/local/243039_crabfishing01.html

220. Ibid.

221. Kenner, Robert. *Food, Inc.* Hungry for Change, 2008.

222. Ibid.

223. Philpott, Tom. "A Reflection on the Lasting Legacy of 1970s USDA Secretary Earl Butz." *Grist.* February 7, 2008. [Cited 1 28, 2011.] http://www.grist.org/ article/the-butz-stops-here/

224. Kenner, Robert. *Food, Inc.* Hungry for Change, 2008.

225. Canada's National Farmer's Union. *The Farm Crisis: Bigger Farms and the Myths of "Competition" and "Efficiency."* 2003.

226. Kenner, Robert. *Food, Inc.* Hungry for Change, 2008.

227. Ibid.

228. Ibid.

229. Institute for Food and Development Policy. "The Industrialization of African Agriculture: Answer to Hunger or Gateway to Violence?" *Food First News and Views.* Fall, 2010 Volume 32: 118.

230. Carson, Rachel. *Silent Spring.* Mariner Books: New York, 2002.

231. Cox, Caroline. "Glyphosate Fact Sheet." *Journal of Pesticide Reform*, Fall 1998, Revised October 2000.

232. Carson, Rachel. *Silent Spring.* Mariner Books: New York, 2002.

233. Kerns, Thomas A. *Environmentally Induced Illnesses: Ethics, Risk Assessment, and Human Rights.* McFarland & Co., Inc. 2001.

234. Carson, Rachel. *Silent Spring.* Mariner Books: New York, 2002.

235. Stauber, John and Rampton, Sheldon. "Let Them Eat Sludge." *PR Watch.* 1995. [Cited 1 28, 2011.] www.prwatch.org/prwissues/1995Q3/sludge.html

236. Ibid.

237. Goldman, Lynn R., MD, MPH. *Toxics and Poverty.* John Hopkins Bloomberg School of Public Health. 2002.

238. The Pesticide Action Network of the U.K. "Are Pesticides Linked to Poverty?" 2011. [Cited 1 28, 2011.] http://www.pan-uk.org/general/are-pesticides-linked-to-poverty

239. Center for Food Safety. "True Food Shopper's Guide: How to Avoid Foods Made With GMOs." 2010.

240. Ibid.

241. Seeds of Deception. "Health Risks of GM Foods: Summary and Debate." 2011. [Cited 1 28, 2011.] http://www.seedsofdeception.com/Public/Home/index.cfm

242. Kingsolver, Barbara. *Animal, Vegetable, Miracle.* New York: Harper Collins, 2007.

243. Kenner, Robert. *Food, Inc.* Hungry for Change, 2008.

244. CBS News. "WikiLeaks: U.S. Wanted Trade War Over GM Crops." *CBS News.* January 4, 2011. [Cited 1 28, 2011.] http://www.cbsnews.com/stories/2011/01/04/world/main7211185.shtml

245. Collins, Ronald K.L., "Veggie Libel: Agribusiness Threatens to Stifle Speech." *Multinational Monitor Magazine.* May, 1998.

246. The United Nations. *Agenda 21.* Rio de Janeiro, 1992.

247. Ibid.

248. Ibid.

249. Mosher, Steve. "Too Many People? Not by a Long Shot." *Wall Street Journal.* February 10, 1997.

250. Margolis, Eric and Romero, Mary. *The Blackwell Companion to Social Inequalities.* Wiley-Blackwell, 2005.

251. Ibid.

252. The United Nations. *Agenda 21*. Rio de Janeiro, 1992.

253. Annenberg Public Policy Center, University of Pennsylvania. "Katrina: What Happened When." September 16, 2005, Revised November 8, 2005. [Cited 1 30, 2011.] http://www.factcheck.org/society/katrina_what_happened_when.html

254. Balko, Radley. "When the Catastrophe is Government." Fox News. September 7, 2005. [Cited 1 30, 2011.] http://www.foxnews.com/story/0,2933,168732,00.html.

255. Annenberg Public Policy Center, University of Pennsylvania. "Katrina: What Happened When." September 16, 2005, Revised November 8, 2005. [Cited 1 30, 2011.] http://www.factcheck.org/society/katrina_what_happened_when.html

256. Ibid.

257. Ibid.

258. Balko, Radley. "When the Catastrophe is Government." *Fox News*. September 7, 2005. [Cited 1 30, 2011.] http://www.foxnews.com/story/0,2933,168732,00.html.

259. Ibid.

260. Annenberg Public Policy Center, University of Pennsylvania. "Katrina: What Happened When." September 16, 2005, Revised November 8, 2005. [Cited 1 30, 2011.] http://www.factcheck.org/society/katrina_what_happened_when.html.

261. Ibid.

262. *Camp FEMA: American Lockdown*. William Lewis Films & Gary Franchi Productions. 2009.

263. Robinson, Eugene. "Tainted FEMA Trailers Should be Destroyed, Not Sold." *The Washington Post*. March 16, 2010. [Cited 1 30, 2011.] http://www.washingtonpost.com/wp-dyn/content/article/2010/03/15/AR2010031502291.html.

264. NBC News. "Katrina Victims Blame Racism for Slow Aid." *MSNBC*. December 6, 2005. [Cited 1 30, 2011.] http://www.msnbc.msn.com/id/10354221/ns/us_news-katrina_the_long_road_back/.

265. Brown, D.M. *Hurricane Katrina: The First Seven Days of America's Worst Natural Disaster*. Lulu, 2005.

266. Adams, Sam. *Understanding and Surviving Martial Law*. Solutions From Science, 2009.

267. Ripley, Amanda. *The Unthinkable: Who Survives When Disaster Strikes—And Why*. Three Rivers Press, 2008.

268. Americans Networking To Survive.org, 2010. [Cited 1 30, 2011.] http://www.americansnetworkingtosurvive.org/.

269. Bradley, Arthur T. *Handbook for Practical Disaster Preparedness for the Family.* CreateSpace, 2010.

270. Ibid.

271. Ibid.

272. Koc, Mustafa; MacRae, Rod; Welsh, Jennifer; and Mougeot, Luc J.A. *For Hunger-Proof Cities: Sustainable Urban Food Systems.* IDRC Books, 2000.

273. Nettle, Claire. *Growing Community: Starting and Nurturing Community Gardens.* Department of Health, Government of South Australia. 2010.

274. The American Community Garden Association. "Starting A Community Garden." [Cited 1 30, 2011.] http://www.communitygarden.org/learn/starting-a-community-garden.php.

275. Despommier, Dickson. *The Vertical Farm: Feeding the World in the 21st Century.* Thomas Dunne Books, 2010.

276. Bello, Marisol. "Communities Print Their Own Currency to Keep Cash Flowing." *USA Today.* April 4, 2009. [Cited 1 31, 2011.] http://www.usatoday.com/money/economy/2009-04-05-scrip_N.htm.

277. Gorder, Dan P. Van. *Ill Fares the Land: The Famine Planned for America.* Belmont: Western Islands, 1966.

278. Ibid.

279. *Gone Before You Get There: 77 Items That Instantly Vanish From Store Shelves in a Panic.* Solutions From Science, 2010.

280. Ruff, Howard J. *Famine and Survival in America.* Alamo, CA : Target Publishing, 1974.

281. *Gone Before You Get There: 77 Items That Instantly Vanish From Store Shelves in a Panic.* Solutions From Science, 2010.

282. Americans Networking To Survive.org, 2010. [Cited 1 30, 2011.] http://www.americansnetworkingtosurvive.org/.

283. Kingsolver, Barbara. *Animal, Vegetable, Miracle.* New York: Harper Collins, 2007.

284. *Food Storage Secrets.* Solutions From Science, 2009.

285. Ibid.

286. King, Richard P. "How to Save Your Own Seeds." *Mother Earth News*. October 7, 1977. [Cited 1 31, 2011.] http://www.motherearthnews.com/Organic-Gardening/1977-09-01/Save-Your-Own-Garden-grown-Vegetable-Seed.aspx.

287. Ibid.

288. Ibid.

289. *Gone Before You Get There: 77 Items That Instantly Vanish From Store Shelves in a Panic.* Solutions From Science, 2010.

290. Stein, Matthew. *When Technology Fails: A Manual for Self-Reliance, Sustainability, and Surviving the Long Emergency.* Chelsea Green Publishing Company: White River Junction, 2008.

291. Angier, Brandford. *Feasting Free on Wild Edibles.* Stackpole Books, 2002.

292. Ibid.

293. Ibid.

294. Ibid.

295. Kallas, John. *Edible Wild Plants: Wild Foods from Dirt to Plate.* First Lyons Press, 2002.

296. Murphy, J.J. "Survival Foods: Edible Wild Plants." *Nature Skills.* January 28, 2010. [Cited 1 31, 2011.] http://www.natureskills.com/wild-foods/edible-wild-plants/.

297. Stein, Matthew. *When Technology Fails: A Manual for Self-Reliance, Sustainability, and Surviving the Long Emergency.* Chelsea Green Publishing Company: White River Junction, 2008.

298. Ontario Minister for the Environment. *Guide to Eating Ontario Sport Fish.* 21st Ed., revised, Queen's Printer for Ontario, 2009.

299. *Gone Before You Get There: 77 Items That Instantly Vanish From Store Shelves in a Panic.* Solutions From Science, 2010.

300. Adams, Sam. *Understanding and Surviving Martial Law.* Solutions From Science, 2009.

301. Adams, Sam. *Hide Your Guns.* Solutions From Science, 2008.

302. Ibid.

303. Ibid.

304. Adams, Sam. *Understanding and Surviving Martial Law.* Solutions From Science, 2009.

305. Morris, David. "Improvised Weapons, the Election, and Finding Like-Minded Preppers." *Urban Survival Guide*. October 29, 2010. [Cited 1 31, 2011.] http://secretsofurbansurvival.com/483/improvised-weapons-the-election-and-finding-like-minded-preppers/?utm_source=feedburner&utm_medium=feed&utm_campaign=Feed%3A+Secretsofurbansurvivalcom+%28SecretsOfUrban Survival.com%29.

306. Adams, Sam. *Understanding and Surviving Martial Law*. Solutions From Science, 2009.

307. Adams, Sam. *Hide Your Guns*. Solutions From Science, 2008.

308. Ibid.

309. Ibid.

310. *Camp FEMA: American Lockdown*. William Lewis Films & Gary Franchi Productions. 2009.

311. Adams, Sam. *Hide Your Guns*. Solutions From Science, 2008.

312. Ibid.

ഇ•ര

Index

೫೦•೧೪

W

CPSIA information can be obtained at www.ICGtesting.com
Printed in the USA
LVOW110838020112

261981LV00001B/1/P

9 781937 660048